The Healing
Power of EFT &
energy
Psychology

T0299464

# The Healing Power of EFT & energy Psychology

**Tap into your body's energy to change your life for the better**

## DAVID FEINSTEIN, DONNA EDEN & GARY CRAIG

FOREWORD BY CANDACE PERT, PhD

piatkus

PIATKUS

First published in the US in 2005 by Jeremy P. Tarcher/Penguin (USA)
First published in Great Britain in 2006 by Piatkus Books
This paperback edition published in 2010 by Piatkus

13

A CIP catalogue record for this book
is available from the British Library.

ISBN 978-0-7499-4020-1

Printed and bound in Great Britain by Clays Ltd, Elcograf S.p.A.

Papers used by Piatkus are from well-managed forests
and other responsible sources.

MIX
Paper | Supporting
responsible forestry
FSC www.fsc.org   FSC® C104740

Piatkus
An imprint of
Little, Brown Book Group
Carmelite House
50 Victoria Embankment
London EC4Y 0DZ

An Hachette UK Company
www.hachette.co.uk

www.improvementzone.co.uk

*Dedicated to Jean Houston,*

*a giant in our midst*

The cell is a machine driven by energy. It can thus be approached by studying matter, or by studying energy. In every culture and in every medical tradition before ours, healing was accomplished by moving energy.

—*Albert Szent-Györgyi*
*Nobel Laureate in Medicine*

# ACKNOWLEDGMENTS

A book presenting a method that traces back to a 5,000-year-old healing tradition has a long list of indebtednesses. After a respectful bow to the ancestors, we turn to four contemporaries who paved the way for this presentation: George Goodheart, by bringing the energy perspective of ancient Eastern healing arts into the Western, thoroughly modern form called Applied Kinesiology, provided the foundation upon which this program rests. John Thie, by bringing the principles of Applied Kinesiology to the general public and introducing them as "Touch for Health" to hundreds of thousands of people in at least forty countries, demonstrated that powerful healing methods can be used by laypeople responsibly and effectively. Psychiatrist John Diamond and psychologist Roger Callahan, by independently applying the principles of Applied Kinesiology to emotional issues, fashioned prototypes of the approach presented here.

The immediate predecessor of this book is a training program for psychotherapists and other health-care professionals called *Energy Psychology Interactive: Rapid Interventions for Lasting Change*. The book you are holding synthesizes some of the most immediate and practical concepts and procedures from that program, which David Feinstein developed over a four-year period in conjunction with two primary advisors, Donna Eden and Fred Gallo, Ph.D., and an advisory board composed of twenty-four of the field's pioneers and leaders. These included Joaquín Andrade, M.D., Dan Benor, M.D., Patricia Carrington, Ph.D., Asha Nahoma Clinton, MSW, Ph.D., John Diepold, Ph.D., Jim Durlacher, D.C., Charles R. Figley, Ph.D., Tapas Fleming, L.Ac., Rebecca Grace, Psy.D., David Gruder, Ph.D., Dorothea Hover-Kramer, Ed.D., R.N., Warren Jacobs, M.D.,

Martin Jerry, M.D., Ph.D., Peter Lambrou, Ph.D., Greg Nicosia, Ph.D., Larry Nims, Ph.D., Gary Peterson, M.D., George Pratt, Ph.D., Lee Pulos, Ph.D., Mary Sise, MSW, Larry Stoler, Ph.D., Judith Swack, Ph.D., Sharon Cass Toole, Ph.D., and Helen Tuggy, Ph.D.

Meanwhile, several hundred lay and professional practitioners have been meticulously describing clinical outcomes and sending them for posting on Gary Craig's Emotional Freedom Techniques (EFT) website. Although too large a number to acknowledge individually, that level of documentation is a tremendous contribution to a fledgling field, and some of those cases are presented in this book.

The influence of each of the individuals mentioned above is gratefully acknowledged, along with the courage and inventiveness of growing numbers of practitioners who are successfully applying energy interventions to all manner of settings, problems, and goals. Special thanks also go to Peg Elliott Mayo, MSW, Ron Ruden, M.D., and Joaquín Andrade, M.D., for their valuable comments on earlier drafts of the manuscript. As usual, however, responsibility for this book's content rests solely with its authors.

# CONTENTS

*Foreword*                                                          *xi*

*Introduction: A Revolutionary Approach
to Personal Change?*                                                 *1*

1 · YOUR ELECTRIC BRAIN                                              13

2 · A BASIC RECIPE                                                   28

3 · FOCUSING ON PROBLEMS                                             65

4 · FOCUSING ON POTENTIALS                                         115

5 · CULTIVATING "EMOTIONAL
    INTELLIGENCE"                                                   157

6 · YOUR BODY'S ENERGIES                               196

7 · THE CIRCUITS OF JOY                                238


*Epilogue: The Future of Energy Psychology*            272

*Appendix 1: The Basic Recipe on a Page*               283

*Appendix 2: If the Program Becomes Unsettling*        285

*Appendix 3: Research Evidence*                        291

*Notes*                                                307

*Resources*                                            318

# FOREWORD

Our ability to help people overcome self-defeating emotional patterns, achieve higher levels of psychological well-being, and open their spiritual sensibilities is accelerating at an extraordinary pace. This book introduces you to a powerful development within that unfolding story.

The biochemical underpinnings of awareness—of sensations such as pleasure and pain, drives such as hunger and thirst, emotions such as anger and joy, and "higher" states such as awe and spiritual inspiration—have been identified. "Informational substances" such as hormones, peptides, and neurotransmitters find their way—in one of nature's most stunning designs—to receptor molecules that are on the surface of every cell in the body.

These "molecules of emotion" shape mood and thought. Significantly, it is a two-way process. Emotions and thoughts initiate a series of cascading chemical and cellular events—including the formation of new neurons—that are the basis of other emotions and thoughts. Some studies suggest, in fact, that meditation may cause neurological shifts that are as potent as our most effective medications for alleviating anxiety and depression.

*The Healing Power of EFT and Energy Psychology* is a synthesis of practices designed to deliberately shift the molecules of emotion. These practices have three distinct advantages over psychiatric medications. They are noninvasive, highly specific, and have no side effects. Energy interventions impact the body's intricate electrochemical system as well as more subtle energies. *Subtle energy* is a term born of an emerging paradigm that is still just outside the embrace of Western science, though it has long been central to the worldview of Eastern medicine and spiritual disciplines.

These practices focus on energy systems that still cannot be detected by our scientific instruments, though they are well known to the most sensitive healers and sages of every culture in recorded history. The program you are about to begin teaches you about these natural energies and how to influence them to shift patterns of emotion, thought, and behaviour that are blatantly dysfunctional, or merely self-limiting.

This book is an early formulation of a new field. It brings unfamiliar methods into the therapeutic and self-help arenas, using tapping as much as talk, aiming for energy integration as much as insight. The procedures, as you will see, can look quite odd. The range of appropriate clinical and self-directed applications is still being debated, but my personal impression, based on my own experience, is that it is enormous.

*The Promise of Energy Psychology* grows out of an earlier highly acclaimed work by a team of twenty-seven health and mental-health professionals led by David Feinstein to bring the new tools of energy psychology to psychotherapists. This book brings those methods to anyone who wishes to apply them.

At the same time I was doing my early work on the opiate receptor at The Johns Hopkins University School of Medicine in the 1970s, Dr. Feinstein was there conducting research on psychotherapeutic innovations. Thirty years later his focus has turned to the intersection of psychotherapy and energy medicine. While he has practiced as a clinical psychologist during the intervening decades and in fact pioneered a powerful methodology for helping people transform the internal guidance system he refers to as a "personal mythology," he has also accumulated some unusual credentials for a psychologist. Not the least of these is that he is married to one of the world's most renowned energy healers, Donna Eden, a co-author of this book.

Together with Gary Craig, founder of the most widely used single approach to energy psychology, the three have produced a work that is authoritative, engaging, and refreshingly friendly. You will find it an illuminating companion as you incorporate these wonderfully empowering methods into your life.

—*Candace Pert, Ph.D.*
   *Research Professor, Georgetown University School of Medicine*

# INTRODUCTION

# A REVOLUTIONARY APPROACH TO PERSONAL CHANGE?

*David Feinstein, Ph.D.*

> All truth goes through three stages.
> First it is ridiculed.
> Then it is violently opposed.
> Finally it is accepted as self-evident.
>
> —SCHOPENHAUER

Your emotional health, your success in the world, and your level of joy can all be dramatically enhanced by shifting the energies that regulate them. That is the promise of the fascinating new field of energy psychology.

With it, phobias and stubborn anxieties often fade in minutes. The lifelong grip of an early trauma can frequently be released within one or two sessions. Anger can be managed more reliably. Depression can in many cases be alleviated without drugs. Achievements in sports, school, music, and business can be given a powerful boost. Other complex issues can be separated into a network of self-limiting beliefs and dysfunctional emotional responses that are eliminated one by one. Even elusive physical problems may respond where other treatments have failed.[1]

After more than three decades as a clinical psychologist carefully monitoring the field's developments, I find that the energy approach presented in this book is the innovation that has made the most profound difference in helping my clients. Energy psychology can shift problematic beliefs, behaviours, and emotions so rapidly because it allows the therapist to alter the client's brain chemistry with a precision yet gentleness that is unprecedented within psychotherapy. And while energy methods can be extraordinary tools in the hands of a skilled clinician, perhaps their most important application is how empowering they can be in your own hands.

## WHAT IS ENERGY PSYCHOLOGY?

When James Reston, a *New York Times* reporter accompanying Henry Kissinger on a visit to Communist China in July 1971, had an acute appendicitis attack, Chinese doctors performed an emergency appendectomy. Reston suffered from postoperative abdominal pain, which was treated with acupuncture, a routine procedure in many Chinese hospitals. The publicity surrounding Reston's successful acupuncture treatment, which included a front-page article in the *Times,* is credited with having opened Western minds to the practice of acupuncture. By 2005, the American Academy of Medical Acupuncture had over 1,600 members, and the World Health Organization listed more than fifty conditions for which acupuncture was believed to be effective.

Since the early 1980s, Western mental-health practitioners have been finding ways to apply the principles of acupuncture to psychological issues, patterned initially on the work of California psychologist Roger Callahan and Australian psychiatrist John Diamond. While acupuncture is usually associated with the use of needles, less invasive procedures—such as tapping or massaging specific points on the surface of the skin—can also produce the desired effects. This allows therapists not trained in the use of acupuncture needles to still apply the principles of acupuncture, and it allows you to use them on a self-help basis as well.

Energy is the blueprint, the infrastructure, the invisible foundation for the health of your body. Your body is composed of energy pathways and energy centres that are in a dynamic interplay with your cells, organs, moods, and thoughts. If you can shift these energies, you can influence your health, emotions, and state of mind. These energies include electromagnetic impulses, such as those that can be recorded by an MRI or EEG, as well as more subtle energies, which existing scientific instruments are not able to detect. But cultures that are closer to nature have developed disciplines— such as acupuncture, yoga, and qi gong—for working with these energies. As the field of energy psychology is maturing, it is drawing from these traditional systems while also staying consistent with the storehouse of knowledge offered by contemporary Western science and psychology.

Energy psychology, in fact, builds upon conventional psychotherapies. It works within the context of established psychological principles such as the decisive role of the conditioned response in human activity and the ways that early experiences shape current emotional and behavioural patterns. But energy psychology also has a special card in its deck. Stimulating energy points on the skin, paired with specified mental activities, can instantly shift your brain's electrochemistry to:

- help overcome unwanted emotions such as fear, guilt, shame, jealousy, or anger,
- help change unwanted habits and behaviour, and
- enhance your abilities to love, succeed, and enjoy life

The procedure allows virtually anyone who learns how to use it greater emotional control, inner peace, and effectiveness in the world. But this was not always my assessment of the approach.

## A SCEPTIC'S JOURNEY

My personal voyage into the perspective reflected here occurred over many years and with much resistance. I happened to marry a woman,

Donna Eden, who was destined to become one of the world's most renowned natural healers. For the first nineteen years or so of our relationship, I did not know what to make of her work. I had early in my own career served for seven years on the faculty of The Johns Hopkins University School of Medicine, a fount of innovation in health care, but I'd never seen anything like this. As I witnessed people coming to see her from all over the world with serious illnesses report improvement after a session or two, I explained to myself that these outcomes were a product of Donna's empathy, charisma, belief in the power of her methods, and perhaps a peculiar healing presence. I certainly did not think it was a system that could be taught or replicated, and the "subtle energy" explanations that were bandied about by alternative healers seemed more confusing than clarifying.

Donna was receiving overtures to write a book and she asked me, scepticism notwithstanding, to help her tackle the job. The next two-year period was an amazing process. I interviewed her, day after day. I could not pose a question that she could not persuasively answer from within her energy paradigm. Granted, she had one little quirk that was hard to verify: a lifelong ability to "see" energy as if it were as visible as the print on this page. Repeatedly, she had, by simply looking at a person's body, made health assessments that were later confirmed by medical tests. While her abilities to see and read energies were far beyond anything I'd personally experienced, her explanations remained coherent no matter how hard I tried to poke holes. That, combined with her accurate medical evaluations and impressive cure rate, pushed me to conclude that effective healing forces were somehow being mobilized by her "energy" approach.

Once the ability to derive meaningful information by reading the body's energies is accepted, then Donna's method turns out to have a strong internal logic. Those who can see energy—and Donna is by no means unique in this—report that the material world is patterned on a "blueprint of energetic forms." Medical intuitives who can recognize problems in the flow of the body's energies (a new genre of electronic instruments can also identify such abnormalities[2]) are able to accurately predict the kinds of physical problems that are likely to emerge before any symptoms or other signs have been detected. And they can prevent the brewing illness by restoring the energy flow. Many healing traditions understand this relationship. In some provinces of ancient China, where work with the body's energies was highly refined, you paid the doctor to keep you healthy. The recognition of energy disruptions before symptoms appeared allowed those disruptions to be corrected rather than to progress and finally erupt into a cancer or heart failure or nervous disorder. If you got sick, more intensive treatments were offered, but they were free.

I eventually realized from the discussions with Donna leading to her book that she operates according to principles that are highly empirical, a fact that had eluded me for nearly two decades. Her approach is based on observation (though through an unusual lens) and experimentation. She sees and feels where the energies are not flowing or not in balance or not in harmony, uses her hands or other means to try to correct the problem and, based on what happens, figures out the next step. Everyone's hands actually have an electromagnetic field extending beyond the fingers, so simply holding one's hand over an affected part of the body can have a therapeutic effect, as can massaging, tapping, or holding specific energy points on the skin. Other techniques might include asking the client to move or stretch or contract in designated ways.

Basing her approach on such methods, and also drawing from ancient as well as modern practices—including acupuncture, Applied Kinesiology, and Touch for Health—Donna had formulated hundreds of interventions for correcting specific kinds of problems in the energy system. Why couldn't these interventions be systematized and made available to anyone wishing to learn them, whether or not they have a special facility in sensing the body's energies? This became one of our central objectives in writing *Energy Medicine*. Now, with the book widely distributed (U.S.

sales in excess of 100,000 copies, and a dozen foreign editions) and many students trained, a plethora of reports has come to us that the procedures work whether self-applied or applied by practitioners who do not have Donna's sight.

*Energy Medicine* was released in January 1999, and we headed out for a six-month workshop and publicity tour. I took a sabbatical from my private practice as a clinical psychologist in Ashland, Oregon. As the close of the six months approached, the book seemed to be hitting a cultural nerve and at least one reviewer had already referred to it as the "classic" in its field. Demand for additional talks and trainings throughout the world became compelling. I returned to Ashland and, with strong misgivings, closed what had been a deeply satisfying clinical practice in order to support this new turn in Donna's journey.

While these were exciting developments, I also mourned the loss of my practice and recognized that I might be leaving forever a career I loved. I was already in my fifties, and I had no idea where energy medicine would lead me. Where it led was right back into psychology. Many of Donna's students were psychotherapists who were applying energy interventions to psychological issues. Because of their influence, I began to study with some of the pioneers in this area. Energy psychology had developed independently of Donna's work, though they are both part of the same Zeitgeist. While I was now open to an energy paradigm, as I educated myself about energy psychology, I discovered that despite this being a relatively new area, it was already rife with controversy, incompatible explanations, and deep schisms about procedures and appropriate claims. This reignited my scepticism, which was further fed because the techniques used in energy psychology look exceedingly strange.

Something else happened, however, that in my mind overshadowed the field's odd procedures and lack of coherent explanations. The outcomes I witnessed seemed remarkable. For a relatively wide range of complaints, the results were more rapid and consistent than anything I'd experienced in my thirty years of clinical practice.

One of the first times I publicly demonstrated the approach, following my own training and certification in it, was during a six-day residential workshop I was teaching in South Africa. Many of the participants were leaders in their communities who had come to learn about the unconscious beliefs and motivations that shape a person's life, what I call a "personal mythology."[3] I had been formulating ideas for integrating energy interventions into the personal mythology model, but I was uncertain how to introduce them. At the close of the first evening, an opening appeared. One of the participants told the group, with great embarrassment, that she was terrified of snakes and was afraid to walk through a grassy area from the meeting room to her cabin, about one hundred feet away. Several participants offered to escort her. Sensing that she could rapidly be helped with this phobia, I thought this might also lend itself to a credible introduction of energy methods. I arranged—with her tense but trusting permission—for a guide at the game reserve where the workshop was being held to bring a snake into the class at 10 A.M. the next morning (having the snake there was not necessary for the treatment to work, only to demonstrate that it had worked).

I set up the chairs so the snake and the handler were about twenty feet away from her, but within her range of vision. I asked her what it is like to have a snake in the room. She replied, "I am okay as long as I don't look at it, but I have to tell you, I left my body two minutes ago." She was dissociating, a psychological defense mechanism in which specific, anxiety-provoking thoughts, emotions, or physical sensations are blocked from a person's awareness. Within less than half an hour, using methods that you will learn in this book, she was able to imagine being close to a snake without feeling fear. I asked her if she was ready to walk over to the snake, across the room. As she approached it, she appeared confident. The confidence soon grew into enthusiasm as she began to comment on the snake's beauty. She asked the handler if she could touch it. Haltingly but triumphantly, she did. She reported that she was fully present in her body. A couple of days later, she joined the group on a nature walk, and at the end when someone asked her if it was difficult, given her snake phobia, a surprised look came over her face. She had never even thought about it. Her lifelong fear had evaporated and, on follow-up two years later, had not returned.

I have now worked with many cases that were similarly dramatic and have interviewed dozens of practitioners whose clinical records contain literally thousands of instances that corroborate my personal experiences. This does not constitute scientific proof—case reports never can—but it is not a one-person medicine show either.

## SORTING OUT THE CLAIMS

The conflicting claims and theories among the field's practitioners were still troubling. Here we had a method that had leaped ahead of all available scientific explanations. It was perhaps unprecedented for an approach with so little theoretical or research support to generate thousands of reports of striking clinical results from hundreds of fully credentialled professionals who represented the whole spectrum of backgrounds and theoretical orientations. What was going on?

As a way of sorting through the field's claims and confusion I, along with Donna and Fred Gallo, Ph.D. (author of *Energy Psychology*, the first academic book to introduce professionals to the field), invited an advisory board of twenty-four of energy psychology's pioneers and recognized leaders to carry out a project that focused on one question: What are the essential principles and procedures that psychotherapists new to energy psychology should master before introducing the methods into their own practice?

The project transformed my computer into a lightning rod for the field's controversies. After four years of wrestling with core questions, a consensus was built, and *Energy Psychology Interactive*, a comprehensive home-study course to introduce clinicians to the field, was released early in 2004. It consisted of a forty-hour computer-based training program on CD-ROM, a companion book, and a client self-help guide. While the broader mental-health field had been slow to embrace the energy paradigm, our program received surprisingly positive reviews. In one of them, the journal *Clinical Psychology* called energy psychology "an exciting and rapidly developing realm" and, after describing some of the controversy surrounding it, concluded that "emerging research suggests that these methods are very effective indeed, extremely rapid, and thoroughly gentle."[4] In a landmark review, the American Psychological Association referred to energy psychology as "a new discipline that has been receiving attention due to its speed and effectiveness with difficult cases."[5] The Association for Comprehensive Energy Psychology, a 700-member professional organization, honored the program with its Outstanding Contribution Award.

## HOW THIS BOOK CAME ABOUT

A book based on the authority of the professional training program but designed to bring the new methods to the general reader seemed a natural next step. But it carried some special challenges. By introducing health and mental-health professionals to the field, *Energy Psychology Interactive* had the buffer of each practitioner's professional judgment before the methods were applied with any particular individual. A popular book, however, would not have that buffer.

The person with by far the most experience in bringing energy psychology methods to the general public was Gary Craig. Gary is not a psychotherapist by training, but I had noticed in doing the research for *Energy Psychology Interactive* that many of the leaders in the field would regularly seek his opinion, or direct me towards him, about various professional questions. His kind responses to my requests always offered insightful, practical, experience-based guidance. In addition, he had personally, or through his home-study programs, trained more professionals and nonprofessionals in the basic methods of energy psychology than anyone else; and his training manuals, videos, e-newsletter, and website constituted a significant portion of the field's evolving literature.

The thought of inviting Gary onto the team was almost instantaneous. Trained as an engineer at Stanford, Gary has a remarkable eye for what works and what doesn't work, and he had been one of the early synthesizers of NLP (neurolinguistic programming), self-hypnosis, and other methods for personal improvement. On studying Roger Callahan's "Thought Field Therapy" (TFT), he was stunned to find that simple physical interventions could help people overcome unwanted emotional reactions and conditions with speed, efficiency, and lasting results. He reworked Callahan's approach into the Emotional Freedom Techniques (EFT), making the methods more accessible to the general public. He has now, for more than a decade, been tirelessly advocating the idea that emotional freedom is everyone's birthright and can be reclaimed by skillfully applying EFT's simple set of procedures, which have powerful neurological consequences. A promoter's missionary zeal does not particularly impress me. Yet the closer I looked, the more impressed I was with the ways Gary's training, website, and newsletter were guiding people to use the methods effectively and with a wide range of issues.

Meanwhile, on the domestic front, Donna had in her own way been practicing energy psychology for a quarter of a century, and her methods were quite different from TFT or its derivatives. First of all, she did not separate the physical from the psychological in her approach. Second, while TFT, EFT, and various other methods that fall within energy psychology begin by focusing on an issue or presenting a problem—usually desired changes in a behavioural, thought, or emotional pattern—Donna's focus was on the body as an energy system. Yet her results often yielded strong psychological benefits.

I asked Donna if she would bring her experience with *seeing* how energy moves when dealing with psychological issues to the book, checking the concepts and procedures against her own observations, and introducing methods from energy medicine that might augment the more traditional energy psychology approach (this became chapters 6 and 7). She met the idea with enthusiasm, and the blueprint for the project had been laid. I have written the first draft of each chapter based on interviews with my co-authors and consultation with their earlier writings, combined with my own clinical experience, and they have then reviewed and further revised each chapter

This is a book that can be approached with a "show-me" attitude. Experiment with the methods it presents. Growing numbers are finding them to be potent and rewarding.

# 1

# YOUR ELECTRIC BRAIN

Information transmitted by one neuron and received by another takes
the form of electrical signals generated by charged atoms.

—JEFFREY M. SCHWARTZ, M.D., *The Mind and the Brain*

Every thought or emotion that you experience causes a reaction in a
specific area of your brain. Joy or sadness, love or jealousy—all
have distinctive counterparts in the way your neurons fire; modern electronic imaging technology allows us to view the intricate dance in your
brain's energies that accompanies your every thought and feeling. If you
were to watch the screen of a brain-imaging device such as a PET scan-
ner while you were experiencing substantial stress or anxiety, you would
see specific areas receiving arousal signals that make the screen light up
like a Christmas tree.

If your brain recognizes a similarity between a distressing situation
from your past and what you are seeing or hearing in the moment—even
though there is no current threat or danger—the same distress signals that
you experienced in the earlier situation can become activated. Although it
may seem unreasonable, the emotional response can be overwhelming. Or
it might be more subtle. Perhaps your spouse's voice hits just the tone of

your parent's voice right before you got spanked, and you are suddenly angry at your spouse and fiercely defending actions that weren't being criticized. Though people often are not aware of it, this basic sequence—where a current situation activates an outdated response—is at the root of many of their difficulties, from dysfunctional patterns in their relationships and self-defeating choices on the job to unnamed anxieties, unprovoked bouts of depression, and irrational jealousy, fear, or anger.

Energy psychology shows how you can stimulate specific points on your skin that will send electrochemical signals directly to your brain. If at the same time you hold in your mind a situation that triggers an unwanted emotional response, you can actually *shift your brain's response* to that situation. It is an unconventional approach, yet it frequently produces undeniable improvement in only one session and often works where other approaches do not. You can also stimulate points to help you achieve specific personal goals, like thinking more positively, speaking more confidently, or eating more sensibly. This book shows you how.

## RAPID SUCCESS WHERE YEARS OF THERAPY HAD FAILED

Despite seventeen years of psychotherapy for symptoms of posttraumatic-stress disorder (PTSD) tracing back to the Vietnam war, Rich's[1] insomnia was so disabling that he had checked himself in two months earlier for yet another round of inpatient treatment at the Veterans' Administration (V.A.) Hospital in Los Angeles. When he tried to sleep, any of more than a hundred haunting war memories might intrude into his awareness. He felt trapped in these overwhelming images, and every night was dreaded and interminably long. Every day was clouded with exhaustion and further anxiety. He could not function effectively. He also suffered from a severe height phobia that had developed over the course of some fifty parachute jumps he had made during the war.

Rich was one of twenty patients treated by Gary Craig and his associate, Adrienne Fowlie, during a weeklong visit after a hospital administrator had invited them to demonstrate the effects of energy-oriented therapy on emotional trauma. Rich's treatment first focused on his height phobia. He was asked to think about a situation involving heights. His fear level shot up immediately. He was wearing shorts, and he pointed out that the hair on his legs was literally standing up. At the same time, as he brought to mind the terror of facing a height, he was directed to stimulate a series of electromagnetically sensitive points on his skin by tapping them with his fingertips. Within fifteen minutes of using this procedure, Rich reported no fear reaction when imagining situations involving heights. To test this, Gary had him walk out onto the fire escape of the third floor of the building and look down. Rich expressed amazement when he had no fear response whatsoever.

Gary then focused on several of Rich's most intense war memories, using the same tapping procedure. They, too, were similarly "neutralized" within an hour. He still remembered them, of course, but they had lost their debilitating emotional charge. Gary taught Rich a technique for stimulating energy points that he could apply to his remaining memories outside the treatment setting. He complied with this homework assignment, focusing on several of the more intense memories. Eventually, there was a "generalization effect" in that, after a number of the traumatic memories had been neutralized, the others lost their overwhelming emotional charge. Haunting memories simply stopped intruding into Rich's awareness, even at night. Within a few days his insomnia had cleared, and he discontinued his medication. He checked himself out of the hospital shortly after that. At a two-month telephone follow-up, he was still free of the height phobia, the insomnia, and the intrusion of disturbing war memories.

Most of the twenty V.A. Hospital patients that Gary and Adrienne worked with enjoyed near-immediate, readily observable results for PTSD symptoms that had in many instances resisted years of psychotherapy.

Sessions with six of these men were videotaped and are available for inspection,[2] including the work with Rich.

Successful energy interventions have been demonstrated in a range of difficult situations. In Kosovo, for instance, 105 victims of ethnic violence, after receiving energy psychology treatments from an international team in 2000 over a period of several months (TFT, or Thought Field Therapy, was the primary modality), experienced "complete recovery" (based on self-reports) from the posttraumatic emotional effects of 247 of the 249 memories of torture, rape, and witnessing the massacre of loved ones they had identified.[3] Although such anecdotal accounts are scientifically equivocal, their impact on the local community was profound, with the chief medical officer of Kosovo, Dr. Skkelzen Syla, stating in a letter of appreciation:

> Many well-funded relief organizations have treated the posttraumatic stress here in Kosova. Some of our people had limited improvement but Kosova had no major change or real hope until . . . we referred our most difficult patients to [the international treatment team]. The success from TFT was 100% for every patient, and they are still smiling until this day [and, indeed, in formal follow-ups at an average of five months after the treatment, each was free of relapse].

If your own situation is as tough as or tougher than Rich's or than that of the victims of ethnic violence in Kosovo, you should be using this program only in consultation with a psychotherapist. If not, some important cautions still apply. So in either case, please carefully consider the guidelines presented later in this chapter under the heading "What This Book Can Do and What It Can't Do" before applying its methods.

# RAPID RESULTS, SLOW ACCEPTANCE

You might think based on the outcomes described above that every relief organization and every V.A. hospital in America would be experimenting with these methods. That is not how it played out. In professional practice, as in human history, an old way is not necessarily immediately replaced just because a better one appears, particularly when the new way cannot be understood using familiar concepts. Most relief workers have still not heard of, or at least have not investigated, the methods offered by energy psychology. As for V.A. hospitals, the evolution has been interesting. Initially there did not seem to be *any* curiosity on the part of the treatment staff. Even with the conspicuous, rapid help the men described above were receiving for the stubborn symptoms of PTSD, none of their therapists accepted invitations to sit in on the sessions. None responded to offers to watch the videotapes. And though most of the patients expressed strong enthusiasm and appreciation, no one on the clinical staff indicated any interest in hearing more or learning more.

The V.A.-hospital episode is a microcosm of the way much of the psychotherapy community initially responded to energy psychology and its unconventional techniques.[4] Though unfortunate—people such as Rich who could have been helped haven't been helped—it is also understandable. Seasoned clinicians have learned, through hard experience, to be reluctant about embracing new methods before they have been scientifically substantiated; and the methods discussed here are just starting to command the attention of serious researchers. While the professional atmosphere is becoming more receptive[5]—a number of V.A. hospitals, for instance, were a decade later routinely training their clinical staffs in these methods with good results[6]—psychotherapists are, of course, sceptical upon hearing claims that strange and unfamiliar methods produced near-instant cures of long-standing problems. Beyond suspicion about the odd-looking procedures used in energy psychology, therapy is not believed to be so rapid. Time is needed for building rapport, examining the antecedents of the problem, exploring the meaning of the symptoms in the person's life, assessing which therapeutic modalities are most appropriate for the unique situation, applying them, observing, and revising.

What might account for the contrast between the videotaped outcomes with the patients at the V.A. hospital, corroborated by thousands of similar cases reported by growing numbers of energy-oriented psychotherapists, and conventional wisdom regarding the therapeutic process? If we try to understand the results in terms of the stock concepts of psychotherapy— such as insight, cognitive restructuring, reward and punishment, positive expectation, or the curative powers of the relationship—they make little sense. If we examine electrochemical shifts in brain chemistry that are brought about by stimulating points on the skin that are known for their electrical conductivity, however, a coherent explanation for these rapid shifts in long-standing patterns of mind, emotion, and behaviour begins to emerge.

Brain-scan images can tell the story visually. Scans from Dr Joaquín Andrade's study (see pp. 301–5) showed a patient's progression over twelve treatment sessions, conducted during a four-week period. The treatment involved tapping electrochemically sensitive areas of the skin while bringing to mind anxiety-provoking images. The patient was being treated for generalized anxiety disorder. Where a fear or phobia is a response to a specific type of situation (such as Rich's fear of heights), generalized anxiety disorder is characterized by persistent *free-floating* anxiety, accompanied by symptoms such as tension, sweating, trembling, light-headedness, or irritability (such as the unrelenting nervousness, insomnia, and physical tension that were part of Rich's PTSD). The brain scans showed that the disturbed brain-wave activity found at the start of treatment with the patient suffering from generalized anxiety disorder had normalized by the end of the treatment.

By comparison, matched patients at the same clinic who were successfully treated with cognitive behaviour therapy, a conventional treatment for generalized anxiety disorder, showed a similar progression of brain scans, but it took a greater number of sessions before the brain-wave patterns had normalized and, on one-year follow-up, the improvement was less likely to have held. Patients who were treated with medication also showed a decrease in symptoms, but the brain scans did not show significant changes in the brain-wave patterns, suggesting that the medication had masked rather than treated the disorder. And indeed, in addition to frequent side effects being reported with the medication, symptoms tended to return when the medication was discontinued.

## How Do Energy Treatments Work?

Growing understanding about the relationship between electromagnetic energy and the molecules that carry information throughout the body is causing conventional medicine to rapidly update the old perspective that treats the person primarily as a bag of chemicals and organs. The EEG, EKG, PET, and MRI are diagnostic instruments that allow us to glimpse the dazzling intelligence of the body as an electrical system. Your brain, for instance, consists of some one hundred billion neurons that each connect *electrochemically* with up to ten thousand other neurons in governing your every movement, feeling, and thought. Despite this incomprehensible complexity, powerful treatments are being devised that influence the brain's electrical activity in precisely the ways needed to overcome a range of psychiatric and other medical disorders.

- The magnetic stimulation of specific areas of the brain, for instance, has been shown to help with major depression that did not respond to other therapies,[7] as well as with bipolar disorders.[8]
- The surgical implantation of deep brain stimulators—devices that deliver precisely targeted electrical stimulation in the brain— has helped thousands of patients with Parkinson's disease to

control their symptoms. These "brain pacemakers" are also being used with some success to stimulate the vagus nerve in treating severe depression, obsessive-compulsive disorders, and other neurological conditions.[9]

More closely related to the approach described in this book, because it is based on the client's own efforts, is neurofeedback training. By using EEG biofeedback to teach patients how to alter their brain-wave patterns, improvement has been demonstrated for a wide range of psychological disorders, including attention deficit disorder, hyperactivity, depression, anxiety, migraines, panic attacks, PTSD, seizures, impulsivity, and cognitive performance.[10] Neurofeedback training does, however, require expensive equipment and has a longer learning curve than stimulating points on the skin.

Except for such still-rare and sometimes invasive applications, however, Western medicine has so far produced very few treatments that take full advantage of the ways the body's energies can be directed to mediate the complex flow of biological information that influences health. Energy psychology, on the other hand, is part of a coming wave of such approaches.

While Western medicine may be slow to understand the body's subtle energies and even slower to accept that these energies can be used in healing, other cultures have been working with energy healing for thousands of years. From tribal healers throughout the world to Hindu yogic practices to traditional Chinese medicine, models for working directly with the body as an energy system are plentiful. One of the most elaborately developed systems, and one that has held up relatively well to Western scientific scrutiny, is the practice of acupuncture. Acupuncture is not only among the oldest known medical treatments, extending back some five thousand years, it is one of the most widely used health-care systems on the planet.

In acupuncture, the tips of needles are inserted at specific points in the skin to treat pain or disease. An acupuncture point, or acupoint, is a tiny area of the skin with significantly lower electrical resistance than other areas of the skin.[11] Acupoints also have a higher concentration of receptors that are sensitive to mechanical stimulation; and specific points, when stimulated, send signals directly to areas of the brain that are associated with emotions. The electromagnetic properties of the acupuncture points can be activated by tapping, massaging, or holding them, as well as through more intrusive means such as the insertion of needles, electrical stimulation, or the application of heat. At least 360 acupoints are distributed along a network of energy pathways that is called the meridian system. A more accurate translation (from the Mandarin) than "point" is "hollow," and because of their lower electrical resistance, acupuncture points have been called "windows" into the body's energy system.[12]

These entryways into the body's energy system can be used for restoring physical and mental health.[13] Stimulating an acupoint can send impulses to areas of the body that are far away from the point itself. For instance, an acupuncture needle inserted into a specific point on the toe can be seen in a "functional MRI" (fMRI) as affecting blood activity in the brain,[14] though no nerve, vascular, or other physical connections are known to exist. Another study, also using an MRI, demonstrated that stimulating specific points on the skin not only *changed* brain activity; *it also deactivated areas of the brain that are involved with the experiences of fear and pain.*[15] Stimulating certain acupuncture points also causes the secretion of serotonin,[16] a neurotransmitter that, if not present in sufficient amounts, is associated with depression, anxiety, and addictions.

## A BASIC HYPOTHESIS

The implications of these findings for working with psychological issues are enormous. Here is a *preliminary* explanation for the near-instant, lasting results seen in the snake-phobia case reported in the Introduction and the PTSD cases reported earlier in this chapter. First, the following is an outline of the known biological sequence that is involved when a typical, threat-based, dysfunctional emotional response has been triggered:

1. A harmless sight, sound, smell, feeling, or thought (the trigger) is recognized by the amygdala, a part of the brain that identifies threat, as being similar to a previous experience that involved physical danger or emotional threat.

2. The amygdala sends impulses to the autonomic nervous system that elicit the "fight, flight, or freeze" alarm response. Chemicals such as adrenaline, noradrenaline, and cortisol are released into the bloodstream, causing the heart rate, blood pressure, and other bodily processes to undergo a series of dramatic changes. At the same time, primitive areas of the brain, designed to respond to threat, shape perception and thought. The rational mind has little involvement in this sequence.

3. The physical sensations of the alarm response are experienced as angerlike feelings (fight), fearlike feelings (flight), or an inability to take action (freeze).

And here is an outline of the way we believe energy interventions *interrupt* the above sequence:

1. The triggering image is brought to mind while physically stimulating a series of acupoints that send impulses directly to the amygdala, which inhibit the alarm response.

2. These impulses also cause a reduction, within the amygdala, of the number of neural connections between the image and the alarm response.

3. After a number of repetitions of number 1, the image can then be brought to mind, or the situation can be experienced directly, without eliciting the alarm response.

This explanation addresses the way that stimulating acupoints may help overcome psychological problems.[17] Other research holds implications for the way energy interventions can enhance peak performance and the achievement of goals. It has been established within sports psychology, for instance, that mental rehearsal can improve performance. Vividly imagining fifty successful free throws initiates neurological shifts[18] and increases shooting effectiveness on the basketball court.[19] Reports from energy psychology practitioners suggest that combining such imagery with acupoint stimulation intensifies this effect. Based upon these observations and the above speculation about the role of the amygdala in the treatment, a tentative hypothesis can be formed to explain the rapid improvement that is so frequently reported after energy interventions.

**Hypothesis:** Stimulating specific electromagnetically sensitive points on the skin while bringing a psychological problem or goal to mind can help a person overcome that problem or reach that goal by changing the chemistry in the amygdala and other areas of the brain.

## ARE FEAR AND ANXIETY THE PRIMARY CONDITIONS ENERGY PSYCHOLOGY CAN TREAT?

Do the psychological problems that energy interventions can effectively treat go beyond phobias and other anxiety-related issues? There is to date no published research on this question, but impressions from various clinicians are available. The only systematic examination at this point of the conditions for which energy-oriented psychotherapy is most and least effective (indications and contraindications) is a substudy coming out of a fourteen-year investigation that was conducted in eleven clinics in South America, involving some 31,400 patients (details on p. 301, Appendix 3).

Clinicians who were not involved in the treatment assessed the outcome of energy interventions with a sample of patients that represented a wide spectrum of clinical disorders. They gave each case a subjective score of 1 to 5, estimating the effectiveness of the energy interventions in contrast to the conventional treatments that might have been used (a 5 indicated that the rater believed the energy approach was far more effective than the conventional treatment would have been; a 1 indicated that the rater believed it was far less effective than the conventional treatment would have been).

While highly subjective, these ratings were designed to help the South American clinics generate guidelines as they introduced energy techniques. The staff reports having found that the resulting guidelines were administratively useful and clinically trustworthy. This is, of course, still largely impressionistic, and the degree that the ratings might generalize to other settings is also unknown. But the ratings at least give an early glimpse into the conclusions of one group of practitioners.

Most anxiety disorders received a 4 or 5. These included panic disorders, agoraphobia, specific phobias, social phobias, separation anxiety, post-traumatic stress disorders, acute stress disorders, obsessive-compulsive disorders, and generalized anxiety disorders. The raters believed that the energy interventions were more effective or far more effective than other available treatments for these anxiety conditions. Also receiving a 5—and this is highly relevant for this book—were many of the emotional difficulties of everyday life, from unwarranted fears and anger to excessive feelings of guilt, shame, grief, jealousy, rejection, isolation, frustration, or love pain. Other conditions that were rated as more likely to respond to an energy approach included adjustment disorders, attention-deficit disorders, elimination disorders, impulse-control disorders, problems related to abuse or neglect, learning disorders, and communication disorders.

Cases receiving a 3 indicated that the rater believed that the energy intervention produced a result that would be about the equivalent of other available psychological treatments. This would suggest that maximum clinical advantage would be gained by combining the energy approach with the more conventional treatment. Conditions in this category included mild to moderate reactive depression, learning-skills disorders, motor-skills disorders, Tourette's syndrome, substance-abuse-related disorders, and eating disorders.

Cases where a conventional treatment approach was rated as being likely to have been more effective than the energy treatment included major endogenous depression, personality disorders, dissociative disorders, bipolar disorders, psychotic disorders, delirium, and dementia. Note that each of these conditions has a strong genetic or biological basis. Reports are nonetheless now appearing that people within these diagnostic categories have been helped by energy treatments with a range of life problems that are secondary to their condition.[20] Seasoned healers are also finding ways of adapting energy methods to treat the primary conditions themselves. But the typical practitioner with knowledge only in the rudimentary use of acupoint stimulation should, at a minimum, have special training and experience in working with these conditions before using energy interventions so they can be applied in conjunction with more established methods.

## WHAT THIS BOOK CAN DO AND WHAT IT CAN'T DO

The place of energy interventions within the field of psychotherapy is still unfolding. With some kinds of problems, such as uncomplicated phobias and many mild to moderate anxieties, the energy intervention itself can often overcome the problem. With other psychiatric disorders, energy interventions are being combined with more traditional approaches, and a growing number of clinical reports suggests that they significantly increase the effectiveness of the standard approaches. Therapy is still about insight, intention, positive thinking, cognitive restructuring, and the healing power of relationship, but being able to directly shift the energies that appear to impact the neurology that maintains psychological problems is a powerful adjunct.

The predecessor to this book is a self-help guide that was originally included in the *Energy Psychology Interactive* training program as a resource for psychotherapists to give to their clients to support and reinforce the procedures being used in the office. As substantial anecdotal evidence was accumulating that the methods can be responsibly and effectively applied to a variety of everyday problems without the aid of a psychotherapist, we made the *Self-Help Guide* available to the general public. This book expands upon that earlier work. Its procedures can help you with many day-to-day psychological and emotional challenges, but you also need to be aware of some significant limitations.

*The Healing Power of EFT and Energy Psychology* presents powerful tools for personal development. It does not, however, teach you how to become a psychotherapist, and it is not designed to work with psychiatric disorders without the involvement of a qualified mental-health professional. A small proportion of the population has a physical or emotional frailty so severe that they should not attempt *any* potent healing intervention without the presence and guidance of a skilled professional. The program is also not presented as an independent "self-help" resource for the treatment of such conditions as major depression, severe anxiety, personality disorders, bipolar disorders, dissociative disorders, the aftermath of severe trauma or any substantial bodily injury, substance abuse, or psychotic disorders. Please enlist the help of a qualified psychotherapist if you suffer from any of these conditions. Competent help is available to you (see Resources, p. 318). The techniques presented in this book may supplement the procedures used by a psychotherapist when serious psychological problems are present, but they do not substitute for them.

They may, however, be effective tools for helping you negotiate the ups and downs of daily life and for reaching goals that have eluded you.

They may be used to help you shift self-defeating patterns of thought or behaviour. The methods may assist you in countering emotions that you consider intrusive or irrational, such as inappropriate anger, grief, guilt, jealousy, fear, attachment, self-judgment, worry, sadness, or shame. They may help you reach any of a wide range of personal goals, from healthier eating habits to speaking with greater poise to peak performance in a chosen sport. They may set you on a journey where you learn to respond to your feelings more skillfully, cultivating greater inner harmony and outward success. They are offered with the clear intention of the authors that they provide you with potent tools for navigating your way through life's challenges more skillfully, more effectively, and more joyfully.

---

IN A NUTSHELL: Energy psychology is a contemporary application of methods that are at least 4,500 years old. Specific points on the skin can be stimulated for distinct neurological effects, and this principle can be used for helping to overcome a range of psychological problems. While the research supporting this approach is still in its early stages, reports of effective treatments from hundreds of therapists representing the spectrum of clinical orientations are provocative. This book will provide you with the tools you need to experiment with these methods in your own life.

---

# 2

# A BASIC RECIPE

By stimulating the flow of energy, the body's own healing network
can be activated.

—ROGER CALLAHAN, Ph.D., *Tapping the Healer Within*

I n this chapter, you will learn one of the most basic protocols from
energy psychology for reducing distress,[1] and you will practice it by
applying it to an unpleasant memory. You will begin by giving a rating to
the amount of distress you feel when you bring this memory to mind and
end by assessing the degree to which you were able to reduce the distress.
Once you have developed the ability to reduce the amount of distress
caused by a troubling memory, the following two chapters will show you
how to adapt the same methods to virtually any psychological problem or
goal you wish (within the limits outlined at the end of chapter 1).

If at any point that you are using the techniques presented in this book
you begin to feel overwhelmed, uncertain, or upset, please read "If the
Program Becomes Unsettling" (Appendix 2). You may want to glance
over that material now. As you go through the program, know that it is
there to be consulted at any time you wish. Throughout the book please
also keep in mind the following principle: Tapping on acupuncture points

to decrease the emotional charge around a past memory requires only that *you know* what you are focusing upon—clinical experience has shown that *it is not necessary* and *it is not useful* to immerse yourself in a traumatic memory or in any way retraumatize yourself for energy psychology methods to have their benefits.

Let's begin. Bring to mind an early memory that holds an unpleasant emotional charge. Perhaps it was a time you were embarrassed in front of your classroom. Perhaps it was when a relationship ended. Or your family moved to a strange new place. Or you were betrayed or humiliated. Or a pet died. Or you made a terrible blunder. Or you had to hurt someone you loved. For this first time through, we suggest that you not choose a core traumatic event, say a devastating loss or a memory of physical or sexual abuse. But the loss or betrayal or embarrassment or blunder can be substantial. If you cannot think of an incident from early in your life, choose one that is more recent. Everyone has at least a few, though you may have to become still and go inward to find one. You will need a sheet of paper. On it, write a brief description of the memory—just a sentence or two.

## PRELIMINARIES

You will be exploring a new idea in this chapter. Virtually everyone in the mental-health profession agrees that negative, self-limiting emotions can often be traced back to early life experiences that were emotionally damaging. A current event psychologically activates the early experience, and this results in a defensive emotional response that leads to choices and life patterns that are restrictive and dysfunctional. The new idea is that there is a step between the memory and the emotion, and that step is *a disturbance in your body's energies*. The electrochemical events triggered in the amygdala by the memory are detailed on pp. 291-305, Appendix 3, but to express it very simply:

| A Troubling Memory | leads to → | An Energy Disturbance | leads to → | A Self-Defeating Emotional Response |

Conventional psychotherapy focuses on the memory. Energy psychology focuses on the energy disturbance as well as the memory. Focusing on the memory without changing the energies it evokes can perpetuate rather than resolve the emotional problem, as when some people in psychotherepy delve deeper and deeper into understanding the sources of their difficulties without making any significant changes in their behaviour or lifestyle. Focusing on the energy disturbance, as you will be learning to do in this chapter, can resolve the emotional problem so rapidly that it can be hard to believe that you are not feeling it anymore. The woman described in the Introduction, who walked up to and touched the snake after a lifelong terror of snakes, was amazed that half an hour of tapping on certain points dissolved her phobia. She could have talked about and analyzed her fear incessantly, and it is not likely that this would have changed it. When Rich climbed onto the fire escape after a few minutes of tapping and felt no fear, his surprise was surpassed only by his relief.

We know, based on our combined work with thousands of individuals, that witnessing such changes evokes people's scepticism, and we want to address yours. In demonstrations, people do not question that the change happened. They will see a friend who was terrified of public speaking calmly addressing a large group after a few minutes of treatment during a workshop. But they explain it according to frameworks with which they are familiar: "It was the power of suggestion." "It was a distraction technique." "Positive thinking can do that." "It was mind over matter." "It was the enthusiasm and persuasiveness of the therapist." "The person believed it would work, so it worked." People generally don't have a framework to conclude "Oh, of course, the energy system was being balanced while the person was tuned in to the problem, so naturally the unwanted emotional response was eliminated." But that is exactly what happens.

Fortunately, you do not need to believe it in order for it to work. In fact, people *rarely* "believe in" these techniques until they have seen them work a number of times. So we don't ask that you have any faith or belief in the methods, only that you carry them out precisely as described. Our insistence on staying strictly with the protocol is because, at this point, we hope these basic procedures will become automatic for you. Later in the book, we will discuss modifications and shortcuts.

Another reason people initially feel sceptical about the methods used in energy psychology is that they look strange. And we mean *really, really* strange. The protocol you are about to learn will have you talking to yourself, rolling your eyes around in your head, and humming a song while tapping on various parts of your body. These methods don't even remotely resemble psychology as most people think of it. In fact, the premise that these procedures could be doing anything that has a significant impact might be way beyond your sense of what is plausible. However, once you understand their neurological basis, you may wonder why they weren't discovered earlier (as, of course, they were, by Chinese doctors some five thousand years ago).

## SELECTING THE PROBLEM

While you initially will be working with the disturbing memory you selected earlier, the range of day-to-day goals that could be addressed might involve:

- **Emotional reactions**, such as "to overcome my resentment towards my mother" or "to stay calm and relaxed even when my spouse is treating me insensitively."
- **Physical reactions**, such as "to stop the stress headaches I get at work" or "to keep my heart from pounding so hard when I am about to ask someone out on a date."

Habits of thought, such as "to focus more on my son's strengths and achievements than on his shortcomings" or "to stop dwelling upon unfinished tasks whenever I might have a moment to relax."

Patterns of behaviour, such as "to chew more slowly" or "to stop going to the refrigerator whenever I feel agitated."

## RATING THE PROBLEM

Once you have selected the issue or memory you wish to work on, the next step is to rate it on a scale of 0 (no distress) to 10 (extreme distress, or the worst it has ever been), based on the amount of discomfort you experience when you think about it. Again, it is neither necessary nor desirable to relive a past trauma in order to have a successful outcome using energy techniques. If the issue you are focusing on is particularly intense, a variety of techniques can be used to keep the memory, situation, or feeling "at a distance." You could, for instance, give it a rating by "viewing" the memory or situation through a long tunnel. You could simply think about *what it would be like* to think about the issue. Or you can use the "tearless trauma" technique, where you simply *guess* at what the emotional intensity would be (on the scale of 0 to 10) *if* you were to vividly imagine the traumatic incident.

If, on the other hand, you find yourself having difficulty getting your mind around the problem or accessing your feelings about it, you might take more time to attune inwardly while focusing and breathing deeply. You could visualize circumstances that activate the problem, or replay in your imagination a situation in which you have in the past or might in the future experience the problem. Once more, it is not necessary or desirable to immerse yourself emotionally in the memory—only that you touch into it lightly. This is enough that it will be neurologically active while you are doing the tapping. For instance, think about a scary movie right now and your feelings about it. If the movie were your traumatic memory, that is all the activation that would be necessary. You don't have to relive the movie scene by scene.

Whether it works best for you to keep the memory you will be working with at an emotional distance or to actually make it more vivid, your task at this point is to rate the intensity of discomfort the memory evokes in you *right now*, as you tune into it (as contrasted with what you *think* you would feel if you were in the situation again). On your sheet of paper, write down a number from 0 to 10 indicating the amount of distress it causes you to think about the memory, with 10 being an extreme amount and 0 being none at all. You will be using this rating as a gauge of your progress as you go through the sequence. For some people, children in particular, a more concrete way of rating is preferred, such as indicating the amount of distress by drawing a shorter or longer line or extending both hands with palms facing to indicate "this much."

If your memory has several climactic points, focus on only one of them. These *crescendos* may need to be treated one at a time as separate aspects of the event. If the memory is of a car accident, for instance, the crescendos might include hearing the tyres skidding, realizing an accident is about to happen, the moment of impact, feeling your own injury, seeing others on the ground. You would treat each as a separate memory, but you will find that once you have neutralized your physiological response to a few of them, the rest will probably fall away quite readily. If your memory has several crescendos, select only one for now.

Measure the intensity of your memory as it exists in your body when you bring the memory to mind, *in the moment*, rather than what you think it *would be* in the actual situation. This is because the treatment corrects the energetic and neurological disruptions that occur *while you are thinking* about the problem or memory. Once the troubling emotion has been neutralized in this way, experience shows that this readily translates to situations that in the past might have evoked the emotion.

For instance, if you feel strong and irrational anger every time you encounter a policeman, you might close your eyes and bring to mind the first incident you can recall when you felt angry towards a police officer. You would assess the intensity of the anger you feel, on the scale of 0 to 10, *as it exists now,* while you think about this memory. If you rate it as a 9, for example, then you have a benchmark against which to measure your progress as you go through each round of treatment. When it has gone down to 0, you might work with another similar memory. Once you have removed the emotional charge from the memories related to policemen, you are likely to find that the next time you actually see a policeman, your anger will either not be aroused or will at least be substantially diminished. Of course your awareness of past injustices or other causes for your anger will not be erased, but their emotional grip on you will have been loosened and you won't continue to generalize the bad feeling to other situations just because they are superficially similar.

## A BASIC RECIPE FOR CHANGING AN EMOTIONAL RESPONSE

Our goal in this chapter is to provide you with a simple recipe you can use whenever you want to decrease the distress you feel in response to a memory, a situation as it is happening, or a situation that you anticipate. Derived from the Emotional Freedom Techniques (EFT), it is a recipe for increasing your inner peace and emotional freedom. A recipe, of course, calls for specific ingredients that must be added in a certain order. This recipe has only four ingredients, and two of them are identical. Once you have memorized the ingredients, a round of treatment can be performed in about a minute. The ingredients include:

1. The Setup
2. The Tapping Sequence (with Reminder Phrase)

3. The Nine-Gamut Procedure
4. The Tapping Sequence (with Reminder Phrase) repeated

We are suggesting that you do the steps exactly as we've described them so that the basic procedures become rote for you. But there is also one caveat. Even here as you are learning the method, it should not become so rote that you do not feel an emotional connection with the process. It is better to deviate from our instructions for finding the images or wordings you will be using if that helps you stay more emotionally connected with the procedures.

## INGREDIENT 1: THE SETUP

The first ingredient, the Setup, is a way of establishing a psychological and energetic receptiveness for change. Whenever you decide to change a habit of thought, behaviour, or emotion, the part of you that initially *established* that pattern may resist your efforts. Psychological and behavioural habits are often hard-won compromises, and they become embedded in your energy system, your neurology, and your lifestyle. The moment you think of changing one of these patterns, an energy disruption may occur that, if not effectively addressed, can interfere with any further efforts to overcome the problem.

All psychotherapists are familiar with this dynamic, where an inner conflict about reaching a treatment goal is blocking progress towards that goal. And each therapist must find a way to deal with such conflict when it emerges if the work with that client is to be effective. One of the first clinicians to write of the energetic underpinnings of such conflict was Roger Callahan.[2] Callahan describes the first patient he worked with where he confronted this dynamic.[3] The patient wanted the therapy to help her lose weight after years of failed attempts.

Callahan had been experimenting with a healing approach called Applied Kinesiology. Tests of the relative resistance of various muscles had been devised to determine information about a person's health, from which the treatments follow. The practitioner pushes against the person's arm or leg in ways that reveal what is occurring within the person's energy system. Is the energy that is supposed to be going to a particular organ getting there properly, as indicated by the relative strength of a muscle that is on the energy pathway to that organ, or is this energy in some way disrupted? Is the energy to the kidneys, for instance, flowing properly? This allowed physical interventions to be made that corrected, with precision, the imbalances in the person's energy system. The virtues of that approach for promoting health are another story.[4]

The tangent that is important for our story is that these same tests could be used to discover underlying psychological dynamics. If the person makes a statement he or she believes is true, the muscle will still test strong. Usually. If your name is Nancy and you say "My name is Nancy," the muscle will stay firm. But if there is a conscious or subconscious disagreement with the statement, it will not. If Nancy says "My name is Mary," there is a momentary disturbance in the meridian energies, and the muscle will not hold firm when faced with the same amount of pressure.[5] You can see the applications for the therapy setting, a kind of lie detector for unconscious conflict.

Callahan asked the woman who was coming for help with her weight to picture herself as being thin, just the way she wanted to be, and he then did a muscle test. To his astonishment, and hers, when she was able to successfully visualize herself at her ideal weight, the muscle gave way, signifying an inner conflict about the desired image. He began experimenting with different variations of this, such as having her make the statement "I want to lose weight." Again the test indicated that there was subconscious conflict about this statement. Perhaps this is not surprising. Someone who has dieted a great deal may have become uninterested in reenlisting in the seesaw of losing weight only to watch it be regained. For some, the genuine desire to lose weight is countered by the fear of receiving unwanted sexual advances. For others, there is a comfort or protection in having a rounded body. What Callahan discovered was that an energy disruption accompanied such conflicts about the desired goal.

He began to do the test with other patients. Did they also show an energetic disruption when they thought about reaching their therapeutic goals? "I want to get over my anxiety attacks." "I want a better relationship with my wife." "I want to be a successful musician." "I want to overcome my impotence." He also had them make their statement in the opposite way, such as, "I *don't* want to get over my anxiety attacks." To his surprise, he found that with the muscle test, a large number of his clients grew *weaker* when they thought about getting better, and they grew stronger when they thought about *not* getting better. He called this a *psychological reversal*.

Psychological reversals involve unconscious resistance to the consciously desired outcome. A part of you seems to want the reverse of what you consciously desire, or you do the reverse of what you intend. And the harder you try, the more powerful the resistance that counters your efforts becomes. This resistance is compounded by a disruption in your body's energy system whenever you bring your goal to mind. Remember the toy puzzle in which you stick a finger into each end of a straw tube and the harder you try to pull your fingers out, the more firmly they become embedded? That is how a psychological reversal feels. Your efforts produce the opposite of the result you intend. All effective therapies address psychological reversals in one way or another. Until these are resolved, other therapeutic interventions are less likely to have a deep or lasting effect.

Callahan's recognition that there was an energy dynamic in these conflicts about the treatment goal helped him find a way to address them at the energy level, and it is disarmingly simple. It is, in fact, the opposite of a long, complex analysis, which often results in greater understanding but little resolution. The method Callahan developed was this: You make a statement that acknowledges that the problem you want to change exists (e.g., "Even though I have this unwanted weight") and at the same time affirms that you accept yourself even though you have that problem (e.g., "I deeply love and accept myself"). While making this statement, you work some points that move energy through your body. For reasons that are not fully understood, this seems to resolve the psychological reversal the majority of the time. Or more precisely, the person will usually then be able to make the statement about a clinical goal, such as "I want to stop smoking," without an energy disruption, as shown by the muscle test. And most important, Callahan's experience, and the experience of thousands since, is that it then becomes possible to make progress with that goal using other energy methods, even though progress had been blocked prior to the procedure.

The first ingredient of the Basic Recipe, the Setup, allows you to energetically defuse most psychological reversals about a treatment goal. You state a precisely worded affirmation while stimulating certain energy points. The affirmation statement has two parts:

1) *Even though I have this* _____,
2) *I deeply love and accept myself.*

The blank is filled in with a brief description of the problem being addressed. For example:

- *Even though I have this resentment towards my mother, I deeply love and accept myself.*
- *Even though I have this tendency to get headaches at work, I deeply love and accept myself.*
- *Even though I have this obsession about my son's shortcomings, I deeply love and accept myself.*
- *Even though I eat when I'm anxious, I deeply love and accept myself.*

Any psychological or behavioural problem or goal, from a craving for chocolate to improving your tennis serve, can be translated into this format. While many people are accustomed to stating affirmations only in the positive, in this method, you describe the undesired response exactly as you experience it. For your disturbing memory, the Setup Affirmation might be something like "Even though I have this pain when I think of Mary rejecting me, I deeply love and accept myself," or "Even though I have this overwhelming guilt about the awful thing I did to Bobby, I deeply love and accept myself."

The affirmation is best stated out loud, with feeling and emphasis. Various alternative wordings could serve the same purpose, which is to acknowledge the problem while at the same time affirming your worthiness despite the existence of the problem. Additional strategies for working with psychological reversals are discussed towards the end of the chapter. The format shown in the above examples, however, is easy to memorize and has been used widely with good reports. So on your paper, write your Setup Affirmation in the form of "Even though I have [your emotional reaction about the memory], I deeply love and accept myself." This wording is usually effective, whether or not you believe it.

While the phrase "I deeply love and accept myself" might seem a simplistic and overly pat self-affirmation, it seems to somehow interact with the acknowledgment of the problem in a way that eliminates the energy disruption. Any deep suggestion that fosters self-acceptance, despite the unwanted pattern, made with focus and intent, seems to help people address the problem without the interference of the energy disturbance. "I deeply love and accept myself" is usually effective. However, if this phrase doesn't fit for you, other strong, positive, affirming statements can have the same impact, such as "I know I am doing my best," "I deserve to feel good," or "I know deep down that I am a good and worthy person."

### The Energy Intervention

The Energy Intervention is performed simultaneously with stating the Setup Affirmation. The body's energy system can be affected by rubbing, tapping, stretching, holding, or tracing specific points or areas on the surface of the skin. The effectiveness of the Setup Affirmation can be increased substantially by finding and rubbing points on your upper chest that are tender. Just press in on various points until you find one or more that are sore. This is the area you will rub while stating your affirmation three times. Find a "sore spot" on each side and rub both areas simultaneously. Points that are sore on most people are at the edge of the chest, along the indentation where the arm attaches. You can massage these points with

*Figure 1*

CENTRAL MERIDIAN REFLEX POINTS

Massaging or tapping the central meridian neuro-lymphatic reflex points helps with various energy imbalances and tends to dissolve the internal resistance that is the hallmark of the psychological reversal.

three fingers at a time along the entire indentation (see Figure 1). These points are on the central meridian, they are strongly involved with emotional issues, and they are particularly useful when working with psychological reversals.

The sore spots are neurolymphatic reflex points. The lymphatic system is the body's "other" circulatory system. Like the bloodstream, it circulates a fluid, called lymph, through your body. Lymph contains white blood cells and removes toxins. It flows through the lymph system, which is a network of spaces and vessels between body tissues and organs. But unlike the bloodstream, which has the heart, the lymph has no pump. It is "pumped" when you walk, run, or otherwise exercise your body. The normal activities of daily life keep the lymph flowing. But toxins may accumulate and hamper the lymph flow.

When this happens, some of your body's energies also become blocked. Massaging or tapping the lymphatic reflex points has the effect of getting the lymph moving more freely. These points tend to be sore if the lymph they control is blocked. In the process of stimulating the lymphatic reflex points, you give your energies a boost as well. Rubbing sore lymphatic points on your chest disperses toxins (for elimination) that are blocking the lymph system and opens a flow of energy to the heart, chest cavity, and entire body. While some energy therapists specify the location of specific points, neurolymphatic reflex points are distributed throughout the body, and massaging any that are sore activates a flow of energy. And along with the removal of physical toxins, this also seems to release the energies that are associated with stale habits, thoughts, and emotional reactions (the words following "even though" in the affirmation) and makes room for fresh ones.

Rubbing a sore spot should not cause more than a little discomfort. If it does, apply less pressure. Also, if you have had an injury or operation in that area of the chest or if there is any other reason that you should not be massaging a specific area, work only on areas where you have no cause for concern. If there is a medical reason not to massage chest sore spots, or if

*Figure 2*

THE KARATE-CHOP POINTS

As an alternative to rubbing the chest sore spots, you can tap the point at the fleshy part of the outside of either hand or the entire side of the hand, beneath your little finger.

you cannot find a spot that is sore, an alternative energy intervention is to tap the karate-chop points on the sides of your hands. The part of your hand you would use to deliver a karate chop is located at the centre of the fleshy part of the outside of either hand, between the top of the wrist and the little finger (see Figure 2). You could tap these points vigorously with the fingertips of the index and middle fingers of the other hand, or you could use all four fingers to tap along the entire edge of your hand. Alternatively, you can stimulate the points on both hands simultaneously by "clapping" the sides of your hands together.

To enhance your psychological receptiveness for the desired change, repeat three times an affirmation in the form of "Even though I have [describe problem, such as the emotional response to the memory], I deeply love and accept myself." Simultaneously, rub two chest sore spots, the arm-attachment indentations, or tap the karate-chop points for as long as it takes to state the affirmation three times. Do this now.

## INGREDIENT 2: THE TAPPING SEQUENCE

The Tapping Sequence is designed to restore an optimal flow of energy through the body's "meridians," or energy pathways. There are fourteen major meridians, and each is associated with acupoints on the surface of the skin that, when tapped or otherwise stimulated, move the energy through the entire meridian system. It turns out that, because the meridians are interconnected and stimulating one meridian can affect others, working with points on only a subset of the meridans is all that is usually necessary to get the entire meridian system into enough of a flow that psychological issues can be resolved. Various subsets have been used with good results. The sequence you will learn here teaches you eight points, shown in Figure 3, that many have found to be an effective combination.

1. Beginning of the eyebrows—inside edge of the eyebrows, just above and to one side of the nose.

2. Sides of the eyes—on the bone bordering the outside corner of each eye.

3. Under the eyes—on the bone under each eye, about one inch below the pupil.

4. Under the nose—on the small area between the bottom of the nose and the top center of the upper lip.

5. Under the lower lip—midway between the point of the chin and the bottom of the lower lip.

6. K-27 points—the two points immediately below the "collarbone corners," the twenty-seventh points on the kidney meridian—affect many of the body's energies. To locate these points, place your forefingers on your collarbone and

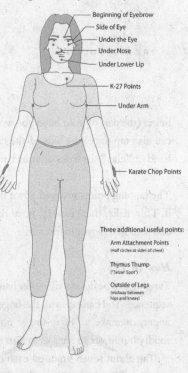

— Beginning of Eyebrow
— Side of Eye
— Under the Eye
— Under Nose
— Under Lower Lip
— K-27 Points
— Under Arm
— Karate Chop Points

Three additional useful points:

Arm Attachment Points
(Half circles at sides of chest)

Thymus Thump
("Tarzan" Spot)

Outside of Legs
(midway between hips and knees)

*Figure 3*

THE 8 EFT TAPPING POINTS

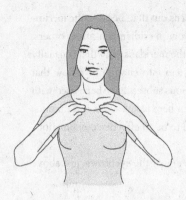

*Figure 4*

THE K-27 POINTS

move them inward towards the U-shaped notch at the top of your breastbone (about where a man would knot his tie). Move your fingers through the bottom of the U. Then go to the left and right about an inch and tap.

7. Under the arms—about four inches beneath the armpit: for men, about even with the nipple; for women, in the middle of the bra strap.

8. Karate-chop points—in the middle of the fleshy part on the outside of either hand, between the top of the wrist bone and the base of the little finger (the part of your hand you would use to deliver a karate chop). You can also tap the entire side of the hand with all four fingers of the other hand or "clap" the sides of your hands together.

The tapping points proceed down the body. Each is below the one before it. This makes them easy to memorize. A few trips through the sequence, and it should be yours forever.

### How to Tap

Tapping can be done with either hand, or both hands simultaneously or in sequence. You can tap with the fingertips of your index finger and middle finger, or make a "three-finger notch" by including your thumb. Tap solidly but never so hard as to hurt or risk bruising yourself.

Tap about seven times on each of the tapping points. You will be repeating a "Reminder Phrase" (see below) while you are tapping, so you will not be counting, and it does not matter if you tap a few more or a few less than seven times. Most of the tapping points exist on both sides of the body. It does not matter which side you use. Many practitioners believe there are benefits to tapping both sides simultaneously.

Some people prefer means other than tapping for stimulating the energy points. One method is to massage the points. In another, called Touch and Breathe,[6] you touch the point lightly with one or two fingers and take a complete breath (one easy inhalation and one easy exhalation, at your own pace, usually through the nose). You can then move on to the next point. For most people, however, tapping is the preferred method, though in a small percentage of cases, other alternatives are required (see "If Tapping Doesn't Work" on p. 218). Take a tour now through the eight tapping points, tapping each one about seven times. Breathe freely as you tap.

## The Reminder Phrase

Memories, thoughts, or circumstances that elicit "negative" emotions cause disruptions not only in the brain but also in the body's energy system. To treat a problem by stimulating acupoints, the energy disruption must be mentally activated. For instance, if the problem from which you want relief is unfounded anger towards your boss, that anger is not present while you are thinking about what to have for lunch. Tapping the points shown in Figure 3 while thinking about the problem not only balances the energy system in the moment, it also retrains your body to be able to hold the thought (or to be in the circumstance) without the energy disturbance and, therefore, without the unwanted emotional response.

You may, however, find it a bit difficult to consciously think about the problem while you are doing the tapping. By continually repeating a Reminder Phrase as you tap, you are able to keep yourself psychologically attuned to the situation that has been triggering the disruption in your energy system.

The Reminder Phrase is a word or short phrase describing the problem. You repeat it out loud each time you tap one of the points in the Tapping Sequence. The statement activates the problem enough to create a reaction in both your energy system and in your brain. The Reminder Phrase is often identical to or very close to the phrase used in the Setup Affirmation. For example, if you were focusing on a memory in which you were humiliated as a child while performing in front of an audience, the Setup Affirmation might be:

Even though I have this humiliation about what happened at the school play, I deeply love and accept myself.

Within this affirmation, the words "humiliation about what happened at the school play" can be used as the Reminder Phrase. Abbreviated versions of the statement, such as "humiliation at the play," or simply "humiliation," will also suffice as long as their full meaning is clear to you. The Reminder Phrase might (referencing back to the earlier examples) be as simple as:

- "resentment towards my mother" (or simply "resentment" or "mother")
- "headaches at work" (or simply "headaches" or "work")
- "obsession about my son's shortcomings" (or simply "obsession" or "Steve's shortcomings")
- "eating when I am anxious" (or simply "eating when anxious" or "anxious eating")

The following additional Reminder Phrases suggest the range of possible areas for energy interventions: my role in the accident, lower-back pain, anger towards my sister, appearing in court, constant hunger, ambivalence about my boyfriend, fired, fear of lifts, missing Mary, stock losses, terrorist attack, divorce. The more specific the Reminder Phrase, or at least the more specific the problem it stands for is in your mind, the more effective the phrase will be.

Some people who have been trained in the use of self-suggestion, or positive affirmations, are puzzled that a phrase that activates the *unwanted* feeling or response, is used in energy psychology. But that is precisely what is required when attempting to eliminate a problematic emotional response, since the energy intervention is only able to rewire the unwanted feeling while it is active. Keeping this principle in mind will help you to craft your Reminder Phrase in the most effective manner. For instance, if the problem you are tackling is your craving for chocolate, "my love of chocolate" would be less effective as a Reminder Phrase than a phrase that activates the feeling of not having chocolate, such as "longing for chocolate."

Formulate the Reminder Phrase you will use in working with your memory and write it on the sheet of paper. Then tap the eight points shown in Figure 3, stating the Reminder Phrase while at each point.

## INGREDIENT 3: THE NINE-GAMUT PROCEDURE

Activities that stimulate certain areas of the brain appear to increase the effectiveness of subsequent energy interventions. Specific parts of the brain are stimulated when the eyes are moved, and various therapies utilize this principle. The most widely used eye-movement technique within energy psychology is Roger Callahan's Nine-Gamut Procedure, an adaptation of techniques used in the field of applied kinesiology. It is introduced here along with the comment that it is one of the more strange-looking procedures even within energy psychology, with the tapping, eye movements, humming, and counting all designed to stimulate specific parts of the brain.

In the Nine-Gamut Procedure, which in itself does not use the Reminder Phrase or directly focus on the problem, one of the body's energy spots, the "gamut point," is continuously tapped while nine simple steps are carried out. The gamut point is on the back of either hand, one-half inch beyond the knuckles (towards the wrist), and in line with the midpoint between the little finger and the ring finger.

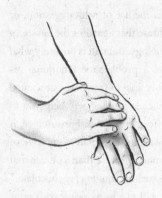

*Figure 5*

THE GAMUT POINT

While tapping the gamut point continuously, perform the following nine actions:

1. Close your eyes.
2. Open your eyes.
3. Move your eyes down and to one side.
4. Move your eyes down and to the other side.
5. Circle your eyes, rotating them 360 degrees in one direction.
6. Circle your eyes in the other direction.
7. Hum a tune for a few seconds ("Happy Birthday," "Row, Row, Row Your Boat," "Zip-a-dee Doo Dah").
8. Count to five.
9. Hum again.

Sometimes the Nine Gamut is ended as follows: Bring your eyes down to the floor and then slowly and very deliberately bring them up to the ceiling, projecting your sight and the "old" energy out into the distance as your eyes move up the arc. Go ahead now and do the Nine-Gamut Procedure.

## INGREDIENT 4: THE TAPPING
## SEQUENCE REPEATED

In the second tapping sequence, you repeat the first one exactly as you did it earlier. Do this now. You can think of the three ingredients after the Setup as making a sandwich:

- The Tapping Sequence (with the Reminder Phrase)
- The Nine-Gamut Procedure
- The Tapping Sequence (with the Reminder Phrase)

## REVISITING THE PROBLEM

When you have completed the second sequence of tapping, you again assess the intensity of the problem: Close your eyes, bring the original memory to mind, and give it a rating from 0 to 10 on the amount of distress it causes you *now,* as you think about it.

If you can get no trace whatsoever of your previous emotional intensity, a final step is to challenge the results (see below). If, on the other hand, you go down to, let's say a 4, you would perform subsequent rounds until, ideally, 0 is reached (getting it down to 1 or even 2 is often all that is required for the problem to essentially be resolved). Even if you haven't been trying out the procedures as you've been reading, you have everything in place to begin working with your disturbing memory. Each round requires just about one minute. Once you've identified and rated your memory, stated your Setup Affirmation while stimulating some of your chest sore spots, and chosen a Reminder Phrase, do the treatment "Sandwich" exactly as described above.

## SUBSEQUENT ROUNDS

Sometimes a problem is resolved after a single round of treatment. More often, only partial relief is obtained and additional rounds are necessary. Two simple adjustments need to be made for these subsequent rounds.

## 1. ADJUSTING THE SETUP PHRASE

A possible obstacle to success during the first round of treatment is the re-emergence of *psychological reversals,* the internal conflicts the Setup Affirmation was designed to resolve.

After treatment has begun and some progress has been made, the psychological reversal takes on a somewhat different quality. A psychological reversal before treatment will prevent *any* progress. A psychological reversal that emerges after the treatment has begun is interfering with *further* progress. The wording of the Setup Affirmation needs to reflect this. The Setup Affirmation is a self-suggestion targeted to the subconscious mind, which tends to be very literal, so the wording should focus on the way the problem is still present. A slight adjustment—the addition of two or three words—accomplishes this. The adjusted format for the Setup Affirmation is:

> *Even though I **still** have **some of** this* _____,
> *I deeply love and accept myself.*

The words "still" and "some" or "some of" shift the emphasis of the affirmation towards a focus on the remainder of the problem. The adjustment is easy to make. The affirmations below reflect adjustments to the affirmations listed earlier:

- *Even though I **still** have **some of** this resentment towards my mother, I deeply love and accept myself.*
- *Even though I **still** have **some** concern about headaches when I go to work, I deeply love and accept myself.*
- *Even though I **still** have **some of** this obsession about Steve's shortcomings, I deeply love and accept myself.*
- *Even though I **still** have **some of** this tendency to eat when I am anxious, I deeply love and accept myself.*

## 2. ADJUSTING THE REMINDER PHRASE

Simply place the word "remaining" in front of the original Reminder Phrase. Here as examples are adjusted versions of the Reminder Phrases presented earlier:

- *remaining resentment towards my mother* (or simply "**remaining** *resentment*")
- *remaining headaches at work* (or simply "**remaining** *headaches*")
- *remaining obsession about Steve's shortcomings* (or simply "**remaining** *obsession*")
- *remaining eating when anxious* (or simply "**remaining** *anxious eating*")

Following each round, you should do a new 0-to-10 assessment of the distress you now feel when you tune in to the original memory or problem. If the level of distress continues to decrease, do subsequent rounds until you reach 0 or until the distress stops decreasing. Do another round now with your disturbing memory, repeating the Setup Affirmation while using the words "still" and "some of," as appropriate, and inserting the word "remaining" into your Reminder Phrase as appropriate (sometimes other wording needs to be slightly revised as well). Again bring the memory to mind and rate it from 0 to 10. If you are still able to activate disturbing feelings in relation to the memory or problem, continue to repeat the Setup and the Sandwich until you are unable to feel distress in relation to your memory, or until you are unable to lower the degree of distress you do feel. At that point you have completed this little experiment. If you noticed a significant reduction in your level of distress, you will be able to build upon the methods in the subsequent chapters. If not, you may find some hints in the following discussion that allow you to use the procedure in a way that is more effective for you.

Sometimes the rating will get down to a 2 or a 1 but will not reduce any further. This is not necessarily a bad outcome. For some problems, you might not be able to conceive of the rating going down to 0, and a 1 or a 2 is essentially a "cure" in your subjective world. In some circumstances, such as taking a test, a small measure of anxiety increases your ability to function. So while 0 might be thought of as the ideal, it is not always realistic or necessary.

If after five rounds a rating is still not down to 0 or near 0, you may need to shift your focus or wording, or you may have identified a problem with which you need outside assistance. There are many possible reasons that improvement becomes stalled. A small proportion of people do not respond to tapping the standard energy points (if you suspect you are one of them, try massaging the points or simply touching each point while breathing deeply). The problem might need to be formulated with more specific or altogether different wording. Internal conflict about resolving the problem might need greater exploration. *Aspects* of the problem that are not being addressed might need to be identified and treated. The aspects of a problem are discussed below. By understanding and working with them, you can laser-focus the techniques in a way that will further reduce the distress you experience when the problem is activated. Other ways of increasing your effectiveness with the Basic Recipe are also discussed below.

Once you do get the subjective distress rating down to 0 or near 0, a final step is to "challenge" it. Try to recall or visualize the situation in a manner that evokes the earlier sense of distress. If the disturbed energy pattern and neurological sequence have been corrected—that is, if the earlier memory, thought, or situation is now paired to a stable response in your brain and energy system—you will not be able to activate your earlier feelings. The speed with which this can often be accomplished is among the most striking benefits of energy psychology. A difficult situation will still be recognized for its inherent dangers, injuries, or injustices, but the stress response in your autonomic nervous system that had been paired with that situation will no longer be triggered.

If you are unable to reproduce any trace of the initial emotional response, the probability is strong that the issue has been deactivated. It might serve to reinforce the gains by going through the Basic Recipe a few more times in subsequent days. Chances are that the internal changes will translate into situations in your life. If they do not, or if there is some slippage, you can do another treatment round or two as the situation is occurring. This often is all that is needed to anchor the changes in your life. Or it may mean that an aspect of the problem still needs attention, as discussed later in the chapter.

## TAPPING INTO TROUBLE AND OUT AGAIN

One of our colleagues was doing a demonstration in front of a large group with a woman who wanted help regarding spells of extreme shyness and a tendency to go silent in certain social situations. Just standing in front of the group, her shoulders slumped, as if trying to make herself take up less space, and her voice became tiny. With the tapping treatment, her stress rating went from an initial 8 down to 6, but it stayed at 6 for the next two rounds. Then surfaced a childhood memory of her and her mother walking into their home while a burglary was in progress. Her mother started to scream, and the intruder began to viciously beat the mother. The girl ran and hid behind some curtains. She was sure the burglar was searching for her and managed to silence her own tears and screams of terror. While she had no previous memory of this incident (she was later able to confirm it with her mother, who had been reluctant to revive the memory), whenever she felt any stress in front of other people, she would have to fight against herself to be able to speak.

Now with the memory rushing back in vivid detail, she went through the same physiological reaction as when the incident occurred, shaking heavily, face blanched, heart pounding, hardly breathing. Of course at this point our colleague saw the symptoms but did not yet know the story. He offered reassuring words while unwaveringly instructing her to continue tapping. By the second trip through the sequence, her breathing had returned to normal and she had stopped shaking. A couple of more rounds of tapping (no Setup Phrase, no Nine Gamut, just the emotional first aid of stimulating acupuncture points involved with the stress response), and she was able to describe what had occurred. Our colleague had one of his assistants then work with her privately for about thirty minutes, focusing on various aspects of the memory and the issue. She then described her experience to the group in full-bodied posture and voice.

The energy methods you are learning here will not create new emotional problems, but it is possible that they may bring to the surface emotional turmoil that has been brewing. Appendix 2 (p. 285) is a primer of steps you can take if the program becomes upsetting. While it would be highly unusual for it to become nearly as upsetting as in the above instance, if you do feel upset, please consult with the Appendix, and also remember two things:

1. You have a powerful tool to calm yourself. Tap the acupoints as you breathe deeply. Continue to breathe and tap through as many rounds as needed until you find yourself relaxing. You will be sending impulses to your brain that strongly counter the emergency stress response.

2. You have a powerful tool for working with the memory or feelings that came up. Rather than continuing to drain your energies or cause defensive maneuvers within your psyche, the Basic Recipe can help you transform a difficult experience from your past into a source of wisdom and strength.

# INCREASING YOUR EFFECTIVENESS
## WITH THE BASIC RECIPE

In the hands of a relatively proficient newcomer, the Basic Recipe seems to produce effective results about 80 percent of the time when applied to reducing the emotional charge on specific difficult memories. While by many standards this is an extremely favourable success ratio, a better percentage is possible when you know how to handle potential blocks to progress. The four most likely impediments to achieving the desired result with the Basic Recipe are:

1. Unresolved *aspects* of the problem
2. Psychological reversals
3. Scrambled energies
4. Energy toxins

## ADDRESSING UNRESOLVED ASPECTS
## OF THE PROBLEM

The most common reason the distress rating would not have gone down to 0 or close to 0 if you followed the instructions precisely is that another aspect of the problem is involved that was not focused upon in the energy intervention. And the most common reason an apparently successful treatment, where the distress rating did go down to 0, won't translate into the actual situation is that a new aspect of the problem comes up in the real situation that wasn't there when you were just thinking about the problem and wording your Reminder Phrase. While many problems are straightforward and do not have multiple aspects, some have a number of physical or psychological aspects that need attention.

The *physical* aspects of a problem include the look, sound, smell, taste, or feel of the situation. Going back to the example involving anger at police officers, suppose that your memory is of a policeman coming to your home, arresting your father, and taking him away. In your tapping, you have a vision of the policeman's face. At first this evokes a level of discomfort that you rate at a 9. You are able to bring it down to 0 by tapping while visualizing the face as you remember it and stating "that policeman." But the next time you see a policeman, your anger is again instant and strong. As you focus on your experience, you realize that the policeman's holstered gun draws your attention. When you were young and the policeman came to your home, his holstered gun was just about at your eye level and was a vivid part of your experience. The tapping may have to focus not only on the policeman's face but also on his gun. The gun is a physical aspect of the memory that needs attention if you are to change your knee-jerk response to policemen. Or perhaps it is an image of the fear in your father's eyes that has stayed with you through the years and needs to be freed of its emotional charge by holding the image while tapping on your acupuncture points.

The physical aspects of a problem may be obvious or may be very subtle, but they can usually be discerned by examining how your experience in the actual situation differs from the scene you imagined during the tapping treatment. Consider, for instance, a fear of spiders. Usually the energy disruptions that occur when thinking about a spider are the same that occur when you actually see a spider. Get the response to the thought down to a 0, and the response to seeing a real spider will be 0. But not always. Perhaps during the treatment, you were thinking of a stationary spider. The spider you imagined was not moving. If movement is an important aspect of the fear, and if it was absent from your thinking during the original rounds of tapping, then a moving spider will still trigger fear. Apply the Basic Recipe next to this additional aspect (*moving* spider) until your emotional response gets down to 0. Once all aspects have been resolved, your phobic response to spiders will have been eliminated. You will be able to stay calm around spiders. The physical aspects of a traumatic event, such as an accident or an abusive situation (the *screeching* of the tyres, the *smell* of his breath, the *look* in her eyes), may be vivid yet go untreated unless you know that they require attention and can be readily neutralized.

The *psychological* aspects of a problem often involve past experiences that carry an emotional charge. Returning to the police-officer example, suppose you can now bring to mind an image of your father's fearful eyes, of the arresting officer's face, and of his gun, each with no emotional arousal, yet the problem is still not resolved. Further exploration reveals that the sight of a policeman elicits at some level your devastation about your father no longer living with you after his arrest. But this, too, will respond to the Basic Recipe. Being able to bring to mind your devastation about being separated from your father without a strong physiological reaction in the current moment is freeing. Again, it does not erase the memory or take away the misfortune, but it does allow you to move forward without emotional baggage that no longer serves a constructive function.

While many emotional issues are just what they appear to be and have no hidden aspects, some problems involve numerous aspects. A recent trauma or loss, for example, can unearth a network of earlier unresolved traumas or losses. These may need to be addressed individually before the emotional response to the situation is reduced or before an apparently successful use of the Basic Recipe proves durable.

Suppose that when you were eight, you were bitten by a dog. This memory has long been forgotten and is apparently resolved. But then you hear of a neighbour receiving a serious dog bite, and you instantly develop a fear of dogs, rated at 9 or 10. This level of fear and physiological arousal suggests more is at play than just having heard a report of a single incident. Applying the Basic Recipe to "fear of dogs" might reduce your fear a bit, but it is not likely that it will be very effective until the childhood incident has been addressed. Having been bitten as a child is an important aspect of "fear of dogs," and it probably will need attention before the fear of dogs that recently appeared can be successfully addressed.

In focusing on the memory, you may find it has its own set of aspects.

This can be a bit like peeling the layers off an onion. Physical aspects of the memory may be haunting and require attention, such as the feeling of your warm blood rolling down your leg. Or you may vividly recall your helplessness upon seeing the dog baring its teeth, about to attack. This might, in turn, tie into other memories of feeling helpless that must have their emotional charge neutralized before the original problem can be fully resolved. Your subconscious mind knows what you are working on, and it will present what requires attention. Our experience indicates that by patiently applying the Basic Recipe to the aspects that emerge and taking them down one by one, most self-limiting psychological problems can be fully and permanently resolved.

For some emotional problems, such as free-floating anxiety or incessant feelings of shame, it is usually necessary to work with specific incidents that were early triggers for the feeling. Each is an aspect of the emotional problem. For a concrete metaphor about the process, think of the psychological issue as a table. If the emotional problem, say anxiety or shame, is the top of the table, the legs are its aspects, particularly specific events that produced similar emotions. By chipping away at the legs, the tabletop will eventually fall away. So rather than beginning with the "tabletop," or global problem such as "I feel shame," you can work with the "legs," addressing the problem's history—specific event by specific event—until the incessant feeling of shame is cleared away.

It is not necessary to remember and treat every aspect that was involved with a problem in order to overcome it. Fortunately, there is a generalization effect. After you address a few related incidents, the effects start to generalize to the broader issue. For instance, someone who has a hundred traumatic memories of having been abused will find that after neutralizing five to ten of them—sometimes as many as twenty need to be worked with, the others will begin to lose their emotional charge as well.

While many issues can be overcome by using the Basic Recipe directly on a general statement about the obvious problem, for other issues you need to be as specific as possible about their aspects. Particularly with an amorphous condition, such as anxiety, it is often necessary to identify specific events. These may be memories from your childhood, more recent incidents, or current situations. If you neutralize their emotional charges, one by one, the relief will eventually generalize to the larger issue.

## PSYCHOLOGICAL REVERSALS

While the standard Setup Affirmation will resolve many psychological reversals, the next most common reason why the Basic Recipe might not be effective, after unresolved aspects, is that the standard Setup wording *didn't* resolve the psychological reversal. Thinking about the goal still triggers a psychological reversal, so the body resists subsequent energy interventions designed to support that goal, such as those in the Basic Recipe.

There are reasons such conflict is often unconscious. Here you have to become Sherlock Holmes on your own trail. There may be "secondary gains" for having the problem—from gaining sympathy to getting disability insurance. There may be costs to overcoming the problem, such as "If I truly learn to relax and not push myself so hard, I won't achieve as much." Keeping the problem may be a way of punishing someone or lowering people's expectations about you. If the Basic Recipe is not working, and you have worked through all the aspects you can identify, looking inward for possible conflicts about overcoming the problem may show you where you are caught. Is there a part of you that does not want to make the change you are working for? If you are able to articulate such a psychological reversal, the "even though [specifics about not wanting to change] I deeply love and accept myself" format paired with an energy intervention will usually resolve it long enough that tapping with the Reminder Phrase will be effective. Some practitioners find that psychological reversals can also be overcome by combining the karate-point tapping or the sore-spot massage with a simple affirmation of the person's intention, such as "even though . . . I want to be completely free of this [state the problem]" or "I will be free of this . . ." Choosing a Setup Phrase that is self-affirming and that resonates with you is more important than the particular format.

Several types of psychological reversals have been identified. Sometimes, for instance, the psychological reversal is not so much about overcoming the specific problem, such as wanting to lose weight. It is more global. Regardless of the specific goal, there is an energy disruption when the person makes a general statement, such as "I want to be happy." In such cases, you may see little progress towards specific goals until this *global psychological reversal* has been addressed. In other situations, the psychological reversal is limited to specific dimensions of the goal.[7] The person may not show an energy disruption to "I *want* to lose weight" but may show an energy disruption to "I *deserve* to lose weight," "It is *safe* to lose weight," or "I would no longer *be myself* if I lost weight." Once such inner conflicts are discovered, the same strategy applies. Find a statement that acknowledges the problem, such as "even though I don't deserve to lose weight," and then, while rubbing the chest sore spots or tapping the karate-chop points, pair it with a statement of self-acceptance, such as "I deeply love and accept myself."

Another format that has become popular is the Choices Method. This approach emphasizes choice and opportunity rather than self-acceptance. "Even though I still obsess about my son's shortcomings, I choose to know that I deeply love and accept him" or "Even though I neglect my body, I choose to know that I deserve to have time for regular, enjoyable exercise." Regardless of the wording, the strategy is to stimulate energy points that help pair a negative self-evaluation with a positive thought or with the recognition of an opportunity. In essence, this programs the negative thought to become a *trigger* for a positive choice.

The Choices Method[8] can be tailored to any situation, even those that are bleak or overwhelming. A depressed client in his first psychotherapy session developed the affirmation "Even though my life is hopeless, I choose to find unexpected help in this therapy." Writing to her colleagues the day after 9/11 on how to assist people in dealing with the psychological aftermath of the attack, psychologist Patricia Carrington suggested using the Choices Method with phrasings such as "Even though I am stunned and bewildered by this terrible happening, I choose to learn something absolutely essential for my own life from this event," or "Even though . . . I choose to be a still point amid all the chaos," or "I choose to have this dreadful event open my heart," or "I choose to sense the Divine intent for a greater good in all this."

While studying some of these more complex ways of thinking about and addressing psychological reversals may help you become more proficient in working with them, the most important thing is to be alert for the possibility of inner conflict about your goal. Once you identify such conflict, you can formulate a two-part affirmation, patterned on those already presented, and combine it with stimulating energy points to eliminate the disruptive energy that is triggered whenever you bring your goal to mind.

## "SCRAMBLED" ENERGY

A third impediment to progress is that sometimes a person's energies are so disorganized that simply tapping a set of acupuncture points is too subtle an intervention to be able to take hold amid all the static. In such cases, it is necessary to work with the energy disruptions pervading the body before focusing directly on precise psychological issues. Chapter 6 offers some methods for accomplishing this. While we would estimate that this has been an absolute necessity in only about 5 percent of the people we've worked with, taking a few minutes to balance your body's energies, particularly your nervous system, prior to focusing on a psychological issue can only be beneficial. A powerful energy-balancing sequence that will in most cases calm the body and the nervous system enough for the Basic Recipe to be effective is presented on pages 206–218 as the "Five-Minute Daily Energy Routine."

## ENERGY TOXINS

Any substance your immune system does not recognize may disrupt your energy system. We are exposed to untold numbers of synthetic chemicals that did not exist while our bodies were evolving.[9] At least fifteen thousand artificial chemicals—from sweeteners to dyes to preservatives to pesticides—may be found in our food alone. We breathe fumes from our cars, from industrial smokestacks, and from the insulation in our homes. Our bodies are continually warding off a relentless onslaught of toxins. While we are brilliantly designed to accomplish this, the barrage can take a toll.

Continual exposure to these artificial substances tends to have a toxic effect on our energy system. While these "energy toxins" do not interfere with most people's functioning in obvious ways, they may be a steady drain on your energies. Methods such as those in chapter 6 will help you establish greater resilience and make you less vulnerable to them. But some people are highly sensitive and may suffer a range of health challenges, from allergic reactions to asthma to autoimmune disorders. Inroads in using an energy approach to address such problems have been appearing.[10]

Regarding energy toxins and the Basic Recipe, there have even been a number of reports where progress was blocked, all other avenues for moving forward were ineffective, and then an energy toxin was removed and progress resumed. The energy toxin may have been the person's perfume or hair spray or shampoo or sweater. It may have been the carpet or drapes in the office. It may have been a food that is part of the person's regular diet. Gary witnessed one case of chronic depression that completely lifted when the person stopped eating wheat. The depression returned when wheat was reintroduced into the diet and lifted when wheat was again eliminated. If the Basic Recipe is not helping you after you have identified and worked with possible psychological reversals and hidden aspects of the problem, and you have done what you can to give yourself a general energy balancing (as in chapter 6), consider the possibility that some sort of toxin in your food or your environment is interfering.

In many cases, the Basic Recipe, used with persistence, will resolve the problem to which you apply it. If it does not, the suggestions in this section can help you identify and address 1) other aspects of the problem, 2) psychological reversals, 3) scrambled energies, or 4) energy toxins. For such an important skill as being able to reprogram problematic emotions and behaviours, the Basic Recipe and the four methods for enhancing its effectiveness are surprisingly easy to master with a reasonable degree of proficiency. The following two chapters will help you further develop that proficiency by showing how to apply the Basic Recipe to a wide range of problems and goals.

---

IN A NUTSHELL: Once you have studied the material presented in this chapter, the following overview can help you to quickly review the principles. Once you are familiar with the basic principles, the list on p. 283 (Appendix 1) can quickly guide you through the Basic Recipe. You may copy it for easy reference.

---

## THE BASIC RECIPE

1. **Identify and Rate a Problem That Is Suitable for an Energy Approach**
   Identify an emotional response, physical reaction, thought pattern, or behavioural pattern you would like to change and rate it from 0 to 10 according to the amount of distress you feel when you bring it to mind (p. 32).

2. **Establish a Psychological Receptiveness for Change**

   State the Setup Affirmation (p. 38) three times in the format of: *Even though I have this* [describe problem], *I deeply and completely accept myself*. Simultaneously rub chest sore spots or tap the karate-chop points.

3. **Initial Round of Treatment (the "Sandwich")**

   - Tap the standard energy points (beginning of eyebrow, side of the eye, under the eye, under the nose, under the lower lip, K-27, under the arm, and karate-chop, as in Figure 3 on p. 43) approximately seven times each, while stating the Reminder Phrase at each point.
   - The Nine-Gamut Procedure: Close eyes, open eyes, move eyes down to right, down to left, circle eyes right, circle left, hum, count, hum while tapping the "gamut point"(p. 48).
   - Again tap each energy point approximately seven times while stating the Reminder Phrase (p. 45).

4. **Subsequent Rounds of the Sandwich**

   Add "still" and "some" to the Setup Affirmation (p. 50); add "remaining" to the Reminder Phrase (p. 51). Repeat up to five times.

5. **Challenge the Results**

   After the distress level is at 0 or near 0, try to bring up the initial emotion. If you cannot, you are done. If you can, do another round of the Basic Recipe.

6. **If the Problem Is Not Responding**

   Identify and address other aspects of the problem, psychological reversals, scrambled energies, or energy toxins.

# 3

# FOCUSING ON PROBLEMS

Many psychological problems can be treated without the need to pass through laborious stages of discovery, emoting, and cognitive restructuring which are frequently considered to be the hallmarks of true psychotherapy.

—FRED GALLO, PH.D., *Energy Psychology*

If you enter almost any psychological or psychiatric problem you can think of into the search engine of the EFT website (www.emofree.com), you are likely to find that someone has worked with it using energy methods and has reported some success. This does not mean that a few thumps on a set of acupuncture points is going to cure schizophrenia,[1] but it does mean that people have found ways to use energy methods to provide some genuine assistance to individuals with psychotic disorders such as schizophrenia, along with an enormous range of other conditions.

How do tapping, rubbing, doing the Nine-Gamut Procedure, and saying the Setup Affirmation and Reminder Phrase combine so that an unwanted emotional or behavioural response stops occurring?

- As you saw in chapter 1, a harmless sight, sound, smell, feeling, or thought (the trigger) leads to a sequence of chemical events in your brain that results in the unwanted emotion or behaviour.

As you saw in chapter 2, activating in your mind the image or situation that triggers the whole sequence while simultaneously doing the tapping seems to send electrical impulses that block the unwanted response.

In many cases, this immediately resolves the problem for which the person is seeking help. In other cases, a web of interrelated triggers must be identified and neutralized one by one. That is the detective work we will introduce in this chapter.

## THE PROBLEMS THAT RESPOND
## THE MOST QUICKLY

The methods of energy psychology can be applied at numerous levels. The core strategy is to extinguish a dysfunctional *conditioned response*. A conditioned response is a feeling or behaviour that is programmed to immediately occur when a particular type of *stimulus* appears (an internal image or external situation). You get on an aeroplane, and you feel panic. You hear the name of your girlfriend's old lover, and jealous rage envelops you. You say "no" when a friend asks you to serve on a committee that holds no interest for you, and guilt plagues you for hours. A TV ad reminds you of your mother, who died in 1992, and you are, for the thousandth time, sent into inconsolable grief. Your spouse's voice gets a bit loud when making a request, and you want to come out swinging.

When there is a clear relationship between an internal or external stimulus and an unwelcome emotion or an automatic behaviour, a fairly routine application of the EFT Basic Recipe will usually interrupt the pattern. To review: You specify the response you wish to change and give a 0-to-10 rating for the level of distress you feel when you bring it to mind. You formulate the Setup Affirmation and state it out loud while massaging points on your chest that are tender. You do the Sandwich: 1) the acupoint Tapping Sequence, while stating your Reminder Phrase at each point, 2) the Nine-Gamut Procedure, and 3) the Tapping Sequence again. You do another assessment and repeat the Sandwich with slight modifications to the Setup Affirmation and the Reminder Phrase. You continue until the distress you feel while mentally holding the image or memory has been eliminated.

Over the next few days, try this with several clear-cut issues, where your response to a situation you sometimes encounter is very specific, such as:

- "When I start to become tired, I automatically turn on the television." (*"Even though I have this weakness for television . . ."*)
- "My clothes wind up on the floor, even though I intend to hang them up when I take them off." (*"Even though I have this habit of leaving my clothes on the floor . . ."*)
- "Every time I sit down to do my taxes, I become anxious." (*"Even though I feel anxiety whenever I start to do my taxes . . ."*)
- "When I see my daughter having fun, I begin to dwell on her poor grades." (*"Even though I have this preoccupation with my daughter's grades . . ."*)

Follow the Basic Recipe exactly as it is described in chapter 2 and you may be surprised by how frequently it is effective in changing your responses. The approach puts into your hands (literally) skills that can free you of emotions that limit you and that make life less enjoyable. Once you have mastered the basic methods taught in the previous chapter, you will be able to change your internal programming in relation to a wide range of issues. One of the comments we hear most frequently from those we train is some version of "I wish I had known this years ago."

The following are actual examples that illustrate the range of issues where simply applying the Basic Recipe gave someone relief: performance fears for a nineteen-year-old gymnast, flashbacks and insomnia a woman was experiencing following two car accidents during a six-week period, a refinery worker stopping smoking after thirty-five years, a woman's extreme anxiety prior to bladder surgery, a six-year-old girl's psychosomatic pains, a mother's fear of flying that was being communicated to her one-year-old daughter, depression suffered by a single mum with two teenage daughters, a woman's intense lifelong craving for chocolate and ice cream, a thirteen-year-old boy's fear of the dark, a boy with an intense allergic reaction to horses, another boy with severe dyslexia, a woman's pain after reconstructive surgery for a damaged knee. You can read details about each of these examples, as well as hundreds of others, at www.emofree.com.

Of course a routine application of the methods will not be effective in every situation. Even in cases where a triggering stimulus and unwanted response can be readily identified, other factors may be involved and need attention. Four considerations for increasing the effectiveness of the tapping protocol were described at the end of chapter 2—aspects of the problem, psychological reversals, scrambled energies, and energy toxins.

In addition, given the complexities of human emotional life, psychological problems do not necessarily break down into a clearly identifiable stimulus-and-response pattern. Careful observation that helps you identify where to focus your attention is often required. Is the progress being blocked by hidden aspects or psychological reversals? Is special understanding required for working with a particular type of problem, such as depression or an addiction? Addressing such questions is the topic of this chapter. It teaches by example, describing how energy psychology has been successfully used with a range of individuals and conditions. It also gives you some insight into the dynamics of each condition. Even if you do not suffer with a specific problem discussed below, some of the principles for overcoming that problem may apply to situations you do encounter, so we encourage you to read each section. The descriptions are written to teach basic strategies and highlight possibilities as much as to address the particular problem. Again, proceed within the context of the discussion of the book's limitations on pp. 25–27, and if at any point in using the techniques presented here you begin to feel upset, please consult Appendix 2, "If the Program Becomes Unsettling."

# FEARS AND PHOBIAS

Energy psychology treatments of fears and phobias are quite familiar, in part because the outcomes are so easy to demonstrate, as when the woman in South Africa triumphantly walked up to and touched the snake that had terrorized her a few minutes earlier. But fears and phobias are by no means the only emotional difficulties that respond to this approach. Energy interventions with traumatic memories, anxiety, depression, addictions, self-defeating habits, and physical conditions will be presented later in the chapter. For each topic, case examples will be followed by a discussion of the principles involved in working with that issue.

## FEAR OF PUBLIC SPEAKING

Sue had a speech impediment that resulted in an intense fear of public speaking. She attended a workshop presented by Gary and his associate, Adrienne Fowlie, and during the lunch break asked them for help with her fear. She showed them a scar on her neck where an operation for throat cancer had been performed. As a result of the operation, she could not speak normally and it was difficult to understand her. Not surprisingly, she was not fond of public speaking. In fact, she was terrified of it and suffered a range of the physiological symptoms of phobia, from a racing heart to feelings of nausea. To make matters worse, she was a sergeant in the Army and frequently had to "public-speak" in front of her troops.

Two rounds of the Basic Recipe were applied, and she overcame the fear in a few minutes—at least to the extent that she no longer felt fear when *thinking* about speaking in front of a group. When the workshop reconvened, Gary asked her to come up on stage to further test the results. As she walked towards the stage, she reported that some fear was upon her again, but it was "only a three," down from the "usual ten." Another round of the Basic Recipe was applied on the stage as she faced the audience, and her fear rating fell to 0. She then grabbed the microphone and enchanted the 100 people in the audience as she told the story of what had happened during the lunch break. She was calm and poised. Her speech impediment was still there, of course, but her fear and the accompanying physical reactions were gone. While eliminating the fear of public speaking doesn't necessarily make someone a great speaker, it does remove the rapid pounding of the heart, the dry mouth, and other symptoms so that the person is then comfortable and able to cultivate the requisite skills.

## CLAUSTROPHOBIA

A thirty-seven-year-old woman who had had a debilitating stroke at age thirty volunteered herself for treatment in a class David was teaching. Shortly after her stroke, she was placed in an MRI machine and became fearful and confused. She panicked when she could not get out, and terror took over. She had been claustrophobic ever since, to the point that she could not sleep with the lights out or even under a blanket, could not drive through a tunnel or get into a lift. Besides being enormously inconvenient, this fear was confidence shattering as she worked to get her speech back.

Within twenty minutes of reprogramming her energy response to enclosed places using the tapping sequence, her anxiety when thinking about being in an enclosed space went from 10+ on the 10-point scale down to 0. To test this, David suggested that during the break, she and her partner return to their room and that she get into the closet. After she entered the closet and closed the door, her partner turned out the lights. She stayed there five minutes with no anxiety. When she returned to report to the group what had happened, she said the only problem was that she found it "boring." The rest of the group, which fifty minutes earlier had witnessed her report that her distress was 10+ when even *thinking* about an enclosed space, was amazed. That evening she slept with the lights out and under the covers for the first time in seven years. Her partner was elated.

Six weeks after this single session, the following e-mail arrived:

> You are not going to believe this! The test of all claustrophobia tests happened to me. I got stuck in a lift by myself for nearly an hour. In the past I would have gone nuts and clawed the door off, but I was calm and sat down on the floor and waited patiently for the repair men to arrive. . . . It was an amazing confirmation that I am no longer claustrophobic!!!!!!!! Thank you. Thank you.

A growing body of clinical evidence indicates that her phobia is not likely to return unless bad fortune retraumatizes her in a situation that involves an enclosed space.

## THE NATURE OF PHOBIAS

You can imagine the years of self-recrimination both women suffered prior to the treatments. We live in a culture that views irrational fear as a character flaw and encourages people to act tough. Both women actually displayed tremendous courage in coping with their fears, but their internal wiring was such that the harder they tried to push through, the stronger the fears became. With treatment that addressed the wiring rather than the feelings or the behaviour, the fears dissolved in minutes.

About 10 percent of the population suffers from one or more phobias. Phobias cause untold misery and often severely limit the lives of those who have them. There are hundreds of possible phobias, but the Basic

Recipe can be effective regardless of what triggers the irrational fear. Because it involves the same neurological process, you use the same strategy whatever the trigger. Among the most common triggers are fears of:

| | | |
|---|---|---|
| Public speaking | Dentists | Telephones |
| Spiders and other | Flying | Bees |
| insects | Speed | Enclosed places |
| Open spaces | Dogs | Driving |
| Bodies of water | Snakes | Rejection |
| Disease | Needles | Men |
| Heights | Bridges | Being alone |

There is a world of difference between a normal fear and a phobia. Fear is a survival mechanism, an evolutionary achievement that helps us avoid danger. It bypasses the rational mind and sets into motion a sequence of automated responses that helped our ancestors survive in the face of mortal danger. If you are driving your car and a truck pulls out of a driveway in front of you, you don't want lots of inner dialogue before your foot hits the brake. Some of our fear-based behaviours are needed to bypass the more well-considered but so much slower rational mind. An automatic fear response becomes attached or "conditioned" to a situation based on a combination of inherited reactions (e.g., the "fight-or-flight" response) and experiences that teach you about what is dangerous.

A phobia, or irrational fear, is a fear that has become attached to an object or a situation that, objectively, does not actually pose a danger or threat, or to a situation where the threat is better managed by normal caution than by a full-blown emergency response. Caution when you see a snake or a spider is adaptive. Either may be dangerous and able to cause you harm. But to experience a pounding heart, headache, nausea, vomiting, sweat, tears, or any of a long list of other symptoms of excessive fear is not only useless, it makes you less effective in the situation. The phobic response, the level of fear that exceeds normal caution, contributes nothing to your safety.

People are often amazed by how quickly a lifelong phobia may vanish. This, of course, does not cause them to step into harm's way. The process doesn't make them stupid; they don't suddenly jump off tall buildings or kiss grizzly bears. Normal caution and concern are not erased by rebalancing the meridian energies in order to neutralize a phobic response. However, people who have eliminated a phobia using energy techniques tend to have less fear in the situation about which they were originally phobic than other people. Almost everyone, for example, has some fear response to heights. Ask 100 people to look down from the top of a tall building, though they are in total safety, and many of them will feel at least a bit queasy. The queasiness is a physiological component of the fear response. By contrast, those who have completely eliminated a height phobia using the tapping sequence don't even feel queasy. The wiring has been changed. They are left with only a healthy caution.

## APPLYING THE BASIC RECIPE
## TO A PHOBIA

It is usually quite simple to establish the Setup Affirmation and Reminder Phrase for a phobia. For instance: "even though I have this fear of heights . . ." (Setup Affirmation) and "fear of heights" (Reminder Phrase). It doesn't matter how intense the phobia is or how long you have had it. This surprises many people because they tend to think that long-standing, intense phobias are "deeply ingrained" and must take months or years to eliminate. Not so with an energy approach. While some phobias do take longer to resolve than others, this is not because of their intensity or longevity. Rather, it is because of their *complexity*. The fear of heights may be a simple conditioned response: Situations that involve height trigger panic based on a single incident, perhaps forgotten long ago. Or it may be more complex, tying into numerous past episodes: a memory of having once fallen from a tree, an image of having seen someone fall from a high place, and having had a panic attack while on a ski lift, for example.

Each is an aspect of the phobia, and these aspects often need to be treated one at a time to completely dissolve the phobia.

For many phobias, it is only necessary to address the most obvious aspect, which is to bring to mind the object of the fear. Just a few brief trips through the Basic Recipe will usually take care of it. But if you are not finding relief after several rounds, focus on an early memory that brings up the fear and apply the Basic Recipe to it. If another aspect emerges—suppose the memory is of a friend who died when a balcony collapsed and you are overcome with feelings of grief—treat those feelings. Work with each aspect of this memory. Remember, your subconscious mind knows what you are processing, and it will present the elements that require attention. Once you have neutralized this memory, see if another comes to mind, and treat it. Of course, when you begin, you do not know how many aspects the problem has. The practical guideline is that you can assume that all the relevant aspects of the issue have been neutralized when you have no more emotional intensity about the original fear-producing thought.

Psychological reversals are less common in phobias than they are in some other conditions, such as addictions, where they are almost always at play. But if your progress in working with a fear or phobia becomes blocked, ask yourself what would happen if you no longer had this fear. On being asked this question, a woman whose fear of flying was not responding to the tapping blurted out, with some embarrassment, "Then I would have to go on those dreadful business trips with my husband." Another woman, whose fear traced to a childhood incident when a man she trusted played a cruel practical joke on her, realized that if she got over her phobia, she might have to forgive him. The subconscious mind works in devious ways. Stay alert for inner bargains you may have struck that keep your fear or phobia engaged for spurious reasons. If you suspect one, formulate a Setup Affirmation that addresses it (e.g., "Even though I have this resentment of Joe that I would rather hold on to than overcome my phobia, I deeply love and accept myself"). State the affirmation three times while rubbing sore spots on your chest or tapping the karate-chop points. Then return to the Tapping Sequence.

## ONCE THE PHOBIA HAS BEEN ELIMINATED, IS THE RESULT PERMANENT?

Strange though it may seem, in our experience and that of many other practitioners, once a phobia has been completely eliminated in the office, the gains usually translate beyond the office, and they usually hold. A fundamental energetic and neurological shift has occurred in relation to the triggering situation, and it does not matter if you are simply thinking about the situation or actually in it. However, if the problem does return, unless an entirely new experience has retraumatized the person, it is almost always because aspects that weren't fully addressed in the treatment are becoming involved. Recall, for instance, the treatment in which the spider's movements had not been part of the initial treatment and had to be addressed in a subsequent round before an actual spider could be viewed with no fear. Stay alert. As you identify additional aspects of the problem, use the Basic Recipe with each of them.

## MULTIPLE PHOBIAS

Sometimes a person suffers from several phobias. The guideline is to treat them one at a time. For example, make sure your snake phobia is totally cleared before you address your claustrophobia. Then make sure your claustrophobia has been completely neutralized before you address your driving phobia. In addition, some phobias, called "complex phobias," are actually several phobias wrapped into one. The fear of flying can be like that. It might involve 1) the fear of being enclosed in a relatively small area, 2) the fear of falling, 3) the fear of turbulence, 4) the fear of taking off, 5) the fear of landing, and 6) the fear of being shut in with people. If you have a complex phobia, treat each component you are able to identify as if it were a separate problem. This may require a number of rounds, but persistent use of the Basic Recipe can permanently neutralize even a complex phobia within a relatively short period of time.

## TRAUMATIC MEMORIES AND OTHER DIFFICULT LIFE-SHAPING EVENTS

Many people are plagued by traumatic memories. These memories may have originated from any shock to the system, such as a natural disaster, injury, accident, or loss. They may also have involved a personal betrayal, such as physical assault, emotional abuse, rape, or other victimization. Reliving or even just being reminded of a past traumatic incident can be intensely painful. The effects can range from relatively mild reactions, such as a headache or a stomachache, to the complete inability to function. Many people experience a variety of symptoms: Their hearts may pound when a traumatic memory intrudes. They may find themselves sweating, crying, or shaking. They may experience sexual dysfunction, grief, anger, depression, or any number of other emotional or physical problems. And even if the memories don't frequently come into their consciousness, they may be doing damage behind the scenes. They may keep the person inhibited or defensive and cause self-doubt, suspicion, anxiety, or nightmares.

Energy psychology, as you have seen, approaches traumatic memories by sending electromagnetic impulses to the brain that interrupt the intense emotional response the memory has been causing. Unlike many other therapies, the emphasis is not on analyzing the memory and its meaning. Rather, you work with the acupoints. You will still, of course, have access to the memory after its emotional charge has been neutralized, but it will no longer create personal mayhem when it comes into your mind. And it will no longer be wreaking psychological havoc behind the scenes.

Some wonder if treatments that neutralize the effects of a personal trauma with almost surgical precision rob a person of the insight and self-knowledge that can be achieved by exploring the problem in depth. Can you even "get to the bottom" of a psychological issue without examining it in detail? In our experience, removing the energy disturbance caused by the memory increases one's self-understanding. When the emotional overwhelm is eliminated, people's attitudes towards their memories change almost instantly. They talk about them differently. Their language shifts from words of fear to those of understanding. Their demeanour and posture suggest an entirely new and more composed relationship to the experience. This is all consistent with the neurological shifts that have occurred. What has changed is that they can now think and talk about the memory without being retraumatized. So rather than circumventing self-examination, they now have more access to their rational facilities and are able to put even the most horrible incident into a realistic and adaptive perspective. Examples of this can be seen in the following two stories.

## A CHILDHOOD RAPE THAT LED TO
## SUBSEQUENT SEXUAL DIFFICULTIES

Sandy and her partner came to one of our colleagues[2] for premarital counselling. Among the issues they were concerned about was their sexual relationship. Although Sandy had been married before, she found herself reacting with uncontrollable negative feelings when her fiancé initiated sexual play. He was willing to be patient, kind, and understanding, and he seemed genuinely interested that sex be a shared experience. While she freely acknowledged that she had no problems with his attitude, she still would usually become upset and turned off by his overtures. They asked for help with this problem, and a private session with Sandy was arranged.

When she came in, the therapist gently asked, "Is there something in your earlier years that you could talk about?" She immediately burst into tears. Red blotches appeared on her skin, and her words were punctuated with heavy sobbing and gasping as she began to relate her story: "When I was seven years old, we lived in [a small rural town]. One day my stepfather took me for a walk down a country road. It was in the summer. We hiked up the side of a hill. Then we stopped. Then he took off all my clothes. Then he took off all his clothes."

At this point she was scarcely able to breathe. The therapist stopped her and said that it was not necessary to go any further. He had her state her distress rating of the memory, which obviously was a 10. He then led her through the Tapping Sequence, at first without even doing the Setup. Her intensity dropped from 10 to 6. At this point, a Setup Affirmation that began "even though I still have some of this . . ." was used, followed by another round of tapping. This time the intensity fell to 2. Then they did another Setup Affirmation beginning with "even if I never get completely over this . . . ," and a last round of tapping.

By this time, Sandy was breathing quietly. Her skin was free of blotches, her eyes were clear, and she was looking at her hands, lying folded in her lap. The therapist said, "Sandy, as you sit there now, think back to that hot summer day when your stepfather took you for that walk down that country road. Think about how you hiked up the side of that hill until you stopped. Think about how he took off all your clothes. Think of how he took off all his clothes. Now, what do you get?"

She sat there without moving for maybe five seconds, then looked up calmly and said, without undue emotion, "Well, I still hate him." The therapist, after agreeing that hating him might be a reasonable response and possibly a useful one to keep, then asked, "But what about the distress you were feeling?"

Again she paused before answering. This time she laughed as she said, "I don't know. I just can't get there. Well, that was twenty years ago. I was just a little girl. I couldn't protect myself then the way I can now. What's the point in getting upset about something like that . . . I never let that man touch me again, and my kids have never been allowed to be near him. I don't know, it just doesn't seem to bother me like it did."

After this single session, she no longer experienced negative feelings in response to her partner's sexual advances. On a two-year follow-up, she reported that the problem was "good and gone"; and her partner, now her husband, confirmed that there was no sign of the former difficulties. Notice, also, that by the end of the session she was speaking of the trauma almost casually, and she was placing it into a self-affirming framework: "Well, that was twenty years ago. I was just a little girl. I couldn't protect myself then the way I can now." Such shifts in relation to a traumatic memory that has been emotionally cleared using an energy intervention are typical.

## PEELING AWAY THE LAYERS OF SEXUAL ABUSE

The above case is presented because it is so straightforward that it is easy to follow what occurred. One traumatic incident. One aspect. Instant results. The path is not always so direct. Rachel told her therapist[3] that she had worked through her childhood sexual-abuse history in therapy, but she still felt that fears and other emotions got in the way of her intimate relationships. She said she "keeps people at bay" and "loses her centre" when she gets involved, and she explained that this was why her relationships have always "backfired."

The therapist did not automatically accept her assurance that she had "worked through her childhood sexual abuse" in her previous therapy. Energy therapists quickly learn that when a client who has been in conventional treatment makes a statement like that, it doesn't necessarily mean the emotions have been resolved. The issue may still cause a reaction in the brain that triggers a dysfunctional emotional response. It is not that they are lying. *"Working through it"* often means they have talked about it repeatedly in therapeutic sessions to gain insight and understanding and hopefully to feel better about it. They may have learned to cope with or repress the emotional response, or to change the subject when the topic comes up. But ask them a pointed question that gets to the heart of the matter and you will often get cringing, tears, physical upsets, and other symptoms of a still-unresolved issue. Taking a clue from Rachel's continuing difficulty with intimacy, the therapist made a first guess that the emotional aftermath of her sexual abuse had not been adequately resolved.

She asked Rachel how she felt talking about her relationships, and Rachel described a physical reaction: "My stomach feels gurgly and gassy. It's holding on to something, not letting go. Something is not being processed the way it should be." The therapist soon had her tapping, using a Setup Affirmation that began "although there's something I can't digest and process . . ." Rachel's stomach calmed with the tapping, and the therapist next asked, "If your digestive system could say what it is that it can't digest and process, what would that be?" The answer Rachel offered was "too much excitement. I just can't process it. I get overwhelmed." Rachel then tapped on "although I get overwhelmed . . ." This led to an insight: "Yes, part of me hates that feeling . . . but another part of me craves it. It's like teen energy. I love the excitement."

The therapist asked her to tune in to what it is like to have these two opposing parts, asking if it set her up for tension or anxiety. Rachel responded that she wanted to learn to contain it all, to enjoy the excitement without being overstimulated. She next tapped for "although I tend to get overstimulated . . ." This was followed by her getting images of herself as a child. She became aware that as a child, if she felt good about anything, she couldn't contain it. She had to "go out and burn it off." This had been true in adulthood, too. Feeling good made her "want to go out and party."

Next the therapist asked her to close her eyes, think about feeling good, and notice her response. Did it give her a calm feeling? Did it give her anxiety? It was as if a light had come on in Rachel's head. She realized that this was the core of her inability to have successful relationships.

Whenever she got close to someone and began to enjoy the pleasure, the anxiety would be so strong that she would sabotage the relationship.

So Rachel tapped on "although feeling good makes me anxious . . ." Tears welled up in her eyes. She realized that as a child, at times "the sexual abuse felt good, but it was bad." She was still carrying that strong inner message that it wasn't okay to feel good. She tapped for "although I learned that feeling good was bad . . ." and "although my child believed that feeling good was bad, I deeply and completely love and accept my child and I know she was a good girl and it wasn't her fault." This was all very moving, the first time she had truly felt compassion for how confused that part of her had been. She next tapped on "releasing this belief that feeling good is bad."

The ninety-minute session did not end there. Rachel next tapped on the pain of how there was no one to tell (about the abuse) and no one to help her. She also worked with her grief over all she had lost by not being able to bond in relationships with others during adulthood. Then, at a certain point, she got in touch with some very positive childhood memories: For example, she remembered that she excelled at a certain sport and felt great about her body when she was really in the flow, "feeling good and calm at the same time." Her therapist showed her how to reinforce the feeling of being fully alive yet not overstimulated by "rubbing in the positive," using the chest sore spots while recalling this memory and stating, "Just calm and in the flow."

At their next meeting, Rachel reported: "Connections with people feel different. I feel an easiness being with people. I just feel closer. It's like the anxiety all went away. There's a part of me that feels really peaceful now. And I've been really energetic!"

While it is beyond the scope of any book to suggest that a history of sexual abuse can be overcome without outside help, this case is instructive in several ways. For one thing, it illustrates how guilt is often a component of unresolved abuse. People tend to focus on their anger and victimization, but Rachel's dilemma that "feeling good is bad" is not uncommon.

Sexual abuse involves our pleasure zones. In some cases, it felt good as well as horrible or confusing. This is not a popular notion. Social pressure actually causes people who were abused to focus on their anger and victimization rather than their guilt. Anger and other feelings about having been victimized can be directed outward, towards the abuser, and that is certainly appropriate. But if guilt is there, it must also be confronted. Guilt is an "inside job." It requires taking personal responsibility for an ongoing problem. For this reason, people often resist working on their own guilt. Those who were abused, however, sometimes need to develop internal permission to recognize that feelings of guilt are involved if they are fully to resolve the ongoing emotional problems caused by the abuse.

## APPLYING THE BASIC RECIPE
## TO A DIFFICULT MEMORY

Additional principles illustrated by Rachel's case include:

1. how many aspects *may be involved* in a complex issue such as relationship difficulties,
2. how resolving one aspect can point to the next one if you simply notice your internal responses,
3. how current issues often lead you to earlier memories, and
4. how rapidly each aspect may be resolved by using the Basic Recipe. Again, each round requires only about a minute.

Rachel's case notwithstanding, many traumatic memories can be resolved without treating any aspects beyond the main memory. A few trips through the Basic Recipe and the energy disturbance and subsequent emotion no longer occur. The memory will lose its emotional charge, and in many cases the change is permanent.

Other traumatic memories, however, have several aspects. They require more time because you need to identify the aspects and then work with each one. But even if extra rounds of the Basic Recipe are needed, the time required to defuse a traumatic memory can still be relatively brief. The most challenging task is identifying the relevant aspects of the memory.

A technique that can support you in identifying the relevant aspects of a memory or a problem is to make a mental movie of the memory or the situation on which you are focusing. This helps the relevant issues become clearer. A traumatic memory is actually already like a short movie that runs in the theatre of your mind: There is a beginning, there are main characters and events, and there is an end. Usually such "movies" play in a flash and finish with a familiar unwanted emotion. Because the movie plays so fast, we are often unaware that it may have different aspects which each contribute to the negative emotion. The emotional reaction seems to come from the movie as a whole.

If you run the movie in slow motion, however, the different aspects can be located and then addressed. And that is exactly the technique we are suggesting: Run the movie in slow motion, examining it scene by scene. If you are concerned that it might be traumatic to reimagine the movie, there is an important in-between step: Begin with the "tearless trauma" technique (p. 32), where you guess *what it would be like* to think about the issue, and use the Basic Recipe to remove some of the charge from the memory until you can psychologically enter the scene without too much discomfort.

Then, run the memory as a short mental movie (perhaps one to three minutes). At the same time, narrate the movie. Describe it *out loud*. Tell it to a friend or a mirror or a tape recorder or simply the space in front of you. And, most important, tell it in detail. This automatically slows the movie down because words are much slower than thoughts.

As you tell it in detail, each aspect will make itself known to you. Stop as soon as you feel *any* intensity (remember, this approach is designed to be adapted in ways that minimize pain) and perform the Basic Recipe on that part of the story as though it were a separate traumatic memory. Actually, it *is* a separate traumatic memory; it just got lost within the larger movie. Continue through the movie, stopping at each aspect. Bring each one to zero, until you can tell the whole story with no negative emotional impact whatsoever.

Again, many traumatic memories have only one aspect. Others have two or three. More than three is relatively rare. Whatever the number, be persistent. If you have several traumatic memories, use the same strategy you would use for several fears or phobias: Treat them one at a time. Take the most intense memory first and bring it to zero before going on to the next one. Then take the next, until each has been neutralized. In the process, you will likely feel a sense of freedom, which may actually border on euphoria. It is a tremendous relief to unload useless baggage. Some people, like war veterans or victims of ritual abuse, may have hundreds of traumatic memories. As they begin to neutralize some of the memories working with an energy-oriented practitioner, the generalization effect (p. 15) eventually comes into play. Once they have completely cleared between five and twenty of the memories, they are likely to notice that after a certain point they have little emotional intensity about the remaining ones. The generalization effect will have neutralized them. So even if your troubling memories run in the dozens or more, relief need not be far away.

## ANXIETY

The 9 percent of people who during any six-month period are afflicted with an anxiety disorder share at least one common trait—they hunger for relief. While fear is an emotion designed to cause us either to flee from danger or to be fully focused and motivated in situations that demand effective action, if the emergency response lasts for a prolonged period of time, the experience can be hard to bear. Fear is a core, visceral survival response designed to cause you to take action. Anxiety is fear without a specific target or action plan, yet it can readily attach itself to all manner of perceived threats. It not only fills the mind with panic, dread, consuming fright, excessive worry, terrifying flashbacks, or seemingly likely horrific scenarios; it can also permeate the body causing shakes, nausea, a racing heart, stomach upset, aching muscles, fatigue, numbness, restlessness, or insomnia. Beyond this psychic and physical distress, anxiety can interfere with a person's ability to function. In the circular grip of chronic anxiety, fear of the next episode becomes yet another source of anxiety. This is not a condition people can ignore. And it also is one they cannot usually just *will* themselves out of, though they may wish to do so with all their strength.

## A TODDLER'S TEMPER TANTRUMS

Fortunately, anxiety disorders respond particularly well to energy interventions. You do not need to identify the target of the anxiety, which is a good thing since anxiety is often free-floating and doesn't have an identifiable target or is triggered by pop-up targets, readily jumping from one perceived threat to another. The following scenario, while not about anxiety per se, illustrates how the methods can be effective even when you don't exactly know the source of the problem.

A three-year-old boy, Evan, had uncontrollable temper tantrums whenever he could not have his way. Evan's parents were both busy doctors, and he was often cared for by other people. Gina and her husband, a couple who frequently had this job, brought Evan along when they visited a friend, Blair, with the intention that they all take a walk in the woods. Evan was very shy when they arrived at Blair's home and turned away from his greeting, but he opened up as they walked along the trail and was in great spirits by the end of the hike. Then they all sat alongside a creek near Blair's home, tossing rocks into the water.

When it was time to go, Evan didn't want to leave and went into a violent temper tantrum. Gina carried him up a hill as he screamed and sobbed, struggling in her arms. Then she put him in his car seat and left the door open. He continued screaming as the adults moved away from the car to talk.

Blair asked what they usually do when he gets like this. "We can't do anything," Gina said. "He just has to have his way. If I talk to him it gets worse and we end up fighting, so I have to leave him alone." She went on to explain that Evan was seeing a psychotherapist and a speech therapist. Blair asked what the professionals suggest doing during this kind of episode. "Nothing," Gina replied. "They just let him cry himself out."

Blair,[4] although not a professional therapist, had some training in EFT. He asked Gina's permission to "try something," and Gina had no objection. He walked over to the still-screaming child and said, "It's okay. I know it's hard for you right now." He reached down, took Evan's little hand, and started tapping on his karate-chop point as he said, "Even though you're really upset right now, we all love you." He tapped around Evan's eyes. "Even though you're really upset right now, you're okay just the way you are." He tapped on the boy's face, then his chest, and the crying stopped. Evan began smiling, and wiped his tears away. Blair finished the round, tapping the back of Evan's hand, held it for a moment, then let go. Evan sat quietly. Gina was dumbstruck. "What did you do? He can't listen to anything when he gets like that, and touching him makes him really mad! What did you do?"

This story (and many others like it) suggests that the Basic Recipe works whether or not you believe it will and whether or not you understand the cause of the feelings. The tapping sent signals to Evan's brain that interrupted the tantrum, and his angry feelings ceased. Because he was already in the midst of the emotion, no Reminder Phrase was necessary.

## AN OBSESSIVE-COMPULSIVE DISORDER

Diane was, in her late teens, diagnosed with obsessive-compulsive disorder (OCD), an anxiety condition that may involve ritualized behaviour, repetitive thoughts about questions such as "Did I lock the front door?" and difficulty in adjusting to new situations. Now thirty and wanting to become pregnant, she wished to go off the medication she had been taking for a decade. Whenever she tried to discontinue her medication in the past, however, extreme anxiety had caused her to resume taking it. At this point, fortunately, she had good support and was highly motivated. While remaining in the care of her treating psychiatrist, she consulted David Lake, M.D., with the hope that energy work would help her to discontinue the drugs. He reports:

> I considered her request a tall order because of the severity of the condition, my limited success using EFT with severe OCD, and the potential complications for her. Nevertheless I thought that using and teaching her to use meridian stimulation would be worthwhile. I did not know whether Diane would be able to cease medication at all—and I told her this. I notified her psychiatrist that I was teaching her a relaxation and stress-management technique that could in some cases have additional benefits as well.
>
> Her symptoms included severe compulsive "checking" of details about the house when going out, and re-checking in most instances as she "forgot" whether she had really been certain of a detail. The process might take an hour. She also suffered panic attacks and generalized anxiety. She had recently developed a fear of flying and was due to fly shortly. I told her that we would make an experiment using EFT and see how much benefit it returned to her.
>
> Initially I taught her the variation of meridian stimulation I call "continual tapping" (see www.eftdownunder.com/articles_EFT.html# Continual) with good results. She noticed a great lessening of the compulsive urge and was particularly pleased to know a self-help technique. After a week, we began to explore her limiting beliefs about her OCD using formal EFT and also using the provocative style that Steve Wells and I have found brings great focus and leverage to a problem. Some of

her greatest fears were that she would never get over this and that she would have it forever, that there was nothing she could do about it, and that it could get worse. Sometimes the fear during an anxiety attack was "paralyzing" and "terrifying"; her ultimate fear was that "I can't be reassured." There were several such intense panic incidents that needed a lot of work to desensitize with tapping, using Gary's excellent "Tell the Story" technique.[5]

Diane continued her practice at home mainly using continual tapping for convenience. She used the tapping I taught her more often and more effectively than anyone I can remember.

At the end of the third session she told me that she had ceased her medication since she felt so well using EFT. I was alarmed, since these medications should be ceased gradually, but because she seemed well we pressed on. She told me that her fear had once returned but it was manageable and subsided with the tapping after half an hour. Her fear of flying was also "95 percent gone" when she next flew in a plane.

On another occasion about six weeks into our treatment, she had a panic and anxiety attack lasting many hours, which did not respond so well to EFT. This was a setback to her; nevertheless, we continued the experiment. There was another episode like this a few weeks later.

Diane remained in control of her symptoms thereafter, using EFT. Her confidence increased and she functioned with a better balance, more accepting and less self-critical. Her old checking habits and anxieties were still there in a minor way, but did not interfere with her life. We had some six EFT sessions over three months, and she became pregnant about six months later. She did have what I would call ordinary anxieties about becoming pregnant and being a good mother. During the later stage of her pregnancy, she did come to see me about an anxiety she "couldn't shake," related to whether her worrying would harm the baby, and if the baby was in fact all right. We dealt with the new fears in the same way as all her original fears and presenting worries—a lot of continual tapping and traditional EFT on every specific aspect we could think of. There was also the fear of the "unknown," of looking after a dependent baby, and whether she would cope with the responsibilities.

Considering how universal these fears are in mothers-to-be, I was struck by how "normal" their degree was for Diane. She did not lose control and she did face up to the reality very well, learning more coping skills and just understanding how other people cope too.

Her progress from the beginning was surprising to me. I have not had this kind of rapid success before in such a severe case of OCD, and with relatively few sessions.

Again, this is a clinical example, and it is appropriate that a therapist be involved with any case of severe anxiety. By seeing how a more extreme situation was handled in a clinical setting you gain deeper insight into how to apply energy methods to everyday anxieties.

## TREATING DISABLING ANXIETY

Rikki, a twenty-five-year-old woman with a five-year history of agoraphobia (a fear of being in open areas or public places) with severe panic symptoms, was referred for psychotherapy[6] by a health-care professional who had been attempting to treat the anxiety using homeopathic remedies. Rikki refused to see a psychiatrist because she was unwilling to consider taking traditional antianxiety medications. Despite having a twenty-two-month-old daughter, she had rarely left her house in the fifteen months prior to entering therapy. She was overwhelmed with disabling anxiety and fears of just about everything. She had not driven a car or left her block in all that time and had food and other supplies delivered.

Given these circumstances, the therapist made home visits and supplemented them with phone sessions. After Rikki learned the tapping procedure, the phone became a viable alternative for the therapist to coach her in applying the method as new situations emerged. Rikki's anxiety about "unsafety in the world" was triggered and fuelled by a multitude of negative thoughts and belief systems that all started with a *"what if . . ."* followed by a *"then . . ."* statement that included a worst-case scenario. For example, "What if I start to drive to my grandmother's house and then I get stuck in traffic at the corner of Main Street and Elm, and I have to go to the bathroom, and I get nervous, and I'm stuck there, and then I can't get back home again." Rikki was aware that her thoughts fuelled her panic, but she had no way to stop them.

The therapy began by tracking her thoughts and her complex system of negative beliefs. With each discovery of a new "nagging" thought, the Basic Recipe was used to eradicate it. While she responded well, she would also frequently mention another fear: that simply acknowledging her worries would escalate her anxiety. At these times, the therapist would have her stop and tap on "even though continuing makes me feel a little nervous . . ." Then she could continue. Rikki began to feel empowered by the process of uncovering her negative thought patterns and having a way to disengage them.

After the initial session, she was able to walk out of her house without feeling anxious. After the second session, she drove the three blocks into town, took her daughter to the library, and began daily brief excursions. Her life was beginning to normalize. Even after she uncovered a core issue and the anxiety returned, she was still able to go out into town.

The core issue had to do with an LSD trip she experienced when she was sixteen years old. She had been traumatized by the "stuckness" of not being able to stop the hallucinations and distortions she experienced for twelve interminable hours. She described her shame and guilt about having taken the drug, as well as the traumatization. The work on this incident required two sessions. The Basic Recipe was first used on her shame and guilt. Then it was applied to the fact that she was allowing herself the memories and verbalizing them, since she believed that talking or reliving the emotional experience would trigger an acid flashback. Next was the feeling that it was unsafe to do this work and the fear that she would uncover something that would propel her into even greater pain. She and her therapist became partners in the process of uncovering and addressing her fears about doing energy work on relieving the trauma of the acid trip itself, and then on her complex system of negative beliefs. It was a profound experience for this young woman to free herself of her agoraphobia and panic attacks by making peace with her "nagging anxiety thoughts and all those what-ifs."

## APPLYING THE BASIC RECIPE TO ANXIETY

Again, the point here is not to encourage you to treat yourself for a serious psychiatric condition without the help of a qualified professional. Rather, by seeing how a severe case of anxiety was successfully treated using the Basic Recipe, you will have a stronger basis for applying the essential principles to help yourself with the normal anxieties of everyday life.

And most of us face anxiety-provoking circumstances every day. Turn on the news. Think about your worries concerning your children, your health, your retirement. We don't have to enumerate; you know it all too well. But it is also not necessary, or useful, to dwell on what can go wrong. Hanging out in anxiety and pessimism does not keep bad things from happening or make you any more effective if they do. Keeping the anxiety at bay is an important skill in these troubling times. In fact, activating your optimism, rather than causing you to be off guard and vulnerable to more bad things, has the effect of making you more resilient and effective in managing life's challenges.[7] Energy methods can help you to turn off unnecessary anxiety and to transform negative, pessimistic thinking—as you will see in the following chapter—into an outlook that highlights and promotes possibilities that are desirable and realistic.

Notice that with Rikki, a traumatic memory was one of the core aspects of her anxiety, but equally harmful were her intruding "what-if" thoughts and negative beliefs. Remember how even as the energy methods were working, fears would emerge about the process itself. She worried that "simply acknowledging my worries will escalate my anxiety" or "just thinking about my LSD experience will cause a flashback." As these negative thoughts intruded, circling back on the treatment itself, the therapist patiently had *them* become the focus of the tapping treatments. You can do that for yourself as well. As you focus on your anxiety, the aspects most likely to emerge are memories from the past that contributed to current feelings of anxiety and negative thoughts that feed them. Both will be responsive to the Basic Recipe.

## DEPRESSION

An estimated forty million people in the United States alone are clinically depressed, and the numbers are increasing. Depression can cause persistent sadness and lethargy, a sense of personal worthlessness, negative thoughts and perceptions, a loss of interest in normal activities, changes in diet and sleep patterns, and frequent thoughts of death. Although medication successfully treats the symptoms of depression in millions of people, the precise causes and mechanisms of the disorder remain elusive. Patients often must go through a period of trial and error before the best drug regimen is identified, and even then the medication may not be as effective as hoped, and will often cause mild to severe side effects.

What is well understood is that if you are depressed, your brain operates differently than it does when you are not depressed. Restoring proper brain function is the goal of all treatments for depression—whether directly, as with medication, or indirectly, as in the development of more life-affirming behaviours, attitudes, and habits of thought. By sending electromagnetic impulses to the brain while focusing on various elements of the depression, energy psychology can *sometimes* restore normal functioning quite readily.

If a person who is going through a difficult and seemingly endless series of challenges becomes depressed, you can certainly understand it. Periods of depression serve a function. Sometimes called "reactive depression," these episodes force you to slow down, turn inward, and adjust to a loss or difficult circumstance. It is either a healthy response that can leave you stronger and more resilient, or it can become self-perpetuating, trapping you in a cycle of negative thinking and self-doubt. When this occurs, the Basic Recipe can be applied to the recent experiences that initiated the depression ("Even though I miss Bill terribly . . .") as well as to various other aspects of the depression, such as negative thought patterns ("Even though I keep dwelling on the missed opportunities . . .") or unresolved early experiences ("Even though this reminds me of how devastated I felt when I was eleven and Grandma died . . .").

## A WOMAN TREATS HERSELF FOR LONG-STANDING DEPRESSION

Maggie was fifty-eight and all her life had suffered from a "low grade" depression that she said would never go away: "It has always been there in the background, and at times it was very intense." She had tried every healing modality she could find short of medication, from primal therapy to acupuncture to nutritional counselling. None had helped sufficiently. She did report some benefit from giving up alcohol, coffee, and tobacco, but she still hurt inside most of the time. Though strongly resistant to taking psychiatric medication, she was considering it when she discovered EFT. Within two days of learning and applying the method based on a home-study course that teaches the principles and techniques presented here, she reported that she "had healed stage fright, and I started in on all my sad and angry feelings." Within a month, she was no longer feeling depressed. Her friends began to comment on the changes they saw in her. She then focused her attention on her "denied creativity," and the poetry she at one time enjoyed writing began "flowing again." She commented that her new "healthy attitude" had started to seem so normal that she would "tend to forget how bad things used to be. That's real progress!"

## MAJOR DEPRESSION

Not all depression is a reaction to life events or negative thinking. Some people's neurochemistry predisposes them to be depressed. This kind of depression tends to run in families and often has a genetic basis. The gene that influences whether you are more or less vulnerable to becoming depressed after a traumatic event, for instance, has been identified.[8] In addition to genetics, early experiences, extending all the way back to conditions in the mother's body during pregnancy, can also predispose a person to depression.

The more the basis of the depression is in the genes or in early experiences, the more difficult it usually is to treat—regardless of the clinical approach. In the treatment of long-standing major depression, most psychotherapists, including energy-oriented practitioners, supplement psychotherapy with psychiatric medication.[9] Psychologist Patricia Carrington explains that otherwise, it can become "a test of endurance" when, time and time again, the therapist may have helped the client become symptom-free by the end of a session, but by the next appointment the gains seem to have evaporated.

Carrington illustrates this by relating her work with Maria, a woman she describes as being highly intelligent and strongly motivated to overcome her irrational feelings of fear and helplessness. However, they discovered early on in the treatment that although Maria would often make excellent progress using the Basic Recipe, even dealing with core issues that were central to her life, the therapy was still unable to "stem the tide" of the depression. The despair and fear were just too much for her, and were undermining her progress. Bringing medication into the treatment made it possible to systematically work with Maria's irrational thoughts and sense of helplessness without the results being dashed by the next wave of depression. The medication was introduced with the aim of phasing it out as soon as Maria had built up her inner strength. Combining Prozac with a tapping approach led to "transformational work," in which Maria "has been able to explore the deepest issues, some of them so early in origin as to be wordless, and one by one to resolve them. And, with the support that she has obtained from the medication—which didn't in itself solve her problems but did enable her to work on them diligently in therapy—she has rebuilt a 'self,' has restructured her relationships to people and the world. . . . She has voluntarily taken herself off of all medication and is doing remarkably well in an exciting new phase of her treatment."

Clinical research supports this strategy. For patients with chronic depression, a combination of medication and psychotherapy seems to prove more helpful than either treatment alone, both in terms of reducing the symptoms[10] and improving overall functioning.[11] Carrington concludes: "Without the help of the drug we couldn't have done it, and similarly, if she had had the drug alone without the therapy . . . at best the drug would have held her in a holding pattern."

## APPLYING THE BASIC RECIPE TO DEPRESSION

The conventional psychotherapy that has been used most successfully in the treatment of depression is Cognitive Behaviour Therapy (CBT). CBT teaches people to interrupt such maladaptive thought patterns as ruminating on everything that might go wrong, seeing the glass only as half empty, or blaming themselves for things over which they have no control. This approach has much in common with energy psychology, where you separate complex reactions into their component thoughts, feelings, and behaviours. But energy psychology adds a means for sending electromagnetic signals that directly shift the neurological sequences involved in maladaptive thoughts and attitudes, often deactivating them with surprising speed and precision. The successful treatment of depression also often includes a number of commonsense lifestyle modifications that can be supported with use of the Basic Recipe, such as increasing rest, decreasing stress, introducing more physical exercise, and developing a better interpersonal support system.

A powerful combination of energy interventions with Cognitive Behaviour Therapy has been developed by Hank Krol,[12] a psychotherapist in Pennsylvania. He gives his clients standardized checklists for assessing depression.[13] They rate themselves on a scale of 1 to 4 for each of nineteen symptoms, according to the frequency of the symptom. Among the symptoms on the scale are:

- feelings of guilt
- irritable mood
- less interest or pleasure in usual activities
- withdrawing from or avoiding people
- finding it harder than usual to do things

Another checklist helps his patients identify the negative beliefs that accompany their depression, such as:

- "I'm no good."
- "I will always fail."
- "Things will never get better."
- "No one can help me."

Identifying these specifics separates depression into its cognitive, affective, and behavioural aspects. Each can then be targeted with energy interventions, using the Basic Recipe much as you learned it in chapter 2. Krol will generally select only one aspect for a single session, two at the most. He will verify that it is important to the patient that distress around this particular issue be reduced. If so, he will (unless the person happens to be directly experiencing the issue at the moment) ask the person to recall a recent situation when the symptom was experienced at a high intensity. The patient applies the Basic Recipe, reducing as much as possible the rating on this aspect of the depression during the session. Homework is also assigned to continue the process between meetings.

In the next session, another memory involving the same symptom or negative thought is identified, rated, and treated if necessary. The patient keeps a focus on this same aspect of the depression until it has been brought down to a 0 or near 0 or a different aspect requires attention before it can be reduced further. Once it has been cleared, another aspect is selected and worked with until it has been neutralized. Krol has found this approach to be quite effective with many of his patients, but doing the suggested self-treatments between sessions seems important to its success.

Different types of depression need to be approached differently. Sometimes a depression simply disappears with a few minutes of tapping. This can be very dramatic, but it is not usually the case, particularly with a serious depression. More often, the depression appears to be caused by numerous unresolved emotional issues such as guilt, shame, fear, grief, or anger. These more complex or persistent depressions usually require work with a skilled counsellor who is able to identify and focus on the core emotional issues. Even more challenging are long-standing depressions where there is reason to suspect a strong biological component. Here, even the best psychotherapy sometimes needs to be supplemented by medication.

Again, for major or ongoing depression, consult a health-care professional, perhaps one who will support you in using an energy approach as an adjunct to the therapy. In applying the Basic Recipe to the more usual mood swings all of us must negotiate, the feature to adapt from Krol's approach is to *be specific*. If stating the generic problem such as "even though I have this depression . . ." does not give you distinct and lasting improvement within a few rounds of the Basic Recipe, separate your depressed mood into aspects like negative thoughts, earlier times when you felt depressed or engaged in negative thinking, other instances when you tended to withdraw, et cetera, and treat them one by one. As the core aspects of *this* depression lose their grip on you, not only will the depression tend to lift, but also you will be building a resilience that makes you less vulnerable to falling into future depression.

## HABITS AND ADDICTIONS

Beyond being able to apply the Basic Recipe to each of the psychological aspects of addiction—such as the cravings, the emotional dependencies, and the personal history that led to the particular object of the addiction—energy therapists are able to shift the dopamine and serotonin imbalances that underlie addiction. The biochemical signature of a person who is predisposed to addiction includes low levels of serotonin (a brain chemical that transmits nerve impulses) combined with a tendency to too readily secrete dopamine (another "neurotransmitter," whose actions are very different from those of serotonin).[14] The correction of this serotonin/dopamime imbalance using energy interventions exemplifies the way that energy psychology can build on scientific understanding of the precise brain mechanisms involved in difficult disorders for formulating effective treatment strategies, and we will discuss in some detail the chemistry of addiction and the application of an energy approach in its treatment.

### THE NEUROCHEMISTRY OF ADDICTION

The neurochemistry of addiction has been closely studied and, to a reasonable degree, mapped. While the following is a vast oversimplification, the basic ingredients of addictive behaviour are rooted in the same mechanisms nature created to motivate us to do the three essential activities necessary for personal and species survival: eating/drinking, avoiding harm, and reproducing. Our motivation to perform these actions is regulated by a small structure in the primitive brain called the "nucleus accumbens" and by a dance within it between two brain chemicals—dopamine and serotonin. Dopamine motivates you to do what is required to obtain food, ensure safety, and procreate. Once you are full, safe, or satisfied, serotonin is secreted. Serotonin restrains the action of dopamine, turning off the compelling motivation to address a primal need. According to Ron Ruden, M.D., Ph.D., in *The Craving Brain*, dopamine sends the message "Gotta have it—go get it," and serotonin sends the mission-accomplished message, "Got it."[15]

When you are hungry, for instance, the nucleus accumbens is sensitized to anything associated with food or with ways to get food. When it recognizes something that can assuage your hunger, it secretes dopamine to motivate you into action to obtain the food. Meanwhile, if you are really hungry, your brain serotonin levels have become low. When serotonin levels are down, the effects of dopamine are amplified, making its call to action an imperative. You can think of little other than food. Once you have eaten, signals originating in your digestive system increase your serotonin levels, your hunger subsides, and you feel a sense of satiation and contentment.

Because we evolved to be able to keep ourselves fed in as many circumstances as possible, it is more than the mere presence of food that releases the dopamine which causes you to spring into action. Images of food, plans for preparing a meal, thoughts of the family at the dinner table, turning onto the street of a favourite restaurant, or a television advertisement featuring chocolate may lead to the same sequence of internal events that the scent of a rabbit initiated in your ancestors. And therein lies the vulnerability to addiction. It is not only the presence of food, danger, or a desirable sexual opportunity that sets the serotonin/dopamine dance into motion. Anything *associated* with food, danger, or sexual opportunity can, when serotonin levels are low, cause high-enough dopamine levels to evoke the same focus and strength of motivation that nature designed for critical survival situations.

Since the mind can associate anything with anything, the possibilities for addiction are endless. All that is necessary is that the triggering substance, situation, or symbol can cause the release of dopamine within the addict's landscape of low serotonin. While the object of choice will depend on a complex of the addict's neurochemistry, environment, and history, dopamine levels may be sharply raised simply by thoughts of alcohol, cigarettes, narcotics, cocaine, marijuana, food, or the behaviour sequences involved in gambling, sex, work, or shopping, as well as anything that becomes symbolically associated with these substances or behaviours. Any of these may take a leading role in the addictive drama of a person whose brain is predisposed with low serotonin levels and a nucleus accumbens that secretes dopamine too readily.

An addiction—an excessive physical or psychological dependence on a substance or a behaviour—is characterized by three successive states: 1) sobriety, 2) relapse, and 3) compulsive, repetitive, coordinated behaviour to obtain the substance or carry out the activity that is the object of the addiction. For an addict, serotonin is low during the craving state that precedes relapse, the nucleus accumbens is sensitized to finding the object of the addiction or anything associated with it, high levels of dopamine are secreted, and sobriety has moved into relapse. From there, the individual feels compelled to pursue the addictive substance or behaviour.

When the object of the addiction is a behaviour such as gambling, sex, or shopping, the behaviour takes on a compulsive quality, performed without a sense of choice, sometimes literally *against one's own will*. An addiction may also be deeply entrenched in a person's self-concept or even be part of a cultural imperative. If you grew up with the Marlboro Man as an image of masculinity, or if you primarily hang out around people who smoke, quitting will be harder than if you idolize the Dalai Lama and are trying to break the habit while spending a month at a yoga retreat.

## DOPAMINE/SEROTONIN IMBALANCES

One of the most intriguing observations to come out of the first large-scale investigation of energy psychology treatments (p. 291, Appendix 3) is that stimulating certain acupuncture points on the skin appears to increase serotonin levels in the brain. While the potential implications of this finding are just beginning to be explored clinically within energy psychology, a related area, neurofeedback training, has already demonstrated measurable success in altering the brain chemistry of addicts.[16] Dr Joaquín Andrade's study (see p. 18) showed the progression of brainwave changes as a tapping protocol was administered to a patient with generalized anxiety disorder. Neurofeedback produces the same kinds of changes.

Rather than using tapping, neurofeedback training involves connecting the person to an EEG (electroencephalogram), an instrument that measures brain waves. By receiving in-the-moment information about the brain's wave patterns the person is, somewhat remarkably but quite reliably, able to willfully change those patterns in desired ways. With desire, effort, and time, this training is capable of producing permanent changes in brain chemistry that 1) reduce the amount of stress in the brain's primal survival mechanisms—presumably allowing the levels of serotonin to increase naturally—and 2) appear to make the nucleus accumbens less reactive to the desired object—less poised to secrete the dopamine that causes one to obsessively pursue the desired object. Clinical reports now suggest that the tapping protocol with addictions may have similar effects. In fact, Dr. Ruden, a pioneer in treating addiction by altering serotonin/dopamine imbalances without the use of medication, is finding that variations of the EFT Basic Recipe seem more effective than neurofeedback training for dealing with cravings and as effective in establishing better serotonin/dopamine balances by altering the person's stress-response patterns.[17]

## THE BASIC RECIPE AND ADDICTIONS

Can the Basic Recipe, simply applied to an addiction or to a deeply in-grained pattern such as "this gambling habit," overcome the addiction? There's no harm in trying, but it usually cannot. Less complex habits and cravings, however, may be more responsive. A craving is an intense desire for a specific substance or activity. Sometimes, all that is nec-essary is to treat the craving. Cases have been reported in which crav-ings for coffee, soft drinks, or chocolate have been completely and permanently eliminated (and occasionally the substance actually becomes repulsive) after a single session using the tapping protocol. For instance, the Setup Affirmation "Even though I have this craving for choco-late, I deeply love and accept myself" would be followed by tapping on the Reminder Phrase "longing for chocolate." You can initially mea-sure the distress around the issue by saying, for instance, "I'm quitting chocolate" and then giving the 0-to-10 rating on the discomfort or anxi-ety this causes you. Continue subsequent rounds until the rating is down to 0.

While it is relatively rare for this procedure to permanently undo a well-entrenched habit in a single sitting, it is at least a powerful tool for overcoming immediate, in-the-moment cravings so that a more compre-hensive approach can gain ground. The one-day-at-a-time attitude towards addictions advanced by Alcoholics Anonymous and other addic-tion programs emphasizes the importance of staying alert for an addic-tion's sudden pull, and the Basic Recipe is an effective tool to have in your back pocket 24/7.

When energy interventions are systematically applied to the different aspects of an addiction or self-destructive habit, their power is greatly ex-panded.[18] They can loosen the addiction's grip and frequently free the person from it completely. Among the dynamics that can be targeted with energy interventions are:

- elevated dopamine/reduced serotonin imbalances in the brain, as discussed above
- mentally generated stressors (e.g., guilt, hate, anger, envy) that lower serotonin levels
- the anxiety or emptiness that arises when the substance or activity is not supplied
- the ways the addiction is tied into the person's self-concept
- the ways the addiction is tied into the person's lifestyle
- the physical suffering of withdrawal (see "Physical Ailments," p. 108)
- the cultivation of other sources of primal pleasure

The tapping protocol can be adapted to address each element of the addictive syndrome. Again, this often requires skilled guidance and may need to be combined with other methods, such as AA-type support groups and relaxation or meditation training. But the overview provided here can at least help you with milder habits, and it demonstrates the underlying principles for approaching any addictive behaviour.

## TREATING A FOOD ADDICTION

Carol Look is a psychotherapist who has been particularly successful in using an energy approach to help people overcome addictions such as smoking and overeating.[19] She describes Ann, a woman who was referred for weight loss by the doctor who was treating her for back pain (caused by severe sciatica) and knee pain (following knee-replacement surgery a year earlier). When Ann first called, she reported feeling scared. While she was embarrassed about being overweight and knew her excess weight was exacerbating her physical pains and undermining her overall health, she hadn't felt ready to tackle this issue. In the first session, Ann identified three emotional reasons for her overeating: 1) to soothe a sense of emptiness she could trace to her upbringing with a cold mother and absent father, 2) to comfort her when the physical pain was overbearing, and 3) to fill a void from feeling starved of emotional and physical affection from her husband. Over four months of treatment, Dr. Look helped Ann address each of these areas with EFT. During this period Ann lost twenty-five pounds without pressuring herself to change her eating patterns.

With the EFT treatment, unlike her experiences with dieting, Ann reported that she was thrilled because she didn't feel deprived by the changes in her eating habits. She was still able to eat her favourite foods, but she had a new awareness about what her body needed. She no longer had to "eat to fill the [emotional] starvation" she had always felt. Ann described how food was no longer central in her life: "I eat moderately and am more conscious of when I'm full and what I need. . . . I enjoy not cramming food down my throat anymore."

Addressing and neutralizing the underlying emotional states that drove Ann to binge and overeat in the first place were central to her treatment. Each of the three emotional reasons Ann identified for her overeating was addressed in depth. Her mother, for instance, continued to be an active player in Ann's emotional turmoil. Ann had been overweight most of her life, and she described how she sometimes used food to "stick it to" her mother. By eating when she was irritated with her mother, she could show that she was "in charge." She understood that this was self-defeating, but she found herself unable to stop using food in this way when she was feeling angry or resentful. In her words, "I eat to squash the turmoil." In their adult relationship, Ann felt as if her mother were the child. She never felt heard or understood. In one confrontation, her mother told her she didn't think Ann was likable. Meanwhile, Ann was still as hungry for her mother's love and acceptance as she had been while a girl. As a result, she was chronically angry at her mother, and their ongoing relationship difficulties were intertwined with Ann's overeating. Here are some of the Setup Affirmations used in Ann's treatment to address her relationship with her mother:

- "Even though my mother doesn't even like me, I completely like and accept myself."
- "Even though my mother doesn't think I'm good enough, I choose to believe I'm lovable and good enough."
- "Even though I use food to comfort my loneliness, I deeply and completely accept myself."
- "Even though my mother has never understood me, I accept her for who she is."
- "Even though my mother is too selfish to hear me, I accept my own feelings anyway."

Other sequences focused on her physical pain and her relationship with her husband. In each, the core issue and its aspects were reduced to 0. Sample Setup Affirmations around the physical pain included:

- "Even though I feel enraged by my pain, I deeply and completely accept myself."
- "Even though my pain reminds me of my mother, and I feel resentful, I deeply and completely accept myself, including the pain."

Affirmations that addressed her marriage included:

- "Even though I'm not appreciated for what I do, I love and appreciate myself anyway."
- "Even though I feel angry when he doesn't listen to me, I choose to listen to myself.
- "Even though I feel rejected and it feels painful, I deeply and completely accept myself."

Along with having lost the weight, by the end of the four months of treatment, Ann reported that she was no longer triggered by her mother or her husband, and she felt much more at peace with her childhood and its emotional deprivations. While recognizing that neither her mother nor her husband had changed in any way during the four months, she felt confident that she could identify and process all her feelings in relation to both of them. She harboured no desire to abuse food as a way to suppress her feelings or avoid the realities of these relationships. In the late afternoons, when Ann used to binge on cookies and sweets, she was now taking the time to be by herself, read, think about her feelings, and tap.

## APPLYING THE BASIC RECIPE TO
## HABITS AND ADDICTIONS

The emotional baggage carried with any addiction or difficult habit can be systematically addressed, as you saw with Ann. Early in the treatment, Dr. Look asks her clients to identify the *downside* of overcoming their addictions. The answers often point to psychological reversals and other emotional aspects of the pattern. For instance, a downside Ann identified in relation to stopping her afternoon food binges was that she would feel dissatisfied and angry all the time and wouldn't know what to do with those feelings. She also said she feared that she would have to come to terms with all the turmoil in her life, and she acknowledged that the extra weight was being used as protection against years of emotional pain and feelings of rejection and abandonment.

Along with healing the emotional components that underlie an addiction, energy interventions can provide a way of dealing with cravings as they occur in the moment. While we know of no laboratory studies that track this specifically, we suspect that tapping on a specific craving impacts the dopamine/serotonin imbalances discussed earlier. In working with smokers, Look asks her clients to take out a cigarette, smell it, and rate their current desire, craving, or urge on the 0-to-10 scale. Then the Basic Recipe is used to reduce the craving as it exists right then in the office: "Even though I have this craving to smoke now . . ." She then asks her clients to identify three or four times of the day when they most like to smoke and will apply the Basic Recipe to bring down each of them. If smoking with their morning coffee is one of their favourite times, Look has them imagine having their morning coffee and giving a rating to how much they want a cigarette. Then the Basic Recipe is applied to each of these situations where the trigger for the addiction is strong, using a Setup such as "even though I want to smoke when I drink my morning coffee . . ." or "even though I have this urge to smoke after dinner . . ."

Once these urges have been brought down, Look reverses the situation. Clients are asked to imagine themselves having their morning coffee without a cigarette; then they rate the level of anxiety or upset they feel. This can subsequently be treated using the Basic Recipe, but it is a time to stay particularly alert for additional emotions that keep an addiction in place. Once these aspects of the addiction can be identified, they can be treated one by one. Among the feelings that often come up when people think of quitting their addictions are:

- fear or anxiety
- emptiness or boredom
- sadness about giving up the substance or activity, which then triggers other grief
- the loss of secondary gains—such as in an addiction to work, the accomplishments gained by keeping the addiction, or with smoking, the islands of relaxation or a defiant sense of power over one's spouse

A final consideration in stopping a physical addiction is withdrawal. Every smoker or coffee drinker who has ever tried to stop knows that the symptoms of physical withdrawal alone can keep them hooked. Sometimes it is necessary simply to tough it out. With some addictions, such as to drugs like heroin, medical intervention may be required. But with most withdrawal symptoms, energy interventions can again help. You want to keep your body's overall energy system in the best possible balance, as we will discuss in chapter 6, but you can also apply the Basic Recipe to specific physical symptoms of withdrawal, as discussed in the following section.

## PHYSICAL AILMENTS

Most physical ailments have an emotional component. Even if your illness was not *caused* by your emotions, you cannot help but become emotionally involved with any sickness that overtakes you. The Basic Recipe can address this emotional dimension of physical illness, and more often than you might expect, it can be a force in helping to overcome the physical problem. Studies show that the majority of visits to a doctor's surgery are for complaints with no apparent organic cause,[20] so on closer examination, this may not be so surprising. While sound judgment and caution are certainly called for—in other words, seek competent professional health care when you need it—the tools you have been learning about can help create an internal emotional atmosphere that is conducive to healing.

Reports found on the www.emofree.com site suggest that basic tapping methods have resulted in improvement in headaches, back pain, stiff neck and shoulders, joint pains, cancer, chronic fatigue syndrome, lupus, ulcerative colitis, psoriasis, asthma, allergies, itching eyes, body sores, rashes, insomnia, constipation, irritable bowel syndrome, eyesight, muscle tightness, bee stings, urination problems, morning sickness, PMS, sexual dysfunction, sweating, poor coordination, carpal tunnel syndrome, arthritis, numbness in the fingers, stomachaches, toothaches, trembling, and multiple sclerosis among many other physical conditions. This is not to suggest that the Basic Recipe replaces medical care, but it is interesting that an approach designed to address emotional problems is so frequently reported as helping with physical problems as well.

## EXAMPLES OF PHYSICAL CONDITIONS

A therapist[21] who was having her home remodelled noticed that one of the construction workers had a strange skin condition on his arms. She asked him about it, and he said, "Oh, that's my psoriasis. Had it for years." He turned his arms around to show her that from his wrists to his shoulders, his skin was a bubbling ocean of peeling skin with sore red tissue and fluid beneath it. She replied, "Ooh, that must be painful. How did you get it?" "Well, I don't know," he replied, "I guess it started about three years ago, when my girlfriend told me she was pregnant." The therapist asked if he might like to try a new treatment she knew. He was dubious. His doctor had told him there was nothing to be done. The therapist replied, "Ah, yes, what he meant was, there's nothing to be done with pills, ointments, and injections. Your mind created this, and so only your mind can take it away again." He nodded and she showed him just a bare-bones procedure, suggesting that three times each day he do three rounds of tapping to the statement "I want to get over my psoriasis." Within two weeks, his skin had healed on both arms, down to a small patch the size of a coin on his elbows. In addition, he has since used the approach to overcome lower-back pain that had troubled him for years.

A woman who had suffered from carpal tunnel syndrome for about eight years received some training in EFT. After having had extensive chiropractic and physical-therapy treatment, she thought she was about as healed as she was going to be without surgery. Even though she felt better in general, the chronic pain still wore her down occasionally. After being introduced to EFT and being guided through a tapping sequence for about ten minutes, she had absolutely no pain! She reports, "I couldn't believe it! I kept mentally searching throughout my body for the pain. It just wasn't there! I had actually taken a few minutes to tap on the corner of my eye, my hand, and other simple, easy-to-reach places on my body and had shed this pain with which I thought I was destined to live!" Next she applied it to grief that had burdened her for many years. Within minutes, she recounts, "I felt the weight lift from me. I have been able to remember my sister fondly and nostalgically, but with no pain of grief, ever since!"[22]

A man[23] who had recently been introduced to EFT convinced his wife to apply it for her severe lactose intolerance (an inability to digest a type of sugar that is found only in milk and milk products), with which she had suffered for more than a decade. Even small amounts of lactose would cause her pain, gas, diarrhoea, and embarrassment. Hypnosis had not helped, and there is no established treatment except to avoid milk products. Here is the husband's report:

> We decided to give EFT a try. I told her to buy some ice cream (she hasn't had any in years because of what it does to her). We chose Friday morning (Christmas Eve) for the tapping so that if it didn't work, she would be close to the toilet for three days. We dished out the ice cream, and I had her look at the bowl of Chocolate Truffle. She rated her anxiety about eating it at an eight. We tapped until that was zero. Then we picked up other aspects (fear, silliness, etc.) for another five minutes.
>
> Once it seemed as though we had covered everything, she enjoyed that bowl of ice cream and braced herself for the worst. The first hour passed. Wow. No problem. Then half the day passed. Double wow! Still no problem. In the afternoon, she went out and ran some errands. That night for dinner, she had ranch dressing and ice cream for dessert. Still no problem. Now it has been four full days and she's had cream of broccoli soup, more ice cream, milk chocolate, and more.
>
> Shirley and I didn't expect to have any results with EFT, based on what we've been told about the condition. As we understand it, a person only has "so many" enzymes in their lifetime, and once you use them up, that's it. Your body can't produce any more. Based on this belief, I knew

EFT probably wouldn't work, but it only takes a few minutes, so why not try it? Those of us without this problem take these things for granted, but my wife has been set free. I hope this inspires someone else to become free of unnecessary pain, discomfort, and embarrassment.

A woman trained in EFT[24] was at an elegant dinner party when one of the guests began to go into anaphylactic shock. Anaphylactic shock is a rapid and severe allergic reaction to a substance (most often a vaccine or penicillin, shellfish, or insect venom such as a bee sting) to which the person has been sensitized by previous exposure. It can be fatal if emergency treatment, including the administration of epinephrine injections, is not given immediately. Apparently, this man was severely allergic to shellfish and he was unknowingly eating crab-stuffed ravioli. As his face and throat began to swell, the host jumped up to call for help. The woman immediately took the man into another room and began to treat him with EFT. Before her eyes, the swelling in his face and neck began to go down and in just a few minutes he had returned to normal. He rejoined the dinner party and the emergency call was cancelled as all his symptoms completely vanished. All this occurred within a ten-minute period.

## GETTING TO EMOTIONAL CAUSES

In each of these cases, little attention was given to the emotional causes of the physical condition, yet a simple tapping routine was sufficient. In other cases, emotional aspects are central in the treatment. Gary was making a presentation at a conference when a participant named Janet asked if she could have a private session to help with her nearly constant pain from fibromyalgia. She had already been tapping sporadically for three or four weeks prior to the conference. At best, she would get temporary relief for an hour or two but then the pains would come back. Gary decided to focus on the emotional causes of Janet's condition. He asked her to pick out an intense emotional issue from her past. She chose one that was so intense that she rarely discussed it with anyone. She quickly rated it at a 10 and had strong bodily sensations at the mere thought of it.

To apply the tapping with minimal emotional pain, Gary had her make a mental movie (as described on p. 83) of the event, and narrate it. Because the suggestion to verbalize the event caused Janet to go into an emotional reaction, they did a few rounds of the Basic Recipe even before she began the narration. These preliminary rounds began "even though I'm anxious about telling this story . . ." Eventually Janet was ready to narrate the story as though it were a movie. As she did, Gary had her stop whenever she came to any part of it that increased her emotional intensity. They stopped several times and tapped on various evocative scenes. They actually went through the story two or three times, and each time they found different aspects of the problem that required individual attention. It took between thirty and forty minutes, including restful conversation in between the rounds of tapping, before Janet was able to tell the story with relative calm. Even then there were a few areas where a bit of an emotional reaction would come up, but because Gary had another appointment, they did not have time to cover the aspects involved with those parts of the story. All the aspects were down to near zero, however.

While they didn't focus again on her fibromyalgia symptoms, Janet seemed much lighter by the end of the session and she left knowing substantial emotional headway had been made. A couple of weeks later, Gary received the following note from Janet: "The EFT is working just great for me. It is night 13 of falling asleep without the pain of the Invisible Chronic Illness [fibromyalgia] and this is a phenomenal record for me. Since 1991, the onset of this illness, I have not had two pain-free nights in a row . . ." On a follow-up phone call, Gary learned that Janet was continuing to use EFT with underlying emotional issues and she was essentially pain-free all day and all night. Occasionally she would wake up in the morning with a little stiffness, but she just "taps it away." She reported some pain when she had a massage because it involved pushing on her body. Under normal circumstances, though, she said, "I forget what pain is about."

## APPLYING THE BASIC RECIPE
## TO PHYSICAL PROBLEMS

In medicine, a basic guideline is to apply the least invasive treatment that might remedy an illness before moving to more invasive measures. The Basic Recipe is about as noninvasive as an intervention can be. It is easy to apply. It is self-administered. It is gentle. It takes very little time. Hundreds of reports exist of its being effective with long-standing physical conditions where other treatments were not. The relief from symptoms is often immediate. And if it does not work, all other options are still available.

So as a first intervention with physical conditions, there is good reason to use a method that simultaneously addresses the emotional basis of physical conditions and rebalances disturbances in the body's energies. The Basic Recipe could be part of every healer's tool kit. Gary is fond of saying, "Try it on everything." It won't hurt. It may help. But here are three caveats:

1.  For any serious medical condition or suspicious symptom, work in conjunction with a qualified health-care professional.
2.  Even if you completely clear your symptoms, consult with your doctor before you discontinue the use of a medication.
3.  Be aware that pain is a signal from your body and if a pain you have subdued using the tapping routine keeps returning, be sure you understand the medical basis of that pain.

"Trying it on everything" may also lead to subtle improvements that help other treatments to be more effective. Bringing balance to the energies disturbed by a physical condition and addressing its underlying emotional causes can only be beneficial. For help with immediate symptoms, apply the Basic Recipe ("even though I have this headache . . .") whenever you want relief. You will get instant feedback on its effectiveness.

For an illness, you might apply the Basic Recipe to every specific event that may have been involved in the onset or emotional foundation of the illness. Ask yourself, "If there were an emotional contributor to this condition, what would it be?" If you don't know, guess, and treat whatever comes up. As you work with the illness, additional memories or emotional involvements may occur to you. Persistence pays when addressing serious or long-standing physical problems. Gary often has students who are addressing an illness go through the Basic Recipe ten times every day, spread throughout the day. You can remember to do the procedure by tying it in with routine activities such as waking up, going to bed, eating, or going to the bathroom. Although this is an uncharted area in terms of scientific investigation, there is enough totally unexpected anecdotal evidence to warrant a bit of experimentation, particularly before introducing more invasive measures.

---

IN A NUTSHELL: The Basic Recipe can be applied to virtually any psychological problem and to physical problems as well. Balancing the meridian energies that have been disturbed by an emotional or physical condition and addressing the underlying emotional causes can only be helpful. When using a general statement is not enough, you can increase your effectiveness by treating past incidents that might be involved in the current symptom. Stay alert for hidden aspects, psychological reversals, or secondary gains. Be specific. Persistence pays.

---

# 4

# FOCUSING ON POTENTIALS

*Making your goals happen is exhilarating.*

—JOHN KEHOE, *Mind Power*

You've seen how a simple tapping protocol can be effective in over-coming a variety of emotional challenges. Does the same strategy apply when you want to go from solving an emotional problem to actual-izing a personal potential? Part of the human condition is to know that we *could be* better than we are. We can always see beyond where we can cur-rently reach. Can energy interventions help you attain an important per-sonal goal? Can they help you become a more loving person? Can they increase your effectiveness in the world? Can they help you achieve your maximum potential? We believe they can. This chapter shows you how.

Directed psychological change is not only about healing old wounds and repairing emotional difficulties. The skilled psychotherapist uses lan-guage to inspire, to open the perception of new possibilities, to counter limiting beliefs, and to expand self-concept so that latent potentials may flower. With energy psychology, you initiate such shifts in consciousness by combining the use of words and images with the stimulation of energy points. Stimulating these points alters your neurochemistry in ways that enhance the impact of the words and images you focus upon. This can provide the missing link that turns commonsense approaches for personal improvement into truly effective strategies.

In the previous chapter you learned how to change the internal wiring in relation to a clear-cut problem or symptom. This chapter begins by focusing on obstacles to living fully that may be less obvious but that, nonetheless, hold you back. You will be examining how your self-image, core beliefs, and unresolved hurtful experiences may be getting in your way. The chapter then moves on to ways of envisioning what is possible for you and manifesting it through the use of affirmations, visualizations, and mental rehearsals—each augmented by energy techniques.

## CORE BELIEFS AND THE SENSE OF SELF

The clinical uses of hypnosis, guided imagery, cognitive restructuring, and related procedures have demonstrated that suggestion and self-suggestion are powerful interventions for changing feelings, beliefs, and behaviour. Combining words or images with the stimulation of energy points appears to send signals to the brain that further boost the potency of these methods. But, with or without energy interventions, the use of positive images and affirmations is often not effective if there is a contradiction between the person's self-image or core beliefs and the intended change. *When such a contradiction exists, the self-image or core belief tends to prevail.*

### TRANSFORMING YOUR SELF-IMAGE
### AND CORE BELIEFS

One way to transform an internalized image or belief that is holding you back is to identify the self-limiting messages that are connected with it. These inner voices can be likened to backseat drivers in your car telling you to stop and get fuel though the tank is full, to watch out for monsters on the road, or to turn left when your desired destination is straight ahead. They operate according to maps that are no longer valid and perhaps never were. Can you identify a persistent internal message that makes it harder for you to get where you want to go? Most people can. Here are some examples:

*Women like me cannot manage money.*
*We men have to be strong no matter what.*
*My parents did permanent emotional damage to me.*
*People who take risks get hurt.*
*If something good happens, something bad always follows.*
*Born poor, die poor.*
*I have never been in a good relationship, and I never will be.*
*I may make a good start, but in the long run I never succeed.*
*I never seem to have the right words.*
*I'm too old to learn how to use a computer.*
*I don't know how to have fun.*
*I have a weak constitution and pick up every bug that comes around.*

The EFT Basic Recipe is a way of getting these "backseat drivers" out of your "car." Apply it to them, as illustrated below, whenever you hear their voice. If you can remove them, along with their "luggage" (i.e., any aspects that emerge as you focus on them), they usually do not get back in. And without them in your car, you will simply be able to navigate more effectively. So a way to become more successful in your life is to identify the internal voices and images that block you and, using the Basic Recipe, confront them, one by one.

## USING THE BASIC RECIPE TO OVERCOME
## A SELF-LIMITING BELIEF

You can use the Basic Recipe to challenge and overcome a self-limiting belief by:

1. giving a 0-to-10 rating on how true the statement sounds to you at this moment
2. using a Setup phrase such as "Even though I believe I have a weak constitution, I deeply love and accept myself."
3. using a Reminder Phrase such as "This belief about my constitution . . ."

A broad spectrum of goals can be approached by focusing on the self-limiting beliefs that interfere with the goals.

A straightforward example is that of an athlete who improved his performance by challenging the belief that he could not do well under specific circumstances. Raul Vergini, M.D., an Italian doctor who uses EFT, describes a consultation with a championship motorcycle racer. The man had recently placed fifth at the most recent world championship for 125cc motorcycles. The problem he wanted help with was that he always raced poorly in the French and Brazilian competitions. Although he was the winner or a strong contestant in most of his races, he had never placed better than eighth in those circuits in his five years of competing in them.

He could not identify a strong emotional feeling about this that would lead to a clear 0-to-10 intensity rating, so Dr. Vergini focused on a self-limiting belief. He asked, "How true is the affirmation 'I never can do better than eighth in the French and Rio circuits,' on a zero-to-ten scale?" The answer was 9 (very true). The treatment was used to bring this statement down to a 0, and then to focus on a statement having to do with winning those races.

The treatment actually took an interesting twist. After the first round of tapping following the Setup "Even though I never can go better than eighth, I deeply love and accept myself," the believability of the self-limiting statement went down to 7. With some minor wording changes to address possible aspects of the issue, the score went down to 5, then 3, then 2, where it then seemed stuck. At this point, however, Dr. Vergini had a hunch that the meaning of the statement had shifted for the man. It turned out that the believability rating of the statement that he could never do "better than eighth" had gone down to a 0 several rounds back, but had been automatically replaced in the man's mind with a statement about an inability to place first. This kind of shift is not unusual and simply needs to be noticed. Dr. Vergini explains, "We laughed and quickly zeroed in on 'I cannot WIN in France and Brazil,' which, of course, was already at a low two" and readily dropped to 0. While changing your belief that you can't win isn't the only ingredient necessary to becoming a champion, it is an important one.

## TRANSFORMING A DAMAGED SENSE OF SELF

Having access to a mechanical procedure that, as it did for the motorcycle racer, shifts a deep belief that somewhat dampens your performance in an arena where you already excel is a handy tool. Being able to change dysfunctional beliefs that run to the core of your sense of who you are can be life changing. To illustrate how a person's self-concept can be shifted, we will focus on an extreme situation, where a victim of ritual abuse is working with a therapist and parts of her sense of self that interfere with her healing are addressed. We are presenting a case involving ritual abuse not because we want to encourage you, without a psychotherapist, to treat disabling traumatic memories. Rather, we want to illustrate that even with very difficult traumatic memories, or whatever may be in your background, you can systematically move from one aspect to the next to the next to update core guiding internal images. This synopsis is worth studying[1] because it demonstrates several important principles that can be applied to a broad range of issues:

1. how the Basic Recipe can be used to address a deeply embedded and severely limiting aspect of a person's self-concept
2. how to divide a complex issue into its aspects
3. how to be guided by what just occurred as you choose the next step
4. how to be specific
5. how to approach emotional issues with an attunement to their physical components (notice the frequent references back to bodily sensations as the therapist carefully tracks the woman's experiences)
6. how to tailor the Setup Affirmation to reframe a problem (reframing a problem is understanding it in a context that highlights its positive purpose and often reveals an unrecognized solution)
7. how to test the resilience of your results

Glenda, fifty-six, was ritualistically abused as a child. Her therapist had been using EFT and other methods with her for several years, and she had made a great deal of progress. While there were literally hundreds of terrible memories that might intrude into her awareness at any moment, she had learned to work with them using the tapping protocol. When a memory or flashback would intrude, and she treated it, it generally would not intrude again. She might later get another piece of information about the incident, but the exact same picture she tapped on would not torment her again.

## "TOO DAMAGED TO HEAL"

A memory emerged while her therapist was out of town that Glenda was not able to make progress with on her own. She contacted Gary for help.

Before the memory became clear, she had intruding thoughts that she "would never completely recover emotionally," "would never heal," and that she was "too damaged to heal." When she went inside to explore these thoughts, a memory became vivid that involved physical abuse and the use of electric shocks. The perpetrators would shock her and then implant thoughts within her by using repetitive statements. One of these statements was "You'll never heal; you're too damaged to heal."

Gary[2] asked Glenda to describe what happened emotionally when she said "They shocked me electrically." She reported that her chest tightened and she felt fear. She gave the chest tightness a distress rating of 6 or 7 on the 10-point scale. She used the Setup Affirmation "Even though I have this electric-shock tightness in my chest, I deeply love and accept myself," as she tapped the karate-chop points. Gary also sensed that an integral step in Glenda's healing was to deeply recognize that the perpetrators were ill and that she had responded as any child would to such a horrific experience. He addressed this with a second Setup Affirmation that combined an assertion that the perpetrators were ill with a statement about Glenda deeply and completely accepting herself. This was followed by a round of tapping using the Reminder Phrase "electric-shock tightness in my chest."

When Gary asked Glenda if the tightness in her chest was still a 6 or 7, she indicated that the chest tightness had improved but her body would "jump, like I was being shocked." Now when Gary asked her to say "They shocked me electrically" and rate the distress level, it was up to 10. This did not mean that tapping on the chest tightness didn't work but that it removed a layer and allowed a deeper distress to surface. In Glenda's words, "It moved from being a memory to when my body starts feeling it." So the next round used Setup and Reminder Phrases centered on "even though I have these electric body jumps . . ." and this brought the distress level down from 10 to 4.

## THE POSITIVE MESSAGE IN THE SYMPTOM

The next round used the same phrase but introduced the words "still" and "some of," as the Basic Recipe indicates for subsequent rounds working on the same issue (p. 49): "even though I *still* have *some of* these electric body jumps . . ." Gary also introduced a new concept. The second part of the Setup Affirmation used one of the usual phrases, "I deeply and completely accept myself," the first time through. But Gary then changed it to "I honour them because they're giving me a message and allowing me to heal them. If they didn't show themselves to me, I might not even know they were there, except for the fact that they screw up my life, so I honour them." Notice that rather than being a deviation from the formula, the new phrase simply shifts from a general statement of self-acceptance to a statement that specifically accepts and honors the symptoms and their constructive purposes. Many physical and psychological symptoms grow out of the body's or the psyche's efforts to solve a difficult problem.

The next round of tapping used the Reminder Phrase, "remaining electric body jumps." This brought the memory "They shocked me electrically" down to a reported distress level of 2. Here Gary asked how she knew it was a 2. Glenda answered that there was a tight spot in her back. Gary explored with her whether this was different from the "body jump." While she believed it was also related to having been shocked, she realized it was not the same thing. The body-jump sensations were no longer there, so the focus now shifted to the tight spot, which she rated as a 2. The new phrase was "even though I have this electric-shock reaction in my back . . ." Here Gary was simply keeping Glenda attuned to what was happening in her body, to the ways her feelings and sensations were changing.

## REFRAMING PAST EVENTS/EXPLORING THE MEANING OF CURRENT SENSATIONS

Now when Glenda said "They shocked me electrically," the spot in her back was down to 0, but she noticed tightness in her tailbone and hips, which she rated as a 4. The next Setup combined this new sensation with the important concept introduced earlier about the perpetrators being ill: "Even though I still have some of this electric shock in my body, and it is a tightness in my hips and tailbone, I fully accept that the perpetrators were ill." After checking that this statement made sense to her and that he hadn't "put words" into her mouth, Gary asked her to tap to the reminder phrase "ill perpetrators in my hips and tailbone." Then he asked if the tightness in her hips and tailbone was still at a 4, and she indicated that the tightness was gone.

This was not the end of the session. Next, Gary gave Glenda the instruction to create a movie in her mind about one of the times when she was shocked, a specific incident, and to run through the movie, but without dwelling on it in detail. Once she came to the end of the movie, she was asked to describe her emotional response on the 0-to-10 scale. Energy interventions are decisive enough that it is typical to test or challenge apparently successful results in this manner. Glenda reported a distress level of 2, based on her body having tightened somewhat. The next round of tapping used the Setup "Even though I still have some residual electric-shock body tightness, I deeply and completely accept myself and I recognize that the perpetrators were ill." The Reminder Phrase was "Remaining electric-shock in my body and the perpetrators were ill."

## RETURNING TO THE LIMITING CORE RELIEF

Following this, Glenda went through the movie again, and she reported no distress. So Gary returned to the original statement, asking her to say "I am too damaged to heal." This was at a 6, from the initial 10. The focus now shifted from her stress response around the memory of the electrical shocks—which had by all available indications been cleared—to the perpetrators telling her she was too damaged to heal. While she felt this scenario had occurred many times, she worked with one specific flashback that involved three men. One of them in particular had made the statements about her being too damaged to heal. Some discussion ensued. Gary explained that what they did to her had elements of mind control as it is used in methods ranging from advertising to brainwashing, where statements are repeated continually and paired with an emotional charge, like an advertising jingle. She found it helpful to think of "You are too damaged to heal" as a "silly advertising jingle." Her next round of tapping was with the words "Here's my silly jingle. You're too damaged to heal." After this round of tapping, her distress rating after saying "I'm too damaged to heal" had gone down to 0. She reported having heard an internal voice say "not true" as she said these words aloud.

## TESTING THE GAINS

To test these results, Gary asked Glenda to again go through a mental movie of the electric shock and the "You're too damaged to heal" indoctrination. This time, rather than running it through briefly, he challenged her to play it vividly in her mind, actually exaggerating the sights, the sounds, the feelings, literally trying to make herself get upset about it. The instructions were clear that if she did get upset, she was to stop immediately. The point was not to cause unnecessary pain. Rather, this was a practical test to see if they were done or if there were additional aspects of the memory needing their attention. And while she could bring up very little distress, it was still at a 2 and she reported a spot under her eye that had begun to hurt.

Glenda next used the Reminder Phrase "this 2 feeling" as she tapped. Gary asked her if there was a particular part of the movie that caused the

"2 feeling" while she was replaying the memory. There was. In addition to programming her that she was too damaged to heal, another phrase they used was "You're beyond help." Gary gave her the Setup "Even though I have another jingle that says 'You're beyond help,' I deeply and completely accept myself." This was used along with the Reminder Phrase "You're beyond help." Gary also re-emphasized the illness of the perpetrators and Glenda's vulnerability as a little girl. After this round of tapping, Glenda was able to vividly replay the movie without feeling distress. She rated it at 0. Gary asked her to once more go through the movie, this time trying to make herself feel upset, exaggerating the sights, sounds, and feelings. This brought her distress level back up to a 3. In this replay, she jumped high when she received the electric shock and remembered how much it had hurt. After some exploration, the Setup Affirmation "Even though I really jumped because it really hurt, I deeply and completely accept myself" was used and paired with other statements recognizing that she had no choice but to jump. The Reminder Phrase for the tapping sequence was "big jump." Next, when she went through the movie and tried to become upset by exaggerating some of the most difficult moments, she said she could watch it and she could watch it with compassion. While she of course wanted the scene to stop and be different, she no longer had a bodily reaction while replaying the scene, and she could not manufacture one.

The final test was for Glenda to again say "I'm too damaged to heal." This time her response when asked to rate it on the 0-to-10 scale was to calmly say "No, that's not true." Gary acknowledged that it was not true logically and asked if it was also not true emotionally. She responded, "It doesn't feel true emotionally either." She expressed enormous relief and gratitude by the end of the session, which, despite its complexity, only lasted forty-five minutes.

## HOW WAS THAT POSSIBLE!

Is it possible to bring about lasting change to deep issues such as self-concept and core beliefs in the space of forty-five minutes? The features of the Basic Recipe that make this approach plausible are, again:

1. Each round of tapping requires only about a minute.
2. While you need to identify the hidden aspects of an issue, they
   a) do tend to reveal themselves as you proceed and
   b) are finite in number.
3. Once you have the sense of having fully resolved an issue, it tends not to return, and if it does return, you have the tools to focus on any aspects of the issue that still remain.

## CHIPPING AWAY AT YOUR OWN
## LIMITING MEMORIES, BELIEFS, AND
## EMOTIONAL REACTIONS

It is not necessary for most people to search very hard to find obstacles to developing their full potential. Recognizing them can cause you to feel bad about yourself (leading to avoidance, denial, or self-deprecation), or they can be a step towards helping that potential unfold. If you have tools that allow you to use such realizations constructively, you begin to welcome them, and the Basic Recipe is such a tool. When you identify a feeling, thought, or behaviour that limits you, apply the Basic Recipe to it. You will find it surprisingly powerful and freeing. Treat each aspect of the self-defeating feeling, thought, or behaviour as it emerges. Resolve any psychological reversals. In identifying the areas that are ripe for your attention, you probably don't need to make a list. For most of us, life presents them every day; we need only recognize them.

# THE "PERSONAL PEACE PROCEDURE"

However, you *can* make a list. In Gary's Personal Peace Procedure, he suggests making a list of every bothersome *specific event* from your past and every unwanted *emotional response,* and systematically applying the Basic Recipe to them, one at a time, until they no longer exert a negative emotional impact. Rather than starting with a problem and seeing where it leads, you aim for a deep psychic cleansing. You might think of each self-limiting emotion or event from your past as having left a stagnant pool that is leaking toxic substances into your psyche's "water supply." Whatever their origins—such as past failures, losses, rejections, abuses, fears, or guilt—cleaning them up, one at a time, is going to gradually purify the water.

Let's assume there are 100 of these toxic pools on your property. You clean out one of them. While you are likely to gain some noticeable emotional relief around the issue of concern, you still have 99 pools draining toxins into your water supply. But what would happen if you methodically cleaned one pool each day? Eventually, your well would be refreshed, with your self-esteem taking leaps, and a new, more positive self-image emerging.

Fortunately, you do not even have to clean all 100 pools to get this effect. Pools with similar origins are connected by an underground system of waterways. If there are ten pools in the area called "failure experiences," take the dirtiest and deepest one first, and clean it and all its aspects. Then go to the next one. Once you have fully cleaned three or four of them, you will have effectively cleaned all ten of them because the underground system connecting them will no longer be overwhelmed and will be able to use its own natural filtering system for keeping the water clean. This is the same type of generalization effect we have seen in clearing traumatic memories and other issues (p. 58). Then go on to the next theme. Perhaps it is "rejections" or "abusive experiences." Begin to clean these interrelated pools, and again the generalization effect will ease the task. In this way, all 100 pools may be cleared by working directly with perhaps only 20 or 30 of them.

Does this lead to enlightenment? Does it purify the well so you are free of emotional toxins forever after? Personal development has sometimes been likened to an upward spiral where you revisit the same issues, again and again, but because it is an *upward* spiral, you meet them from a new vantage point, a new level of development.[3] The more effectively you dealt with each issue during the previous round of the spiral, the more the issue becomes a source of experience and wisdom rather than limitation. Cleaning all your pools over the next two months cannot ensure enlightenment or that new psychological challenges will never again emerge. But by systematically addressing every issue you can identify, you can shift personally limiting elements of your self-image, remove the roots of many emotional problems, and greatly enhance your personal level of inner peace. This is of course a substantial undertaking, and we are not suggesting that you stop reading the book until you have completed it. Subsequent concepts and techniques do not depend upon your having completed the Personal Peace Procedure. But there may be a time that is right for you to undertake such an "emotional cleansing," and when that time comes, the following instructions can guide you.

## THE FIRST STEP

The first step is to make a list of all the past unwanted emotions or troubling experiences you can think of. Include every time you can remember having felt fear, rejection, guilt, anger, betrayal, jealousy, etc. Write down everything you remember, no matter how big or small. Organize your thoughts and emotions into categories or themes: e.g., humiliations, losses, accidents, relationship failures, etc. Within each category, put the most intense experience or emotion at the top of the list. By neutralizing it first, you take better advantage of the generalization effect. You probably won't think of every relevant incident or feeling in one sitting. You can add to the list as new incidents occur to you as you go through the process. If it is too difficult for you to organize the list into themes, you can skip the use of categories and organize it solely by intensity, placing the most intense items at the top and working your way down to the least intense.

## THE SECOND STEP

Choose a category from your list and apply the Basic Recipe every day to the first memory or emotion within it or, if your list isn't divided into categories, begin at the top and work your way down. Work with each item separately. Bring your response down to 0 or near 0, neutralizing aspects and psychological reversals as necessary. Some items will require several days. Others will respond so rapidly that you may be able to clear two or more at a single sitting. Once an item is down to 0, go to the next item in that category. Continue one item at a time until there are no additional issues in that category and you can think of none to add. Then move on to the next category you are drawn to address. Clear each item and all its aspects one at a time, until every item has been resolved, either by the tapping routine or the generalization effect.

## OBSERVE CAREFULLY

Because improvements occur much more rapidly with issues such as phobias than the deeper shifts in self-image and core beliefs that will result from the Personal Peace Procedure, observe carefully how your life changes. While the results of cleaning out each area will immediately be evident in your feelings about the specific issue, more far-reaching changes may require closer observation. They tend to be more gradual and subtle, and you may not even realize significant shifts are taking place. Notice, however, how you handled a recent rejection more matter-of-factly than before, or how you speak up more often, or how you are taking better care of yourself, or how your conversations are finding a more positive tone. Noting such changes reinforces them and helps update your core beliefs and guiding images more rapidly. Remember: Practice this every day; work with one incident at a time; each round takes but a minute; changes last; and greater emotional freedom is the prize.

## CONSIDER WORKING WITH A PARTNER

While some people can carry out this process independently—making the list as if writing in a journal and moving forward with little external reinforcement—a good way to approach this periodic cleansing of your psyche is to find another person and support one another as you both move forward. Discuss and build your lists together. Reflect with one another on your experiences as you apply the Basic Recipe to each emotion or memory. Even if you do not meet every day, check in by e-mail or phone to describe what happened with that day's session. Share your observations about subtle or deeper changes. This can be a powerful and important exercise for you. Working with a partner will help keep you on track and can add invaluable support.

# THE NEUROCHEMISTRY OF THE "SELF-FULFILLING PROPHECY"

Beyond removing limitations in your self-image and core beliefs, you can create shifts that aim directly at bringing out the best in you. Medical studies show that believing a drug can help overcome a physical illness will, *on its own*, reduce the person's symptoms in up to 50 percent of the cases. Pills with *no medically active ingredients* have the desired effect up to half the time, depending upon the illness. This is known as the *placebo effect*. Medical science attempts to control for this "complicating variable" so that research can establish that it was the action of the drug rather than the placebo effect that brought about the observed benefits. A more pertinent challenge, however, may be to *harness* rather than work around the powerful self-fulfilling force of a belief that something good is about to happen. The drug studies have unwittingly established that, in some situations, "believing it" really does make it so.

This principle holds true for every area of your life, from your professional success to your relationships to your health. People who believed they were prone to heart disease were nearly four times as likely to die from it as people with the same risk factors—including age, blood pressure, cholesterol, and weight—who did not hold this belief. Patients who were given aspirin or blood-thinner medication and warned of possible gastrointestinal problems—one of the most common side effects of the medication—were three times as likely to experience stomach discomfort as those who were not given this warning. In medicine, this is called the *nocebo effect,* the "placebo's evil twin."[4] Believing that something negative will happen has, it turns out, an even stronger impact than the placebo belief.

For better or for worse, your expectations release a flood of chemicals in your brain. Every sensation, emotion, and passing thought cause millions of neurons to fire together, shaping your next response to whatever life presents. For example, patients with Parkinson's disease who were given inactive pills as their "medication" released dopamine, exactly the neurological reaction the active medication would have produced. In another study, a group of college students were told a small electrical current would be passed through their heads and that it might cause a headache. Though not a volt of electricity was actually used, two-thirds of the group reported headaches. In another study, people who were allergic to roses started wheezing when a convincing artificial rose was brought into view.

While each of these examples describes an expectation that was created in a moment and that had an immediate effect, core beliefs such as we have been discussing carry expectations that are far-reaching, decisive, and every bit as much part of your neurochemistry. If you want to improve your relationships, increase your success, or enhance your *joie de vivre*, cultivating more self-affirming and optimistic core beliefs may be the first place to target. If you *know* you are a person who fails at relationships or money or career, *positive thinking* or *trying harder* can be but puffs of noble intention breathed into the wind. Until self-limiting core beliefs are transformed, all other efforts hit against an invisible ceiling, crumbling into oblivion like so many unkept New Year's resolutions before them. On the other hand, instilling core beliefs that support your natural capacities for love, joy, and success can be a decisive step towards deep fulfillment.

## How to "Uplevel" Your Self-Image and Core Beliefs

A plethora of pop-psych books combines affirmations, visualization, and positive thinking to attempt to change the core beliefs that psychologically shape most everything else. This approach seems to make good sense. If you can deeply program yourself so your self-image and core beliefs are organized around the idea that you are an excellent tennis player, when the ball comes over the net, you are more likely to get yourself into the right position, more likely to swing well, and more likely to place the ball where your opponent isn't than if you deeply believe that you are not very good at tennis and usually miss your shots. While it is of course also true that your performance shapes your self-concept, the feedback loop goes both ways: *Your self-concept shapes your performance.* You can improve your performance by changing your core beliefs.

## IMAGES AND WORDS THAT EVOKE
## YOUR POTENTIALS

Inner disposition shapes experience. Two people witnessing the same accident often give substantially different accounts of what happened, even though the actual facts are identical for each. More so with those facts of life that are subtle and ambiguous, as most psychologically relevant facts tend to be. Vivid positive visualizations and affirmations can change your "inner disposition." They pull you in their direction. They seem to do this in at least three ways:

1. *They attune you to opportunities for behaving in a manner that is consistent with the image or belief.* As the tennis ball speeds towards you, your focus may be on how it is travelling awfully fast and how your opponent is a better player than you anyway, or it may be on how to get into position so the ball will meet the sweet spot of your racquet, just as you expect it to. Life gives us endless opportunities to find the sweet spot, and our self-concept and deep expectations determine whether or not we get ourselves into position to take advantage of them.

2. *They mobilize your biochemistry,* or as medical commentator Norman Cousins put it, "Beliefs become biology."[5] Core beliefs and images are neurochemically coded, and they also provide a foundation for the ways you code new experience. You tend to filter out perceptions that do not conform with your deepest notions. And you tend to organize the perceptions that do filter in according to those notions. Your core beliefs also mobilize your biochemistry in the most tangible physical ways, sending chemical messengers to your nervous, endocrine, and immune systems. We saw this in the greater incidence of deaths from heart disease among people who believed they were

prone to heart disease compared with those with equivalent risk factors who did not hold this belief.

3. *They attract circumstances that bring the deep expectation into being.* You have probably noticed that people who have a more optimistic outlook seem to attract more positive circumstances to themselves than people who have a more pessimistic outlook. While this may be explained in terms of their perceptions, expectations, and past experiences, other intangible forces may also be at play. For instance, the number of well-designed scientific studies demonstrating the impact of thought and intention on physical events is persuasive for anyone who really looks (see pages 291–305, Appendix 3), and if our intentions themselves do indeed impact the world, it is well worth the effort to marshal them wisely.

## AIMING AT THE RIGHT TARGET

Nonetheless, the pop-psych use of affirmations and visualizations often proves unproductive and discouraging. While the methods are powerful and potentially effective, they are often applied incorrectly. Principles for using them effectively follow. But an even more fundamental reason why they do not work is that affirmations often inadvertently aim at the wrong target.

A frequent problem is that what is *actually* affirmed is not what is stated. It is, in fact, often the opposite. If the affirmation runs counter to a core belief, the psyche simply tags the core belief to the tail end of the stated affirmation. "I'm an excellent tennis player" is the conscious statement; but, mentally, you continue, "but I'm too uncoordinated ever to play well." This mental note that we add on after the affirmation is called a "tail-ender." As with a psychological reversal, you say the affirmation and you inadvertently reinforce the tail-ender, or core belief, instead of what you are stating aloud. This is all subtle and outside your conscious

awareness, yet the effect is powerful. So before introducing other principles for creating effective affirmations and visualizations, we will focus on
how to identify and take aim at these "tail-enders."

## IDENTIFYING THE TAIL-ENDERS

Positive affirmations are often stated in the present tense, as if they have
already occurred. Gary had the experience nearly three decades ago of
permanently losing thirty pounds with the only intervention being a
vivid, consistent affirmation that said, "My normal weight is eleven stone,
and that is what I weigh." He never dieted. His cravings and his biochemistry changed to conform with his "normal" body weight.

This same strategy can, however, activate a tail-ender and have the
opposite effect. Donna describes in *Energy Medicine* how a woman who
was trying to lose twelve pounds *gained* eighteen pounds while stead-
fastly, but without supervision, using a technique Donna had taught her
that included an affirmation. When she finally met with Donna and
angrily announced the outcome of having so faithfully used this new
and apparently promising technique, Donna asked her to notice what
thoughts were following the affirmation, whether her mind was wander-
ing, or if any images were entering her awareness. It turned out that
every time she said the affirmation, images of herself as an overweight
woman intruded along with the thought "Oh, hell, I've got a Slavic body,
I'm always going to have a Slavic body, and I'm going to end up looking
just like my [fat] Aunt Sophie." She was doing this five times *every day*.
And it was working! She had gained eighteen pounds.

The woman did eventually shed those eighteen pounds along with the
twelve pounds she originally wanted to lose, all without dieting. A series
of energy interventions was used for working with her self-image as well
as her metabolism. But addressing the tail-ender involving her Aunt Sophie was the first step in making the other procedures effective.

Often tail-enders involve a limiting self-image that instructs you that the desired state is not possible, you are not capable of it. "I inherited a Slavic body," and that's that. But they can also involve unacknowledged or unwanted consequences of reaching the goal. Staying with weight examples, unrecognized tail-enders that might show up at the end of a positive affirmation designed to bring a woman to her ideal weight might include:

- "But if I lose the weight, men will hit on me and expect sex."
- "But if I lose the weight, I will weigh less than Mum, and she will be jealous and angry."
- "But if I lose the weight, I will feel emotionally vulnerable."
- "But if I lose the weight, others will expect me to keep it off."
- "But if I lose the weight, I will have to give up the comfort and pleasure of eating what I want."
- "But if I lose the weight, I won't know if a man loves me for myself or for my body."

The list of possible tail-enders is endless. The outcome, however, is that the affirmation that you think is aiming at your goal ropes in the tail-ender, and what is affirmed is not so much your goal as the reasons your goal cannot or should not be reached.

Think about a goal that you have held for a long time but that you have not achieved. It can be one you are actively pursuing or one that just kind of stays in the background. Most people have at least one, even if only dimly recognized. Bring it to the front of your awareness and put it into words. Write it down. Then describe what comes to you, if anything, as you think about completing each of the following statements:

- The thing about me that makes it impossible for me to reach this goal is . . .
- The thing about my past that makes it impossible for me to reach this goal is . . .
- If there were an emotional reason for my not reaching this goal, it would be . . .

- If I did reach this goal, the consequences would be . . .
- In order to reach this goal, I would have to . . .
- What I really want, rather than just this goal, is . . .
- Thinking about this goal reminds me of . . .
- I would be more willing to reach this goal if first . . .

These statements can bring the hidden tail-ender or tail-enders into view. They may reveal a chain of events, beliefs, and attitudes that is keeping the goal from becoming a reality. If you are not big on lists, one of our colleagues simply asks, "How do you plan to sabotage your goal" and reports that people "generally know." If the goal is important to you, you can use the tapping protocol to remove the emotional charge on each of the tail-enders. You state your goal, identify any tail-enders, and neutralize each using the tapping protocol.

## REMOVING TAIL-ENDERS

Therapists generally do not work with friends or family members because the relationship itself is part of the healing process. The therapeutic relationship needs to be kept as objective and as untainted by conflicting interests as possible. Even an excessive desire to help can get in the way, interfering both with the therapist's best judgment and with the client's motivation. The experiences reported by energy therapists, however, are a bit different. Because the techniques can be taught and self-applied, some practitioners view bringing them to their own children as part of the educational role of parenting. A seasoned therapist with a great deal of experience in using energy interventions tells the following story about her twenty-three-year-old son, Jonathan:[6]

> Jonathan works for a banking company as a customer service representative. He's the guy you talk to when you call about your credit card. He takes about 120 calls during his shift and helps resolve issues for customers regarding late fees, interest rates, lost cards, credit limits, etc.

He finds the job to be fun and challenging. Except he hates to sell! One of his responsibilities is to offer eligible customers the opportunity to accept a "balance transfer." This means that the customer can transfer his or her balances from other credit cards to Jonathan's company and get a very low interest rate for a six-month period.

The banking company encourages its people to offer balance transfers. In fact, they offer monetary incentives to people for achieving a 20 percent rate of successful balance transfers a month. That would mean averaging about 10 balance transfers a day for the entire month. Jonathan was averaging about two a day.

On his own, he'd managed to "force" himself to get about six a day, but he hated every minute of it. He felt stressed out. He had a headache. He hates to sell!

Four days before the end of the month, when he realized that he was eligible for a monthly bonus in every other area of his work, but would not achieve that bonus because of his statistics in balance transfers, he asked me to help him. So, I asked him to tell me what's been his "hang-up" in this area. He told me the following:

"I don't like selling."

"No one wants to hear about it."

"I think about asking when I'm on the phone with a customer, but I just don't do it."

"People are upset when they call about a late fee, and they don't want to hear about anything else."

"I get rejected when I ask."

"I'm afraid I'll get rejected."

"I wouldn't want someone to do this to me if I were calling in about something else."

"I'm irritated by this aspect of the job."

"I don't think it's fair that I have to do this in order to meet incentive."

We tapped for each of these tail-enders. He loved the session and laughed a lot as we worked. And then I decided to do some energy testing with him [a technique used within energy psychology to assess the body's energetic response to a question or other input]. I asked him how many balance transfers he thought he could accomplish now. Remember, he'd never gotten more than seven in a day and usually got about two.

He said he now felt confident that he could achieve forty balance transfers a day. I asked if I could ask the body about that. He gave me permission. As I tested his arm, I had him say, *"I can easily achieve ten balance transfers a day."* The arm stayed strong. I had him say, *"I can easily achieve fifteen balance transfers a day."* Still strong. "Twenty" was strong, too. "Thirty" was strong. The body took us to thirty-six! The body said that Jonathan could achieve thirty-six balance transfers a day!

I reminded him that having a goal does not always mean that we "get" exactly what we've pictured, but that our goals "move us in a direction." He was very satisfied with that observation.

The next day, Jonathan achieved thirty-seven balance transfers! Every day until the end of the month, he averaged about the same number! He met incentive and received a bonus for his work. He said, "What have you done to me? I'm blowing them away here! They [his bosses and colleagues] can't get over the change in me! This is amazing!"

# A Four-Part Strategy for
# Reaching Your Goals

As in Jonathan's case, simply erasing the tail-enders with the tapping protocol (starting with the first one on his list, using the Setup "Even though I have this 'I don't like selling' attitude, I deeply love and accept myself" and the Reminder Phrase "this 'I don't like selling' attitude") is often enough so you find yourself moving towards your goal with a whole new spirit and strength. Affirmations, visualizations, and mental rehearsals can further propel you towards a goal you wish to achieve. If applying the Basic Recipe to tail-enders is the knife that cuts the cord to the dead weight that was holding you back, applying it to further energize your affirmations, visualizations, and mental rehearsals is the magnet that pulls you towards your goal. After formulating a goal and eliminating any tail-enders, the next step in this four-part strategy is to formulate affirmations, visualizations, and mental rehearsals that will be effective with a particular goal. The four-part strategy is to:

1. state the goal
2. identify and neutralize the tail-enders
3. formulate affirmations, visualizations, and mental rehearsals
4. use the Basic Recipe to further empower them

## AFFIRMATIONS, VISUALIZATIONS, AND MENTAL REHEARSALS

After more than a century of modern psychotherapy, Cognitive Behaviour Therapy has taken its place as one of the most effective clinical approaches available for people who are motivated to overcome anxiety, depression, and numerous other psychological difficulties. Providing people with tools for effectively shifting the self-talk that is at the basis of their feelings and actions is among its greatest strengths.[7] Often our internal talk is so quick and automatic that we don't even notice it. It seems that the external situation is causing our feelings, but it is actually our interpretations about what we are experiencing that shape our reactions. According to psychologist Edmund Bourne:[8]

> Emotional reactions usually occur without our noticing what we said to ourselves just before we reacted.

- We usually can see the connection between our self-talk and our feelings only after we take a step back and examine what we've been telling ourselves.

- Self-talk is often in shorthand, where a word or image contains a whole series of thoughts, memories, and associations; so identifying our self-talk may require unraveling several distinct thoughts from a single word or image.

- Even irrational self-talk tends to sound like truth—it reflects beliefs we are scarcely aware of—so habitual irrational self-talk tends to go unchallenged and unquestioned.

- Negative self-talk perpetuates avoidance. You tell yourself a situation is dangerous and avoid it, and by avoiding it you reinforce the belief that it is dangerous.

- Negative self-talk is a series of bad habits. We aren't born with a predisposition for it; we *learn* to think that way.

- Just as you can replace unhealthy *behavioural habits* with healthy ones, you can replace unhealthy thinking with more positive, supportive *mental habits*.

## COUNTERING NEGATIVE SELF-TALK

Bourne identifies four of the most common types of anxiety-provoking negative self-talk personas. They are the *worrier*, the *critic*, the *victim*, and the *perfectionist*. He suggests that the most effective way to deal with negative self-talk is to *counter* it with positive, self-affirming statements that directly refute or invalidate the negative statements. These positive statements are to be written down and frequently rehearsed. Among the distortions that such positive statements need to counter are the following types of self-talk:

- "what if" thinking, which overestimates the likelihood of a negative outcome,

- "catastrophizing," which overestimates the consequences if a negative outcome were to occur, and
- "pessimistic self-appraisal," which underestimates your ability to cope.

Affirmations introduce positive self-talk, which can impact your self-image and core beliefs. The first step in using affirmations effectively, as you have seen, is to neutralize the tail-enders or negative self-statements that go along with them. If each time that you state the affirmation you are also triggering highly charged doubts, objections, or counterarguments, you reinforce the opposite of what you intend.

## AFFIRMATIONS THAT WORK

Three other reasons, beyond tail-enders, that an affirmation may fail to bring about the desired outcome are that the affirmation:

1. reflects what you think you *should* want rather than what you really want,
2. calls for too large a step or for changes that are too far beyond what you believe is possible, or
3. is being repeated mindlessly or is worded in a way that does not engage your enthusiasm.

Someone who affirms "I'm happy, I'm happy, I'm happy" by rote is not likely to be inducted into the Happiness Hall of Fame anytime soon, even if all the tail-enders have been identified and neutralized. Here happiness is not a driving goal but rather a "wouldn't-that-be-nice" sort of effort that lacks the passion of a motivating vision. For an affirmation to be maximally effective, its focus must reach you deeply and become a compelling force. A goal worth pursuing evokes your passion.

The goal needs to strike a balance between being achievable within your belief system and stretching you to another level, beyond your current limits. Stretching stimulates excitement. The goal of raising your annual income from £30,000 to £31,000 is not likely to get your juices flowing. The prospect of moving up to £50,000 or £70,000 may. Once these levels have been reached, it becomes easier to envision £100,000 or £150,000, and these calibrations hold whether the goal is more money, less weight, better relationships, more vibrant health, or greater achievement.

In working with affirmations in this program, begin with small steps. Develop one goal at a time. Put an affirmation behind it. Adjust it as you move forward. Establish small victories at first and then move on to larger ones. Once you have removed the tail-enders, you have cleared the path for an affirmation to lead to substantial new possibilities. Based on a synthesis of various approaches that use affirmations, including Cognitive Behaviour Therapy, hypnosis, and NLP, here are ten guidelines for constructing an effective affirmation:

1. Affirm a *want*, not a *should* (e.g., you may feel you *should* be pleasing your boss, but that may not be where you *want* to focus your efforts nor may it be the path for your highest development).

2. Affirm your *wants* rather than your *don't wants* (e.g., affirm the achievement of inner peace rather than the avoidance of the obstacles to inner peace).

3. Affirm a goal you believe is realistically possible to attain, or adjust the wording so it is within the range of what you believe is realistic (e.g., if "I am healthy" feels beyond your reach for the time being, you can soften it with a modifier, as in "I am *becoming* healthy").

4. At the same time, affirm a goal that is a "stretch," a goal that is large enough to be exciting (e.g., rather than "I get by in my

job," "I find the challenges in my work and I enjoy meeting those challenges every day").

5. State your affirmation in the first person, present tense (e.g., "I am," "I know," "I feel," "I find").

6. Keep your affirmation short, simple, and direct (e.g., "I make a difference wherever I go").

7. Augment your statement with a vivid mental image or inner rehearsal of the goal already having been attained (e.g., seeing yourself waxing eloquent in front of an enraptured audience).

8. Adjust your affirmation from time to time to eliminate boredom or to aim at different aspects of your goal (e.g., "I am healthy and vibrant" may focus for a while on "My muscles and resilience are growing stronger as I exercise every day").

9. Keep your focus on what *you can do* rather than what you hope *others will do* (e.g., "I am a warm, loving person who attracts love" rather than "John loves me").

10. Keep your affirmations private (except for sharing them with a therapist or growth partner, announcing them to others diffuses their impact, interacts with the other person's agenda for you, and invites premature judgments).

Here are a few examples:

- "I'm at ease around new people and look forward to meeting them."
- "I see the opportunity in every challenge."
- "Peace is my companion."
- "My book is finished, and I'm proud of it."
- "My blood pressure stays below . . ."
- "I am attracted only to healthy food."
- "I have a perfect balance of work and play."
- "I am making a full recovery quickly, easily, and joyfully."

- "I am wealthy" (or for easier believability, "I am becoming wealthy").
- "I appreciate every moment" (or "I am learning to appreciate every moment").

Formulate an affirmation you would like to bring into reality. Go over the guidelines and examples above. State your affirmation with conviction and deep feeling. Bourne reminds us that "getting a new belief *into your heart*—as well as into your head—will give it the greatest power."[9] He recommends becoming deeply relaxed and stating the affirmation slowly, with feeling and conviction. Repetition is another part of the formula. Among the techniques Bourne recommends that utilize repetition are:

1. writing the affirmation five or ten times every day for a week or two,
2. writing the affirmation in giant letters with a Magic Marker on a large sheet of paper and placing it so you see it frequently,
3. putting your affirmations on an audiotape and listening to them once a day for thirty days, and/or
4. having a partner say your affirmation to you (replacing "I" with "you") with conviction while looking you in the eye. Then *you* state your affirmation, looking your partner in the eye.

## ADDING AN IMAGE

The image you pair with the affirmation can heighten its effectiveness. Begin with an experiment. Take everything out of your hands but the book, sit back in your chair, and follow the instructions as you read along.

Hold your free hand out in front of you and imagine you are holding a lemon that has been cut in half. Hold the lemon so you can see the exposed juicy part. Use your imagination as vividly as you can and feel the texture of the lemon with your fingertips. Notice the little indention marks on the outer peel as well as the oily surface. Can you feel that? Now bring it up to your nose and smell it. Can you smell it? Okay, bring it back down.

Next, you are going to bite into this lemon. To do this correctly and get the purpose of the exercise, you must put your vivid imagination into it. That means you must really chomp into this lemon. Not a little nibble. Really bite it. Ready? One, two, three, bite. Now chew it.

Okay, now take it out. Notice whether you salivated? Most people do. By vividly involving your imagination, you create physical changes in your body and your neurochemistry. Your brain treated your imaginary lemon like a real lemon. Sensing a sour acid, it sent saliva to neutralize it. It salivated even though a real lemon was not present. The persistent repetition of an affirmation paired with a vivid image conditions body and mind towards perceptions, thoughts, and behaviours that conform to the newly envisioned reality.

In a study of the effects of imagery and mental rehearsal on basketball performance, volunteers at Ohio State University were divided into three groups. One group practiced shooting free throws every day for thirty days. The second group practiced shooting free throws every day for thirty days, but only in their minds. They did not touch a basketball. The third group was given no special instructions.

After thirty days, all three groups came back to shoot free throws. The ones who did not practice at all made no improvement. The ones who practiced with the actual ball improved 24 percent. The ones who practiced only in their minds improved 23 percent, which is statistically the same as those who practiced on the court.[10]

Vivid imagery and mental rehearsal involve your mind and body in your affirmation in ways that just saying or thinking the words cannot. If your affirmation is "I'm at ease around new people and look forward to meeting them," imagine a situation where you are enjoying meeting new people. Be specific. Use the forms of imagining or rehearsing that are most natural to you. Some people see images easily. Others feel themselves in the situation. Others experience it more like a story. What matters is not which of these styles or combinations of styles you use, but that you be fully and vividly involved in the experience.

Before you move on to the next section, review the goal you selected earlier (p. 140) and the affirmation you developed around it. Be sure the wording of the affirmation follows the guidelines suggested earlier. Then develop an image or mental rehearsal that brings added life to the words.

## COMBINING AFFIRMATIONS WITH ENERGY INTERVENTIONS

Once you have 1) properly worded an affirmation for a goal you consider worthy and realistic, 2) neutralized the tail-enders, 3) amplified the statement by saying it with feeling and conviction, and 4) paired it with vivid imagery, one further step will make it a power tool with few rivals among existing self-help interventions. You have already crafted the affirmation so it is logically and perhaps emotionally believable to you. The final step is to make it *energetically* compatible and more emotionally believable. Once an affirmation is deeply believable and emotionally compatible, changes to your self-image and core beliefs will, according to many case reports, be rapid, deep, and lasting. Conveniently, you *already know* the fundamental skills that are required to make a logical affirmation energetically compatible and more emotionally believable. You will be combining the Basic Recipe with a well-formulated affirmation and accompanying image.

State your affirmation while bringing to mind your mental picture or rehearsal, imagining that your aim has been achieved. In this image, your goal is *already* reality. If your affirmation is "Peace is my companion" and you chose it because the pressures and stresses in your life tend to agitate you, say the words as you imagine staying peaceful and centered in the midst of a potentially stressful event. Then give a rating, between 0 and

10, to how *believable* this statement and image are to you. Notice that in this rating the scale goes in the opposite direction from the distress ratings you have used up to this point. The more desirable the situation, the higher the rating. A 10 means the statement is completely believable; a 0 means it is not believable at all.

## MAKING PEAK FUNCTIONING BELIEVABLE

You will then apply a modified version of the Basic Recipe[11] to increase the emotional believability of your affirmation. The Setup uses a slightly different format: "Even though I only believe [your affirmation] at a [your rating], I deeply love and accept myself." The Reminder Phrase is your affirmation combined with your mental image or rehearsal. Use the same tapping points you learned in chapter 2 and the same "sandwich": the tapping sequence, the Nine-Gamut Procedure, and another tapping sequence. Then again bring your affirmation and image to mind and rate their believability. You may find adjustments in the wording or the image occurring to you between rounds. Incorporate them. Continue with additional rounds until you have increased the believability score to at least 8. Sometimes you need to experience the new response or behaviour in a real-life setting before you can get the believability above 8, but clinical experience shows that once 8 has been achieved, the translation from inner life to daily life tends to be relatively smooth. Here are the steps, along with a case illustration:

1.  State a goal that is important to you.

    *Bill, at thirty-eight, was a self-made success. Born to a poor family, he owned and ran a multimillion-dollar software firm. While his own financial security was assured, he tirelessly tackled new opportunities and took on new projects as if he were still struggling to succeed. He regularly pushed himself beyond the limits of physical endurance and good sense. As a result, he was usually tired, he did not exercise adequately, his blood pressure was too high, his family felt neglected, and he rarely enjoyed an inner sense of peace. The goal he selected during an energy psychology class conducted by David was one he had been paying lip service to for years. He wanted to "slow down, smell the roses, and enjoy my children while they are still children."*

2. Go through the statements on pages 136–137, identify any tailenders, and apply the Basic Recipe to them, one by one.

    *Bill was able to identify many inner objections to slowing down. Following the phrase "If I don't continue to push myself so hard," he listed:*

    *"I will wind up poor, like my parents."*

    *"My employees will think I am lazy and taking a free ride."*

    *"I will not get the satisfaction of innovating new, creative solutions to important problems within my field."*

    *"I will be turning my back on the contribution I am meant to make to humanity."*

    *"Time that is now devoted to important pursuits will just be filled with trivial matters."*

    *"I will find out that I am not as good a parent as I like to believe I would be if I had the time."*

    *Working with a partner during a two-hour session, Bill found he was able to logically counter each of these objections, and he was able to clear their emotional charge using the Basic Recipe. For some of them, he had to address various aspects that arose. The fear that he would wind up poor like his parents, for instance, led to resentment of his father for not having provided better for the family.*

3. Formulate an affirmation of your goal using the guidelines on page 140 and support it with an image or mental rehearsal as if that goal had already come into being.

    *Bill worded his affirmation, "I enjoy an easy balance between my creative professional life and my rich personal life." In his mental rehearsal, he saw himself wrestling with his kids in the living room as his wife looked on with satisfaction, and he had a sense of peace knowing his business was running itself just fine without his micromanaging every detail. He was enjoying his family, undistracted by business concerns.*

4. Rate from 0 to 10 the emotional believability of your affirmation and image.

   *After having removed the tail-enders, the idea of having a better balance between his work life and his home life had become very plausible to Bill, but when he actually said the words and did the mental rehearsal, there was still a sense that this was not going to happen. He gave the believability rating a 2.*

5. Apply the Basic Recipe to increase the emotional believability of your affirmation and image.

   *Bill used the Setup "Even though I only believe I can find a balance between my personal and professional lives at a 2, I deeply love and accept myself." His Reminder Phrase was his affirmation, shortened to "easy balance" and combined with the image of seeing himself playing with his children while knowing all was well at the office. During the first few rounds, the believability only increased to 4. It was at this point that he introduced the part about knowing all was well at the office, and the score went up to 9 the next time through. One of the first things Bill did following the workshop was to hire a personal assistant to whom he could turn over many of the responsibilities that could be delegated. If you change your inner reality, opportunities for changing your external reality that had not occurred to you often become obvious.*

## PEAK PERFORMANCE

You can apply the methods presented in this chapter to virtually any situation where you want to be at your best: You are about to ask your neighbourhood association for an exception to its building code. You want to find the creative twist that will let you bring a perfect completion to the novel you've been working on. You are going to give a solo piano performance of a song you've written for your son's wedding. You are about to visit that high-school sweetheart who dumped you so long ago, and you want to shine. Your church basketball team is going to the finals and you are in the starting lineup.

By combining an affirmation, a mental rehearsal in which you visualize yourself having an optimal response in a challenging situation, and the tapping protocol, you can adjust your energies to support a better performance in any arena that matters to you. Energy psychology practitioners are taking these principles into a wide range of settings, from psychotherapy to parenting to education to disaster relief to business to sports. Work with athletes is particularly instructive because the outcomes are so easy to track. In an athlete's mental rehearsal, a "personal best" performance is often a good initial image. It is believable. It was accomplished before. It is already wired in. The ability has been established. Whether in sports or any other arena that calls for a good performance, the goal can be to make your personal best become your next performance.

Steve Wells, an energy psychology practitioner in Australia who consults with athletes and corporate personnel who want to improve their performance, worked with Pat Ahearne, a baseball pitcher in Australia. Pat gives the following account:

As anyone who has competed in athletics can say, the difference between the average athlete and the elite player is much more mental than physical. In an effort to bring my mental preparation for baseball to the same level as my physical preparation, I was introduced to Emotional Freedom Techniques (EFT) by Steve Wells, a psychologist based in Perth. Before working with Steve, I was able to perform well in training and some of the time in games, but I wanted to access my best performances more often and in the most pressure-filled situations.

Steve and I worked together using EFT to lessen or eliminate the mental and emotional barriers preventing me from consistently producing my best games as a pitcher. The results were astounding. I had more consistency and better command of my pitches, and accomplished it in big games with less mental effort. There is clear evidence in the numbers when you compare my '98-'99 Australian Baseball League season statistics before EFT and after EFT.

Pat pitched 87⅓ innings that season. In the 46 innings immediately prior to his work with Steve, Pat's earned-run average, the most basic statistic for measuring a pitcher's performance (the lower the better), was 3.33. In the subsequent 41⅓ innings, it was a mere 0.87. He gave up 43 hits in his 46 innings prior to EFT, 15 hits in the 41⅓ innings after it; 18 walks prior to EFT and 7 walks thereafter. While these statistics are selective— a pitcher's performance may vary this much with or without any outside help—the difference between his performance in the games immediately prior to his first EFT session and immediately following it was so persuasive to Pat that he incorporated EFT into his regular routine. As he explains:

With EFT, I found the mental edge that raises an athlete from average to elite. I used the techniques to capture the Most Valuable Player of the Perth Heat and the Australian Baseball League Pitcher of the Year awards. I am so amazed with the effectiveness of EFT that I've made it as important a part of my baseball routine as throwing or running or lifting weights.

# SHORTCUTS TO THE BASIC RECIPE

Since each round of the Basic Recipe requires only about a minute, you may wonder why we would even introduce shortcuts. After all, how much shorter than one minute do we need to get? But as you can see from this and the previous chapter, there are numerous situations in which you might need to apply the Basic Recipe many many times.

It certainly will not hurt to use the full procedure. We have not even mentioned the notion of shortcuts until now because you need to have the full Basic Recipe as a foundation for you to effectively introduce shortcuts without undermining the process.

Two advantages of learning the shortcuts are 1) you can deepen your understanding of the Basic Recipe because you have to know the "hows" and "whys" of each piece you are considering deleting, and 2) if you are working on a complex issue where many trips through the Basic Recipe are needed, the process will be nicely streamlined if you can get by with a fifteen- or twenty-second version of the procedure. Shortcuts can be introduced into each of the basic parts of the process:

## 1. ELIMINATING THE SETUP

The Setup Affirmation addresses psychological reversals. But psychological reversals are not always present. While the Setup is not harmful in these cases, it is not necessary. We actually usually do include the Setup because it requires only a few seconds and is often necessary, but when there are multiple rounds, we may see if we can skip it. This is largely an intuitive guess, but you get instant feedback. A psychological reversal will prevent progress. If the distress rating does not go down or stops going down, start doing the Setup again. Keep in mind that a psychological reversal is almost always present in depression and addictions, so the Setup should generally not be skipped when working with these conditions. Also, as you saw in Gary's work with Glenda (pages 120–125), a therapist can use the Setup to accomplish other objectives than countering psychological reversals, such as introducing a new way of thinking about the problem.

## 2. SHORTENING THE TAPPING SEQUENCE

The Tapping Sequence is the main ingredient of the Basic Recipe. While we can't eliminate it, we can usually shorten it. This is because the meridian energies that circulate through the body are all interconnected. Tapping on one meridian will often affect another. The tapping sequence presented in chapter 2 is, in fact, already a shortcut in the sense that it treats only a subset of the fourteen meridians. This subset is usually able to bring the energies in all the meridians into harmony. That sequence can be reduced still one notch further. Through trial and error, we have found that doing only the first seven of the eight tapping points is generally still quite reliable. This minimal sequence includes:

EB = beginning of the eyebrows
SE = sides of the eyes
UE = under the eyes
UN = under the nose
Ch = under the lower lip
CB = K-27 points
UA = under the arms

## 3. SKIPPING THE NINE-GAMUT PROCEDURE

The Nine-Gamut Procedure is also not always necessary. Gary, in fact, often omits it, going from the Setup, to a round of tapping, to a new assessment of the problem, to a revised Setup phrase. Again, this is an intuitive call, and if you skip it but are not finding the progress you might expect, you can always reintroduce it. If the Nine-Gamut Procedure was necessary, progress should resume. By skipping the Nine Gamut when you can, you reduce the "sandwich" to a single slice of bread, a single round of tapping, thereby shortening the process substantially.

## 4. THE FLOOR-TO-CEILING EYE ROLL

This is a useful shortcut when you have brought the intensity of the problem down to a low level, such as a 1 or 2 on the 10-point scale. It requires only about six seconds to perform and, when successful, it will take you to 0 without having to do another round of tapping. To do the eye roll, continuously tap the gamut point (p. 48) while holding your head steady and slowly moving your eyes from the floor up to the ceiling and repeating your Reminder Phrase. You start with your eyes "hard down" at the floor and move up at a rate so it takes about six seconds to make the arc. During this time, breathe deeply and purposefully send the "old" energy outward through your eyes. Some people also routinely do the eye roll at the end of the Nine-Gamut Procedure.

## THE ART OF TAKING SHORTCUTS

Because there is a degree of art involved, it is difficult to put down on paper when and how to introduce these shortcuts. The video and audio demonstrations in the EFT Foundational Course show shortcuts being applied in numerous situations and can give you a better feel for how to use them. Experience is the best teacher. This discussion simply acquaints you with the fundamentals, and you can innovate from there. Virtually every practitioner we know has developed a style that includes a personalized set of shortcuts. Many of these, such as "Turbo Tapping,"[12] are highly innovative and are described on the EFT website. Also, keep in mind that since the Basic Recipe only takes about a minute, you don't really need to do the shortcuts. They are faster and more convenient, but not essential.

The important principles to keep in mind are:

1. Memorize the Basic Recipe.
2. Use it on any emotional or physical problem you wish by customizing it with an appropriate Setup Affirmation and Reminder Phrase.
3. Be as specific as possible and direct the technique at particular emotional events in your life that may underlie the problem (aspects).
4. Remember that persistence pays. Keep applying the methods until all aspects of the problem have been resolved.

And please do not limit your vision of what may be effectively helped by these methods. Try it on anything where it might plausibly work. If it doesn't, nothing is lost. If it does, much can be gained.

---

IN A NUTSHELL: One of the most powerful ways to reach your goals and actualize your potentials is to bring about shifts in your sense of self or in core beliefs that interfere with the goal. The Personal Peace Procedure approaches this by energetically cleaning up the residue of troubling emotions or past experiences that limit you. In a related procedure, where you aim directly at a goal, it is often necessary to neutralize the tail-enders, or subconscious doubts and objections about reaching that goal. This clears the way for the effective use of affirmations, visualization, and mental rehearsal. The power of affirmations, visualizations, and mental rehearsals can also be substantially enhanced by using energy interventions. These methods can also assist you to reach a goal by making it more *energetically* compatible with you, and by helping increase the *emotional* believability that you can reach it. Even the likelihood of achieving a peak performance in a given situation can be enhanced by using the same basic approach that is used to change core beliefs and self-image.

# 5

# CULTIVATING "EMOTIONAL INTELLIGENCE"

Temperament is not destiny.

—DANIEL GOLEMAN, *Emotional Intelligence*

Why is it that the kid with the highest IQ does not necessarily wind up the richest, the happiest, or the most successful?[1] For more than a decade, psychologists have been supplementing the concept of IQ with a recognition that *emotional intelligence* has more to do with predicting a person's success than intellect alone.[2] IQ is usually determined by measuring a narrow band of language and math skills. This second type of intelligence, however, both complements the intellect and operates somewhat independently from it. It includes the capacities to:

1. recognize, understand, and manage your emotions
2. mobilize your emotions so they serve your goals
3. respond to the emotions of others with accuracy, empathy, and insight

This chapter discusses ways of increasing emotional intelligence, particularly as the concept has been popularized by psychologist Daniel Goleman,[3] and it augments Goleman's approach with the techniques of energy psychology. While you will find the methods and concepts presented here useful for enhancing your own emotional intelligence, our focus will be on the critical job of cultivating greater emotional intelligence in children. While such work can be done at any point in a person's life, children are particularly responsive, and the benefits will last a lifetime.

By mentally activating a psychological or emotional issue and stimulating a set of energy points, the neural connections governing that issue can be rewired in desired ways. Deceptively simple to apply, a tool that allows almost surgical precision in changing neurochemistry without causing side effects is somewhat unique within both psychotherapy and education. Its promise is profound, and there is no more profound application to which it could be applied than cultivating emotional intelligence in our children.

Nor is there a more urgent application. Goleman notes that perhaps the most disturbing news in his book on emotional intelligence "comes from a massive survey of parents and teachers and shows a worldwide trend for the present generation of children to be more troubled emotionally than the last: more lonely and depressed, more angry and unruly, more nervous and prone to worry, more impulsive and aggressive."[4] The encouraging news is that, just as we collectively have the means and the knowledge to end world poverty[5]—we need only muster the will to do so—we have the resources to reverse this disaster-bent trend in our children's emotional health. This chapter will demonstrate that we already know how to set up the mechanisms within our families, schools, and neighbourhoods to create a next generation that is able to field the emotional challenges of modern life much more effectively. And it will show you how energy psychology can substantially boost the power of models that are already having a positive impact.

## TAPPING IN SCHOOL

The day Shari Snow met seven-year-old Brandon at the school where she was volunteering, she was told he was going to wind up in a class for students with emotional and behavioural problems. Brandon had experienced difficulty since the day he entered school two and a half years earlier. And he had been considered "at risk" even before entering school. During the current school year, there had not been a day when he had not been sent to the headteacher's office.

This day he had trashed his classroom and was working on trashing the office in anger. He continued to throw things as Shari talked to him about why he was so mad. When he realized she was really listening to him and stopped a moment to breathe, Shari brought her palms apart and asked him to show how angry he was with his hands. He stretched them out as far as he could.

Shari sat down on the floor in the office and said, "This looks really silly, but just do what I am doing." Brandon stopped the "tantrum," sat down, and began to follow the tapping. She tapped with him one round before adding a setup statement for the second round: "Even though I am really mad and nobody will listen to me, I am still a really good kid whom people should listen to."

Two rounds later, when asked how angry he was, Brandon brought his palms together, indicating little or no anger. The school counsellor watching this transformation could not believe it. She described it as "watching the anger melt away." Brandon and Shari talked some more about the issue that had caused the outburst and then, together, they made a plan for the future. When it was time for Brandon to return to class, he asked, "Can I tap at home when I get mad, too?" He had grasped the power of the process within a few minutes.

And he made it a part of his life. Shari reports, "Brandon is now a seven-year-old ambassador of energy therapies. He is tapping on his own and is showing classmates how to tap. He has people around him interested and looking for more information. He is teaching me lessons on how to "get the message" across. He has opened doors I did not expect to open in the conservative rural community I live in."

Brandon has not been back to the principal's office and reports that now he "likes school." His teacher insists that it is a miracle, while Shari counters that it is a powerful message about what is possible for any child. Several weeks after the first tapping experience, Brandon told Shari he was "ready to tell the story for my friends." In the words of a seven-year-old, here is Brandon's report on using energy therapy.

## THE TAPPING STUFF
### By Brandon (as told to Ms. Snow)

*It makes the bad stuff not hurt as much.*

*They look at me funny. But now they know why I do it.*

*My friend got over his dog dying by tapping.*

*I showed him how to help his heart.*

*He told his mum to do it, and she thought it was stupid.*

*I told him to do it anyways, just not let her see it.*

*He made his hands get smaller when Ms. S helped him*

*Ms. Lin [the counsellor] reminds me to tap when I am mad.*

*I can tap in my classroom or ask to go see Ms. Lin.*

*I am teaching Ms. Lin how to tap.*

*She likes to tap by her nose. I like my forehead.*

*I like school now because I am good.*

*I got a treat from the principal for being good.*

*I never did that before.*

*My teachers did not like me because I was bad.*

*I think my teacher likes me now that I am good.*

*I think that is enough.*

*Oh yeah—I do the tapping at home when Nanna yells at me.*

# EMOTIONAL INTELLIGENCE AND
# ENERGY PSYCHOLOGY

Tapping is a simple tool. Cultivating emotional intelligence is a profoundly complex operation. But a trail has been blazed by a growing number of innovative, dedicated educators. Goleman describes a range of programs, from courses in Self Science at the upscale Nueva Learning Center for gifted children in San Francisco to the Social Competence Program at the Augusta Lewis Troupe Middle School in an inner city. The Resolving Conflict Creatively Program, an initiative of Educators for Social Responsibility, has been adopted by 365 diverse elementary and secondary schools in the United States to "ensure that young people develop the social and emotional skills needed to reduce violence and prejudice, form caring relationships, and build healthy lives."[6] The Child Development Project, created in 1981 by the Developmental Studies Center of Oakland, California, has been implemented in 165 schools.

Several large-scale studies over sixteen years compared students from schools that adopted the Child Development Project with students from matched schools that did not participate in the program. These studies covered a spectrum of settings, student populations, and ethnic backgrounds. The outcomes suggest that the Child Development Project brought about significant improvement in a variety of social and ethical measures, ranging from better conflict-resolution skills to decreased use of alcohol and marijuana. School-related attitudes, motivation, and behaviour all improved substantially after the students participated in the Child Development Project.[7]

Goleman summarizes the outcome studies from the various "emotional literacy" programs as having demonstrated improvements not only in emotional awareness but also in the ability to manage one's emotions, to harness them productively, to accurately read and empathize with the emotions of others, and to better handle one's relationships. Within these general categories are *specific skills*, such as anger management, frustration management, self-control, and problem-solving capacities. Behavioural measures of the impact of these programs included fewer suspensions and expulsions, fewer aggressive or self-destructive acts, and improved academic achievement and school performance. How do these programs bring about such outcomes? Among their strategies are:

- having children discuss situations from their own lives in order to increase their understanding of their responses to and their awareness of other options that had been available to them
- using skits and role playing that allow children to explore emotional situations and experiment with new strategies
- showing children how to evaluate their internal talk and encouraging them to adopt self-talk that leads to better choices and attitudes
- going over video footage with children and helping them empathize with others and identify any errors in perceiving social cues
- teaching children to recognize the body sensations that are the root of emotions before interpreting and reacting to them
- adjusting the objectives to the children's age and developmental readiness
- coordinating the lessons of the classroom with the children's other experiences by teaching parents how to support the learnings at home and by creating an emotionally informed culture within extracurricular settings

The programs are ambitious, their tasks challenging, and their goals vital and consequential. And as you will see in this chapter, the simple addition of tapping protocols can make such programs substantially more effective.

# IS TEMPERAMENT DESTINY?

Emotions occur automatically and involuntarily—like reflexes. We do not will them. So is it possible to "educate" people out of their emotional predispositions, however dysfunctional they may be? Solid research on this question comes out of Harvard's Laboratory for Child Development, where psychologist Jerome Kagan has concluded after decades of study that temperamental types such as "bold," "timid," "upbeat," and "melancholy" are wired in at birth. Each reflects a different pattern of brain activity. However, about one of three fearful infants is no longer timid by the time he or she enters primary school. Pointing to this finding, Goleman notes that parents "play a major role in whether an innately timid child grows bolder with time or continues to shy away from novelty and become upset by challenge."

Because several of the brain areas that are critical for emotional life do not fully mature until late adolescence—specifically the frontal lobes, which govern self-control, understanding, and mindful action—the experiences provided by parents, educators, and the social milieu can to a substantial degree counter genetics as well as early emotional deficits.[8] Even the seat of emotion, the limbic system, continues to develop until puberty, so there is, as Goleman notes, a "neurological window of opportunity" while children are still young. The developmental sequence is that the sensory systems have matured by early childhood, then the centers for raw emotion, then the cognitive structures that modulate emotion. The capacity for neural change is also lifelong, though only in childhood is it so explosive. But anything you learn changes your brain, strengthening synaptic connections. Successful psychotherapy demonstrates that new experience and sustained effort can change emotional patterns, behaviour, and brain chemistry. Psychotherapy, Goleman explains, can be "a remedial tutorial for what was skewed or missed completely earlier in life," and the energy methods you have been learning provide direct access for altering neural circuits.

Because the kinds of experiences that enhance emotional intelligence have been mapped, much can be done with children to increase their happiness and wholesome development and to prevent the later need for such "remedial" treatment. A comprehensive five-year study identified the active ingredients of school-based programs that were successful in preventing emotional, behavioural, and social problems. Goleman summarizes the study's central lesson for designing such programs: "The list of key skills [that] should be covered, no matter what specific problem it is designed to prevent, reads like the ingredients of emotional intelligence."

That list can be divided into the three basic categories identified in the opening of this chapter:

1. recognizing, understanding, and managing emotions
2. mobilizing emotions to support goals
3. responding to the emotions of others with accuracy, empathy, and insight

We will address each, with a focus on the ways energy interventions can enhance established approaches to cultivating emotional intelligence in that area.

# 1. RECOGNIZING, UNDERSTANDING, AND MANAGING EMOTIONS

Like too many children, Teddy had been a victim of child abuse and neglect. He spent two and a half years in an intermediate-level residential-treatment facility for emotionally disturbed children. Now about to turn eleven, and after having made a great deal of progress in the program, he was scheduled to leave the following Friday and move into a therapeutic foster home.

He refused to go to school Monday and Tuesday and was again refusing Wednesday morning. His therapist, and other staff who had special relationships with him, tried reassuring him about his upcoming move. He would not be comforted. On Wednesday morning, he threw things, threatened, screamed, and cursed. He had trashed his room several times in the previous two days, but now he physically attacked a staff member. He appeared to be doing everything possible to sabotage his upcoming discharge.

He was placed in an isolation room. The director of the treatment facility, Ann Adams, a social worker who is highly proficient in the use of energy therapy with children, went to see him. In her words:

With brown hair and brown eyes and almost eleven years old, Teddy was considered "cute." But he did not look particularly "cute" when I saw him through the door of the behaviour control room at 9 A.M. that Wednesday morning. He was agitated, angry, and cursing loudly. He had been disrupting the unit for over two hours. Staff had called 20 minutes earlier for a seclusion order after he had been restrained for physically threatening a staff member who tried to calm him after he had trashed his room for the third time that week.

Still cursing, he stared at me as I peered at him through the plastic bubble on the door of the seclusion room. I asked if he thought he had been in seclusion long enough. He glared at me but nodded. I told him I knew a way that helped kids calm down quickly so that maybe he could get out sooner. Did he want to try it? He nodded again, still glaring and hostile. I told him to move to the back wall and I would unlock the door. He did, and I did. I sat down in the doorway, matching his posture.

I went straight to it. "First you tap your hand on the Karate-chop spot," showing him as I spoke. When upset, Teddy was not known for his cooperative nature or his willingness to follow instructions! I knew I couldn't push too hard and that I had a limited window of opportunity. But he wanted out of seclusion, so he tapped. He glared at me as I said, "Even though you did something really foolish today, you are still a good kid."

His eyes got larger and he nodded and tapped the side of his hand. "Even though you trashed your room, you are still a good kid." He tapped and nodded. "Even though you got really mad at staff, you are still a good kid." He tapped and nodded.

Following my lead, he tapped the points. When we were through the points, I held my arms apart as far as they would go and asked, "If you were this upset when I first came in, and, this is not upset at all [hands touching], how upset are you now?" I had not asked this question at first as it was pretty obvious he was a 10. He just stared. I stretched my hands out again all the way and told him to tell me when I get to the right place. I moved my hands in slowly. At about the half-way point, he nodded. He was beginning to look "cute" again!

I said, "Great, this is working good for you, let's try it again." I started again tapping the side of my hand as I said with increasing enthusiasm, "Even though you got really upset, you are still a neat kid." He nodded and tapped. "Even though you are really scared about leaving here on Friday, you are still a wonderful kid." His eyes widened further and he nodded vigorously and tapped. "Even though you are worried about moving to a new place with new people, you are still a super terrific kid." His brown eyes widened even further and he nodded even more vigorously and tapped. He again followed me as we tapped the points.

When finished I moved my hands in slowly. He nodded when I got to about six inches apart. "This works great." I said, "Let's do it again." I repeated the setup as above, adding in a few more adjectives such as *marvellous* and *fantastic* kid. As before, as I said each statement his eyes would widen and he would nod vigorously. He seemed to be taking in each word. We completed another tapping sequence.

"So how upset are you now?" But before I could get my hands out to take a measure, this child, who had wreaked havoc on the unit for over two days, put his hands together in the prayer position and smiled at me. He had not said a word through the entire process.

"Wow!" I said. "Cool stuff. This works really good for you." He nodded, still smiling. "Staff tells me you are refusing to go to school." The smile left his face for a truly visible sign of another aspect. "Can you tell me what the problem is at school?" I figured that even if he would not answer me, I could create possible setup phrases. But he did. "They tease me," he said. We talked a minute, and I mean a minute, about the kids at school. This was a child of few words!

I then conducted setup phrases based on the problems he shared. Each time he nodded at the "super kid" part. After three sets, he put his hands together in the prayer position and said, "I want to go to ISS."

ISS is "in-school suspension" where, during school hours, a child must complete mandated natural consequence "time" for negative behaviour. After calming down from seclusion, a resident has a choice to spend the "natural consequence" quiet time in either the ISS room or the behaviour control room with the door open. Most choose ISS.

He processed with the staff who had secluded him, and we left the unit hand in hand to the on-campus school. Teddy served his "time" in ISS, completed the remainder of the week in school, and was no further problem on the unit. He left on Friday all excited about his new "family." The session required 20 minutes.

## SELF-SOOTHING

In discussing this case with an audience of therapists and other energy practitioners,[9] Adams emphasizes that she cured Teddy of *nothing*. She introduced a technique he can use to manage his emotions when he is upset. If you know how to calm yourself when something throws you, life becomes safer. Not only can you handle disturbing situations as they arise;

you also do not have to be on the defensive, scanning your world for anything that might threaten to upset you. When you are triggered, you know how to care for yourself. Self-soothing is a part of managing your emotions and a fundamental skill in cultivating emotional intelligence.

As we saw with Brandon and Teddy, tapping acupoints while saying soothing words during the heat of an incident can calm a person very quickly. The Basic Recipe is a formula that provides both the words and the tapping points. Brandon and Teddy are hardly isolated cases. To the extent possible within her administrative duties, Adams attempts to teach each child a brief tapping sequence shortly after arriving at the facility. She had done this with Larry. About a week later, she went to his cottage and found him lying on the floor of the Time Out room, screaming "at the top of his lungs." Adams walked over to the new staff person who was monitoring Larry in Time Out and asked how long he had been screaming. "Twenty minutes," she said. Adams walked within Larry's sight. He glared up at her, still screaming. She glared back and tapped on the side of her hand. To her pleased relief, he lifted his hand and began tapping, still screaming. She tapped the acupoints and he followed, still screaming. She tapped the side of her hand again, and he followed her through a second round of tapping, still screaming, but not so loud this time. So "I dared a little smile, and we tapped through the sequence again. Larry stopped screaming and smiled back at me. We had not spoken to each other." The new staff person was dumbfounded, managing to eke out a baffled "*How did you do that!*"

Adams will often tell an upset child in her facility who has not yet been introduced to the tapping method, "I'm going to give you something to calm yourself down, and you don't even have to talk to me." She smiles as she points out to the therapists in the audience that *not asking* a child to talk "sets you apart" from all the other professionals who have tried to help this kid.

## REMOVING THE CHARGE FROM AN
## EMOTIONAL TRIGGER

Something more happened for Brandon, Teddy, and Larry than just self-soothing. With Teddy, his fear of leaving what had been his home to live with an unknown family also dissolved. Adams focused on this directly with the Setup Phrase "Even though you are worried about moving to a new place with new people, you are still a super terrific kid." A Reminder Phrase was not necessary since Teddy was deluged in the emotion being treated, but if one were needed to keep the problem in focus, it would generally be derived from the Setup Phrase, such as "worried about moving to a new place with new people." Teddy's distress about being teased at school was similarly reduced.

Sometimes, even after a simple tapping procedure has calmed the reaction to the triggering situation, the response will still return the next time a similar situation arises. Psychologist Pat Carrington suggests carefully identifying your personal triggers: "Once you know what they are, these negative triggers can become a positive signal for you to start using EFT—right on the spot." While it is notoriously difficult to remember to stop for a moment and use a relaxation technique in the middle of a stress response, you saw with Brandon, Teddy, and Larry that tapping can be highly effective even during extreme reactions. Carrington recommends anticipating your vulnerabilities and tapping on them while you are not triggered, using Setup Phrases such as "Even though I get furious when my teacher [friend, parent, child, boss] criticizes me, I choose to keep a level head at those times and find a response that serves me and helps the situation."

The ability to significantly reduce or remove the charge from an emotional trigger is perhaps one of the most practical self-management skills a person can develop. And why not begin in childhood? The procedure is disarmingly simple. Once you have mastered the Basic Recipe and two related processes—addressing unresolved *aspects* of the problem

(p. 55) and resolving *psychological reversals* (p. 59)—you will be able to defuse the emotional triggers in most of the situations you or your child faces.

## EMOTIONAL HIJACKING

Adams correctly anticipated one of the *aspects* of Teddy's tantrum by addressing his fears about leaving his familiar surroundings to move into a strange environment. She identified another when she noticed that "the smile left his face" when she mentioned that the staff told her he had been refusing to go to school. Adults can often identify the aspects of a problem that are interfering with its full resolution. Children usually need help analyzing these more complex issues.

With Teddy, fewer aspects were actually involved than is often the case with such a major life transition. Unresolved grief about having left loved ones in the past or experiences of not being accepted by someone new in his life might, for example, have been probable issues. After Teddy was fully calm and a strong rapport had been established between them, the stock questions Adams might have asked if the issues weren't getting resolved are:

"*What* does this (situation/feeling) remind you of?" or

"*Who* does this remind you of?"

A strength of the Basic Recipe is that, despite its simplicity, you can quite reliably resolve one issue at a time until all the aspects of a complex problem have been addressed.

Sometimes as you work with an issue, you find that the trigger can be traced back to an early trauma or other emotionally overwhelming situation. Goleman talks about the ways the amygdala may "hijack" the entire emotional-response system. It "proclaims an emergency, recruiting the rest of the brain to its urgent agenda. The hijacking occurs in an instant, triggering this reaction crucial moments before the neocortex, the thinking brain, has had a chance to glimpse fully what is happening, let alone decide if it is a good idea." For instance: Lightning strikes the car park of the restaurant with a loud crash, and the war veteran with unresolved PTSD finds that he has just smashed a chair through the plate-glass window and is poised to kill. The neurological response triggered by the current situation is precisely the response that occurred when the original trauma unfolded, and the behaviour that follows is often regretted. While most people are familiar with less intense "emotional hijackings" from their own experiences, such as when they overreact to a comment by a spouse or co-worker, more extreme instances may be at the root of exceedingly destructive behavioural responses.

Many children who have experienced severe trauma are unable to contain themselves or their behaviour. It is not because they are inherently evil that they follow the too familiar path into juvenile detention and then adult criminal behaviour. Early intervention could prevent this downward spiral. The Basic Recipe can systematically rewire the circuitry that causes the emotional hijackings that lead to destructive and damaging behaviour. Skillfully applying it during a child's formative years, in conjunction with other methods of cultivating emotional intelligence, can be the difference between setting the child on a path towards a productive life and allowing a self-destructive spiral to take its course.

When the original event involved severe loss, pain, or abuse, it of course must be handled with great care. All the cautions discussed at the end of chapter 1 and elsewhere in this book apply to children as well as adults, and methods for keeping overwhelming feelings from intruding, such as the "tearless trauma" technique (p. 32), can also be utilized with children. Professional help is, of course, appropriate in cases where the child is clearly emotionally disturbed. Dan Benor, a psychiatrist in Medford, New Jersey, reports strong success using variations of the Basic Recipe with abused and neglected children. One of his comments, however, also gives a glimpse into how complex the aspects can sometimes be:

Several children with PTSD, whose abusing parents were no longer in contact with them, preferred to stop using meridian-based therapy before the emotions around a hurtful memory were completely resolved. My sense is that they want to keep hold of a feeling-memory of their missing parent. Even though it is a negative one, it is one of the few feeling memories they have of that parent.

Even a conundrum like this can be addressed with tapping, along with wordings such as "Even though my mummy has gone away, I'm a good boy and I'm lovable" to help the child move forward from the grip of a tragic history. Again, tapping is a simple tool. Children can learn to apply it quite effectively for self-soothing and neutralizing emotional triggers. And it can be adapted by caregivers, educators, or therapists for addressing exceedingly complex and consequential problems.

## RECOGNIZING, ASSESSING, AND EXPRESSING EMOTIONS

Among the emotional skills identified in the study of successful preventive programs were the abilities to:

- recognize and label one's feelings,
- assess the intensity of those feelings, and
- clearly express them.

The Basic Recipe is an exercise in developing each of these skills. In order for a child to tap to soothe a feeling, the feeling needs to be *recognized and lavbelled* at some level, even if it cannot be fully articulated. Then the *intensity* of the feeling must be assessed and this intensity *expressed* using a method such as spreading the hands to indicate the strength of the feeling or by drawing how disturbing it is. The intensity of the feeling is also frequently reassessed and again expressed as the protocol is being applied.

Finally, after the situation has been resolved, as well as while resolving it, the child frequently talks about the feeling as well as other experiences the feeling brings to mind. In short, teaching a child the Basic Recipe, and encouraging its use, is in itself a way to exercise the muscles for recognizing, assessing, and expressing one's feelings.

## 2. MOBILIZING EMOTIONS TO SUPPORT GOALS

What trait is shared by Olympic athletes, world-class musicians, and chess grand masters? It is their ability to motivate themselves, to pursue unrelenting training routines and self-discipline.[10] The capacity to harness your emotions to help you achieve what is important to you is *the* "master aptitude," according to Goleman, "facilitating all the other kinds of intelligence." He explains that to the degree our emotions get in the way of *or* enhance our abilities to think and solve problems, plan for the future, or pursue a distant goal, they determine how well we will use our innate mental abilities and ultimately how well we do in life.

Emotions can *get in the way of* our ability to use our mental capacities when they overwhelm our ability to focus and concentrate. But emotions can *enhance* our ability to operate at full capacity when, Goleman explains, we are able to marshal our hopes and desires into the enthusiasm and persistence—in the face of setbacks—that is so essential for all kinds of success. The Basic Recipe can be applied in both areas, helping counter the emotional hijackings that get in our way (in the spirit of chapter 3, "Focusing on Problems") and helping galvanize us to actualize what is possible (in the spirit of chapter 4, "Focusing on Potentials").

## FEAR GETS IN THE WAY

Jane, nine years old, had been studying gymnastics since she was three. She was a local star, but she suddenly became fearful and simply refused to return to practice. Brought to a counsellor who does energy therapy,[11] she revealed that she was learning to do a backward handstand on the balance beam and was afraid that her hands did not know what to do. Beyond this, she didn't know how to fall if she had to while doing this particular routine.

In a single session, she tapped on the fear of falling, on not knowing how to fall, on the fear of being hurt, the fear of having people watch her fall, and the fear of letting her team down. When she reported that one of those fears had been completely eliminated, the next fear was addressed. Once they were all resolved, she mentally practiced each part of the routine (both seeing and feeling herself on the balance beam) as well as how to fall. She saw herself moving backward on the beam, her hands knowing where to go, and her feet landing on the sweet spot of the beam. She saw herself knowing how to fall, how to use her hands, how her knees could bend, and how she could land and remount.

Jane's fear of returning to practice was no longer there by the end of the session. The therapist asked Jane's mother to have Jane review with her coach how to fall safely and to walk it through on the grounded balance beam. Jane returned to the gym and moved up to the next level. At a chance encounter several months later, Jane's mother reported that they had needed to use tapping only one other time and were able to do it successfully.

How many children have never returned to a favourite pursuit because a fear or discouragement came up at a critical juncture and was not skillfully managed? Jane had become fixated on her fear and was already refusing to return to the gym. She was fortunate to have been given a simple remedy. Did such a quick fix rob her of some important developmental lesson? As discussed on p. 77, such interventions can actually lead to increased understanding about oneself, as well as about how one's brain works. Fears, discouragement, lack of confidence, and echoes of past failures can all be identified and addressed, one by one, using the Basic Recipe.

## IMPULSES GET IN THE WAY

Another emotional interference to achieving what we set out to achieve is the intrusion of impulses we cannot restrain. Goleman goes so far as to say "There is perhaps no psychological skill more fundamental than resisting impulse." Many emotional-literacy programs attempt to enhance this ability. Children in the Life Skills class at one of the programs are introduced to a "stoplight" poster, which is displayed prominently, listing six steps for impulse control:

| | | |
|---|---|---|
| Red light | 1. | Stop, calm down, and think before you act. |
| Yellow light | 2. | Say the problem and how you feel. |
| | 3. | Set a positive goal. |
| | 4. | Think of lots of solutions. |
| | 5. | Think ahead to the consequences. |
| Green light | 6. | Go ahead and try the best plan. |

This sensible formula is, of course, easier to present than it is to implement. Combining each of the first three critical steps (from *stopping* to *setting a positive goal*) with an energy intervention, however, opens a door. It is easier to stop and calm down if you can turn off the alarm response by tapping a few neurologically active points on your skin. Deep breathing, progressive muscle relaxation, and various distraction methods are all also effective, but none are, in our experience, *as* effective. As you saw with Brandon, Teddy, and Larry, teaching each to tap even during serious emotional meltdowns quickly calmed them. Brandon even went on to become an ambassador of the technique, self-applying it and teaching it to others.

The second step, which involves naming your feelings, is relatively easy compared with the first. The first is more like stopping a freight train. But describing your feelings carries its own set of challenges. It may or may not be hard to identify and articulate a feeling, but it is often hard not to judge it. We get many messages that we should not be angry, jealous, discouraged, or hurt; and we implicitly convey these messages to our children. Effective emotional-literacy classes, on the other hand, teach that *any* feeling is okay. The challenge is to accept what you feel *and* to be responsible for how you act on the feeling. The feeling is a neurological response to a situation. The behaviour that follows is a choice. The first step of the "stoplight" approach—stopping, calming, and thinking—helps assure that the behaviour will be a considered choice instead of a reflex.

In step two, the trickiest part is that there is some legitimate reason to judge the feeling that you are also instructed to accept. If almost every time someone speaks to a child the child feels criticism or ridicule, which then causes anger, it is a pattern that is well worth interrupting. Accepting the feeling is the right thing to do. But noticing and working with the pattern is also the right thing to do. Emotional-literacy programs teach children about the faulty perceptions and negative self-talk that are at the root of many problematic feelings, and they attempt to get the child to change them. The Basic Recipe gives you a tool for rapidly altering the pattern at the neurological level. It does not replace the need for accurate perceptions and constructive self-talk, but it can speed up the process.

The third step of the "stoplight" method for impulse control is setting a positive goal. Again, several potential difficulties may need to be addressed. When there is a contest between a new goal and a person's self-image, the goal usually loses. However, this is also an opportunity to update the self-image, expanding the child's sense of self to embrace greater success and new possibilities. Often deep beliefs need to be confronted, along with the unresolved emotional wounds that are at their root. Again the Basic Recipe can be applied. The way a goal is stated also impacts how likely it is that it will be reached, and efforts at achieving the goal will be thwarted if certain hazards like "tail-enders" (p. 134) are not dealt with adequately. Then, affirmations, visualizations, and mental rehearsals can all be combined with energy methods to supercharge efforts to attain the goal. All this is the topic of chapter 4, and the methods can be simplified and adapted to help children use energy methods to attain greater success in reaching their goals.

Finally, one of the most potent mind-sets to develop for focusing on your goals is optimism. From the standpoint of emotional intelligence, Goleman explains, "optimism is an attitude that buffers people from falling into apathy, hopelessness, or depression in the face of tough going." Realistic optimism, so central not only in emotional intelligence but also in achieving happiness,[12] can be enhanced by applying tapping methods to defuse pessimistic thoughts and to energize the perception of desirable possibilities.

## 3. Responding to the Emotions of Others

Gary Craig had agreed to do an EFT session with five-year-old Josh during an airport layover in Southern California. Josh's mother reported on the phone, prior to the session, that he had been a very happy, well-adjusted child until he witnessed his grandmother being attacked and her bag stolen several months earlier. Since the mugging, Josh had become "explosive" towards his grandmother. Previously, he loved his grandmother unequivocally but, after the incident, he would say things to her like "I hate you. I hate you. Why don't you go to a jungle in South America and die." His sense of security had been severely violated by the mugging, and seeing or thinking about his grandmother had become a trigger for his agitation. He would also go into tantrums if someone left the door of the house open, and he was constantly on the alert for purses and where they were located.

Josh's mother had told Gary that Josh liked science and aeroplanes and, in the interest of gaining quick rapport, Gary arranged for Josh to go inside the cockpit of an aeroplane and speak with the pilots. So just after he and his mother arrived at the airport, Josh was able to have this adventure. He emerged from the aeroplane with a smile on his face, some sweets in his hands, and—since Gary had set up the experience—he was a bit more open to working with this stranger.

Also in the interest of gaining rapport and establishing positive expectations, prior to the session Gary had asked Josh's mother to show Josh a short videotape about a woman who was afraid of mice and rats who quickly overcame her phobia to the point where she was handling a pet rat after just a few minutes of treatment with Gary. Gary also asked Josh's mother to bring some balloons. Gary blew them up and had Josh squeeze tight on the open end and then release them. The balloons zipped all over the airport, of course, and brought smiles to Josh's face. Then, appealing to Josh's scientific interest, Gary told him that this was how jet engines worked and explained how this helped aeroplanes to fly. He also suggested that the escaping air was like getting rid of "bad feelings," and that is what they would be trying to do. Josh seemed to understand.

Gary asked Josh to tell him about the incident with his grandmother, but Josh didn't want to talk about it. He kept saying, "I don't know." Because it is necessary to have the client "tune in" to the problem for acupoint stimulation to be effective, Gary asked Josh to sit in his mother's lap while she told the story *as though she were Josh*. She was able to relate the events in considerable detail while Gary did the tapping. He threw in a few Setup Phrases such as "Even though this bad thing happened, I'm okay." Whenever Gary sensed that Josh might need a break, he interrupted the session and they would release another balloon. This went on for about twenty minutes. Josh seemed okay with it all, but Gary and

Josh's mother had no idea what effect it was having. There were certainly no outward, tangible signs of improvement; Josh just sat there and listened to his mother while Gary tapped.

They did get a clue, however, when they were well into the process. Josh's mother came to a part in the story that caused Josh to put his hands over his ears, as though he didn't want to listen. This alerted them that this was a particularly disturbing part of the story for Josh. Gary knew Josh could hear his mother, despite his efforts to block the sound, so he nodded for her to keep talking while he kept tapping. Within moments, Josh took his hands off his ears and listened calmly as his mother completed the story. Progress? It seemed so, but the only way they would know for sure was if Josh's behaviour changed.

Another clue that some progress had been made came as Josh and his mother were about to leave. When Josh wasn't looking, Gary took his mother's bag (as she watched) from an adjacent chair and hid it behind him, knowing that Josh had been constantly aware of bags since his grandmother's was stolen. They took their time saying good-bye, thus giving Josh plenty of opportunity to notice that the bag was missing. He even looked at the chair where the bag had originally been placed. He didn't notice it was missing. Even though he had compulsively tracked the location of his mother's bag right up to the session, there was no reaction whatsoever.

As they parted ways, Gary again emphasized to Josh's mother that they had no way of knowing what progress had been made. Only his behaviour would tell. Gary mentioned that the ideal time to tap in the future would be when Josh seemed angry or upset. "At these times, he is 'tuned in' to something important, and this is when tapping would most likely be effective." Four days after the session, Josh's mother reported the following:

1. The door to the house had been left open frequently since the session, and Josh did not seem to notice. Previously, this had been a huge issue. On one occasion, Josh was even asked to

close the door because it was getting cold. He closed it routinely without any reaction.

2. There had been a few temper flare-ups in the meantime, and each time Josh's mother administered the tapping. The problems subsided in moments.

3. While there still were a few heated words directed at his grandmother, their frequency had been substantially reduced. Most recently, Josh had crawled into his grandmother's lap in a loving manner, which his mother interpreted as "major progress."

4. Josh's mother suggested that maybe Grandma should be given a medal for saving the lives of both Josh and his mother. "After all, if Grandma hadn't been there, maybe the 'bad guy' would have come after the other family members instead." This was a classic reframe, of course, and it landed beautifully. In our experience, constructive reframes of complex and difficult experiences are much more likely to take hold after the emotional charges have been neutralized. The end result was that Josh and his mother made a card for Grandma that said, *"Thanks for saving our lives. Love, Josh and Mummy."* The card was Josh's idea. The words were also his.

The final area of emotional intelligence identified in the study of successful prevention programs is *the ability to respond to the emotions of others with accuracy, empathy, and skill.* Josh had to rebuild his empathy and understanding of his grandmother after his terror following the mugging became entangled with his perceptions about her. While this was a dramatic instance, the same principle is at work in many interpersonal squabbles. Something about the other person "pushes your buttons." Perhaps it is the tone of voice, a conspicuous trait, or a resemblance to someone who has hurt you. The Basic Recipe is a way of unwiring those buttons.

## UNWIRING BUTTONS

An eleven-year-old girl idolized her father, but was crushed by many of their interchanges. His statements to her were laced with judgments. In his mind, he told her school counsellor,[13] he was interested only in encouraging her to be a better person. To her ears, she was being told she was lazy, stupid, and uncaring. The father was not interested in participating in counselling or in changing a parenting style that he considered effective and appropriate. The dilemma is not unfamiliar to therapists who work with children.

Unable to impact the father's behaviour, and needing to find a strategy that did not sabotage wholesome elements of the father-daughter relationship, the counsellor suggested the Setup phrase "Even though Daddy tells me I am lazy, stupid, and uncaring, I know he loves me and that deep down he knows I'm a great kid." Not surprisingly, it wasn't that simple. When the girl's distress about the relationship improved only slightly with the tapping following that Setup phrase, a number of memories had to be addressed. There was the time she had wowed the audience in a school play only to be met with her father's "You looked silly in that dress." The emotional charge from each memory was neutralized using the Basic Recipe. This, combined with the counsellor's guidance and the original Setup phrase, served to inoculate her at least somewhat against her father's criticisms and enable her to take in their sweeter moments without having to brace herself for the next hurtful comment.

Often it is a child's playmates who push the buttons, and it is not easy to talk him or her out of being "over-sensitive." Who hasn't been on both sides of that dialogue! The same girl whose father's criticisms had become part of her emotional diet developed a tendency to feel put down by innocent remarks made by her peers. She was devastated, for instance, when her best friend made a comment about a ball going over her head during a game; she interpreted the remark to mean she was too short. She wouldn't speak to her friend, and she went into a funk about her height.

After the charge on her overreaction was neutralized by tapping, the whole interchange came into perspective for her after a little more discussion with her counsellor.

Goleman describes studies showing that the trait shared by both bullies and withdrawn social outcasts is that "they perceive slights where none were intended, imagining their peers to be more hostile towards them than they actually are." Providing children with tools to quell such oversensitivities endows them with a tremendous asset. Bringing the Basic Recipe to triggering situations is surprisingly simple, effective, and empowering.

## DEVELOPING EMPATHY

Unwiring the buttons another person presses in you removes a large obstacle to being able to respond to that person's feelings with accuracy. Empathy, however, is the fundamental skill that is involved. Empathy is built into our neurochemistry and can be seen in other primates and in infants. Goleman describes infants actively trying to aid playmates in distress. A nine-month-old girl had tears well up in her eyes when she saw another child fall.

Empathy also needs to be cultivated—shaped by one's caregivers and early experiences. In addition to being both innate and further developed through interactions with others, empathy builds on our awareness of our own internal processes. The more open we are to our own emotions, Goleman explains, the more skilled we will be in tuning in to the feelings of others. Research subjects who were better able to accurately read the nonverbal cues of others—such as tone of voice, gestures, and facial expressions—were better adjusted emotionally, more popular, and more outgoing. Children who rated high in this ability did better in school when compared with peers of matched IQ who were not as adept at reading the nonverbal cues of others.

When children have effective tools to manage their own emotions, they also learn about the emotions of others. A child who is upset and is then able to self-soothe, whether using tapping or other methods, knows both sides—what it is like to feel inconsolably distressed *and* how empowering it is to overcome that feeling. Remember, Brandon wanted to teach tapping to all his classmates. In the residential facility directed by Ann Adams, along with teaching the basic tapping sequence, she also guides children in teaching the Basic Recipe to others, building on the principle that an effective way to learn something is to teach it.

First the children are encouraged to help their "primary staff person" use the Basic Recipe. Adams describes how one of the facility's most self-absorbed children was using tapping to help her primary staff person work with a personal problem. When the staff member finally put her hands together indicating she had no further emotional charge around the problem, the girl—who had been a slow learner in the school's attempts to teach her empathy—was overjoyed. When Adams asked her how it felt to help someone else, the girl glowed and told her, "It felt *wonderful!*" This was a milestone in the evolution of her empathic skills.

Children who are overly aggressive in elementary school are often entering a trajectory that leads to delinquency and failure. Programs that have been successful in teaching them how to curb their antisocial tendencies build the emotional literacy skills of empathy and self-control. Goleman describes a program at Duke University where primary-school boys who had been identified as troublemakers were taught how to interpret the cues of other children more accurately, how to take on the perspective of other children, and how to know when their own body sensations are signalling that it is time to stop and reflect rather than strike out. Three years later, now having entered adolescence, the boys who went through this program were much less disruptive in school than boys who had been equally aggressive but had not gone through the program. They also felt more positively about themselves and were less likely to be involved in drug or alcohol abuse. Again, introducing the Basic Recipe to such programs can build on all their strengths while adding a decisive tool for emotional self-management that directly shifts the neurological basis of the perceptions and behaviours that are of concern.

## OTHER INTERPERSONAL ISSUES

Self-confidence impacts our relationships with others. A ten-year-old boy was afraid to go to school because he was being teased and bullied for being "nerdy." A counsellor[14] helped him apply the Basic Recipe to his difficulties. The result was that his self-confidence increased to the point where he could shrug off his tormentors, walking away without engaging them. A by-product of this triumph, according to his counsellor, is that he developed a sense that he could cope with most situations involving his peers; and this confidence made him a less desirable target for bullies.

After family, the training ground where children learn about life with others is school—certainly a key area when it comes to emotional intelligence as well as long-term success and fulfillment. From the fear of bullies to losing a loved one, every conceivable interpersonal issue may be encountered at school. When the emotional response is irrational, problematic, or prolonged, and does not yield to logic or love, the Basic Recipe can be the bridge to constructive resolutions.

Susan, a fourteen-year-old high-school student, had been a close acquaintance of one of the girls who was murdered at Columbine. Susan became highly anxious. She was unable to read newspaper or magazine accounts of the massacre or view any TV reporting of it. She was besieged by persistent, frightening images of the killers for weeks before she entered counselling with a therapist[15] who uses EFT.

They applied the Basic Recipe to Susan's fear, grief, profound sadness, and rage, as well as to the images that haunted her. The therapist tried to keep the initial focus on less threatening parts of the horrific visions. Later, after the emotional charge to less evocative images had been reduced, subsequent rounds included more evocative images such as the killers' faces or guns. After two sessions, Susan was using tapping between sessions and reporting some relief around her anxiety. By the fourth session, she was no longer having difficulty functioning and was no longer plagued by unrelenting anxiety. She was also able to think about the tragedy without becoming completely overwhelmed with emotion, and she began to develop some perspective on it. As often occurs, the work around her friend's death reactivated early childhood traumas involving the deaths of two relatives. Over the course of three additional half-hour sessions, confusion, fear, and guilt that had been festering for ten years was resolved to Susan's and her therapist's satisfaction.

Life presents intense emotional challenges. Providing children with the skills for managing them effectively as they occur builds strength for meeting future challenges. The Basic Recipe can be taught to children at virtually any age.

## WORKING WITH THE WHOLE FAMILY

Nancy Gnecco is a psychotherapist who works primarily with adults; Beth Andersen is a child therapist. Both incorporate energy methods into their work, and sometimes they collaborate in working with families.

First the parents meet with Gnecco in a no-cost introductory session. She describes her unique approach, shows a thirteen-minute video of a successful treatment for anxiety, and answers any questions the parents might have. After discussing the energy-psychotherapy modalities, Gnecco stresses the importance of having the whole family participate in treatment. She explains that by the time a family has a child in therapy, the emotional distress has affected all family members. It is relatively easy at that point for parents to identify a personal concern that has a high distress rating (on the 10-point scale). Then Gnecco teaches them the EFT Basic Recipe. She demonstrates the tapping procedure, asks the parents to focus on their own issues, and invites them to tap along with her. This is usually so effective in reducing the distress level (on the 10-point scale) that the parents almost always decide not only that they want to continue with treatment, they are usually willing to undergo treatment along with their children.

The second session begins with both therapists meeting with the entire family. They establish the perspective that the child is a "good kid," even with the problem. They then talk about how "Magic Tapping" might be able to help them with the problem. Andersen takes the child to a separate office where she incorporates Magic Tapping into a play-therapy session. She tells stories about fictional characters who have the same problem as the child, and together they tap for the character. She also has a doll and a stuffed cat who get tapped and, eventually, she gets the children to tap on themselves for different aspects of the problem.

Meanwhile, Gnecco works with the parents, setting up a tapping schedule for the whole family and encouraging the parents to treat themselves before treating the child. She explores the deeper issues involved with the family problem, identifying the aspects that are relevant for each parent and helping to neutralize them using the Basic Recipe.

A follow-up session is scheduled one to three weeks later, and the format is similar to that of the previous session. The therapists first meet together with the family to review what has occurred. Then Andersen takes the children, and Gnecco works with the parents. At the end of this follow-up session, the family decides whether or not to continue with therapy on a regular basis and, if so, whether to proceed with the entire family or just specific individuals.

Gnecco tells of a family with two adopted children. The older, a nine-year-old boy, had recently been diagnosed with Attention Deficit Hyperactivity Disorder (ADHD). He was unable to go to sleep without his mother or father lying down with him. The second child, a six-year-old girl, was just starting school. She had acute separation anxiety and school phobia. She could get to sleep, but she would get up during the night to use the bathroom and then climb into her parents' bed. Consequently, they got very little sleep. The father could not get back to sleep after the child joined them, usually between 3 and 4 A.M., and the mother became depressed, overwhelmed, exhausted, and feeling desperate from lack of sleep. Since the children's sleep disorders seemed the most pressing issue, the family agreed to work on them first with both children, and address the separation anxiety at a later time.

After the introductory session with the parents, in which the mother's anxiety about her children's problems was notably decreased during the brief demonstration, both therapists met with the whole family. Andersen then took the kids off for Magic Tapping while Gnecco worked with the mother, who was very willing to use the Basic Recipe and reported feeling better after just a week. The father was sceptical and didn't really want to participate, but he was willing to for the sake of the children, particularly after seeing the tapping work so well with his wife. A daily schedule was set up that included both the mother and the father tapping with the children at different times of day. The mother also agreed to tap for her own issues several times a day.

The family missed the follow-up appointment, however. When they did not reschedule, Andersen phoned and convinced them to come in at least for the originally agreed upon three sessions. They had had only one actual session and had dealt with just the sleep issue; the separation anxiety had not been addressed because the family's first priority was the sleep pattern.

The children bounced into the therapy office for the next session, and the son proudly reported that he had slept by himself since the first night he tapped. He liked the Magic Tapping so much that he had, with no prompting from his parents, started using it for things that upset him— such as his sister getting into his toys. "This weird stuff really works," he said beaming, as he danced around the office, touching everything and displaying typical ADHD behaviours.

The daughter was feeling shy and wouldn't offer her own report, wanting her brother to do it. He announced that his sister still gets up every night now and goes to the bathroom, and she "doesn't turn the light out," but she does go back to her own bed. She has slept with her parents only twice since they started tapping.

When Gnecco asked about the girl's separation anxiety and school phobia, the parents didn't seem to remember it as the major problems they had originally felt them to be, nor did they credit the energy psychology treatment for the dramatic changes. They believed that she had "outgrown" her fears. This was just three weeks after the initial visit.

Now the only problem the family reported was that Mum had become so accustomed to getting no more than four hours sleep at a time that, even with the children sleeping, she wasn't able to sleep for any longer than that. Gnecco asked her if she had thought to tap on it. She hadn't, but was willing to try. Two weeks later she called to report that she was getting a full night's sleep regularly for the first time in nine years.

# ADAPTING THE BASIC RECIPE
## FOR CHILDREN

While Gnecco and Andersen stress that a child's problems resolve much faster when each family member is committed to treating his or her own issues using the Basic Recipe, children can benefit from the methods independently as well. Many of the principles for adapting the Basic Recipe to children have been illustrated in the cases presented in this chapter.

The child can use a more concrete way of assessing the amount of distress than choosing a number between 0 and 10, such as by the distance between outstretched hands or by the length of a line. You can use fun words like "Magic Tapping" or call the acupoints under the arm the "Monkey Points." You can be playful and make the tapping a game. Gary once helped a five-year-old girl get over a fire phobia (it emerged shortly after a small fire in her home) by having her say, "Stomping out the fire" as she was tapping. She giggled through it, and it was effective. You can adapt the Setup and Reminder Phrases to the child's language, using terms such as "Deep down I know I'm a great kid" instead of "I deeply love and accept myself." You can state the phrases for the child, if necessary, and even do the tapping on the child's acupoints if at that moment the child cannot. You do not need a Reminder Phrase if the child is at the moment fully involved in the problematic emotion. Common sense can guide all these decisions.

## BUILDING RAPPORT

Building a strong rapport is fundamental to doing effective energy work with children. Remember that when Gary met with Josh, he had already arranged for Josh to watch a successful session on video, to get into the cockpit of an aeroplane and talk with the pilot, to release inflated balloons in the airport, and to learn how the balloons' movement related to air flight. All this was prior to any focus by Gary on Josh's problem or the intended treatment. While rapport is vital before introducing energy psychology methods to anyone, it is particularly critical when working with children. You want to be in tune with the child's style and needs. You want the child to cooperate. Without adequate rapport, neither is likely to happen.

Introducing a child to strange techniques can also be a bit tricky. With teenagers, you need to have enough rapport that they can tolerate your having weird ideas and still be willing to work with you. There is probably no way around this. With younger children, it is often enough simply to explain that this is a relaxation exercise that can help them calm down quickly.

Ann Adams observes that most children learn the methods quickly. The key is for the caregiver to help the child remember to use the exercise the next time the child *starts* to become upset. This early intervention is critical in her facility, since these children have a particularly "short circuit between calm and the fight-or-flight response."

## RESPECT THE CHILD

While it goes without saying that children fare better when their care-givers recognize their abilities, goodness, and potentials, many adults seeking to help children are unintentionally condescending. This is particularly hazardous when you feel pressure to know the solution to the child's problem. Adams reminds her staff of five attitudes that go far, regardless of the treatment approach:

1. Respect the child no matter what the behaviour.
2. Admire the child's courage for living the best way he or she knows how.
3. Let go of the outcome so you can stay totally focused on the child, in the here and now, without judgment.
4. Stay creative in your ways of establishing rapport and in whatever approaches you use.
5. Be who you are, congruent in your thoughts and actions. This is critical in the child's assessing whether you are a safe person to deal with.

Adams is sometimes asked by a child to say a bedtime prayer. Her favourite captures the spirit of her work: "Dear God, thank you for this beautiful child. Help us to help him to get along better in the world."

## CALM YOURSELF BEFORE YOU CALM THE CHILD

Many who have taught tapping to children emphasize the importance of being calm and centered before working with a child, particularly your own child. They also stress that the same methods that will help the child can help you. Steve Wells, the energy practitioner whom Pat Ahearne credits for helping him capture the Australian Baseball League Pitcher of the Year Award, counsels people who do energy work with children to "remember, emotions get transferred between people when we interact, and children are often like tuning forks for our emotional states." He recommends that you treat yourself for the things your children do that upset you. Adams echoes this, emphasizing that your own comfort level is critical when it comes to helping a child: "If you are uncomfortable about being with this child, tap on your own discomfort before the session. If the child's issues trigger issues from your own past, tap on these before the session." Sylvia Hartmann, a respected practitioner and teacher in the UK, recommends that the parent use a Setup phrase along the lines of "Even though Sam has this problem, I deeply and profoundly accept him and I love him unconditionally."

## USING THE BASIC RECIPE TO
## REFRAME A PROBLEM

Energy psychology draws heavily on Cognitive Behaviour Therapy, particularly in its focus on specific incidents, feelings, and self-statements, and in its use of affirmations. Both approaches routinely teach people how to make self-statements in order to "change their mind." There is an art to this and an art to formulating Setup phrases that are more sophisticated than the simple structure presented in chapter 2. Various models are available.[16] All of them use the power of "reframing"; that is, they change how a situation is viewed, portray it more optimistically, focus on potential positive outcomes, and recognize the opportunities that are not obvious. Experienced energy therapists often craft the Setup and Reminder Phrases so the client begins to reframe the problem. Children can benefit tremendously from a creative reframe that is tuned in to the complexities of the issue, and working with the problems that lend themselves to energy therapy provides many such teaching opportunities.

Recall how Teddy's eyes grew wide when Adams asked him to tap to "Even though you trashed your room, you are still a good kid." That was a reframe. So was "Even though you are really scared about leaving here on Friday, you are still a wonderful kid." A few reframes from other situations include "Even though I can't control my mother's drinking, I am a good kid"; "Even though this terrible thing happened, I know that God loves me"; "Even though Jenny made fun of me, I'm an awesome kid."

Reframes can be embedded in the Setup Phrase and in discussion of the problem, and that is part of the art in using these methods. After the tapping has been completed, self-damaging emotional responses cleared, and the situation reviewed with the child, the child often sees and talks about the situation in a new way. This can lead to a review-and-consolidation phase in which you draw out the lessons from the situation, consider what might have been done differently, and lay out the steps that can be taken now, including an agreement for ongoing tapping to support what has been accomplished. It is also a time to be alert for other aspects of the problem that might not have been resolved during the tapping. These will often appear spontaneously during the discussion or reveal themselves when the results from the tapping don't hold. This most frequently occurs when hidden aspects still need to be addressed. Again, asking "who or what" the current situation brings to mind from the past is a powerful way of identifying unresolved aspects of the problem.

## NIGHTTIME REVIEW

A systematic way of applying the Basic Recipe to cultivate a child's emotional intelligence is with a nighttime review of the day. While the child is being tucked into bed, the parents ask, "Can you tell me about your good and bad thoughts as well as the good and bad things that happened to you today?" As the thoughts and events are being relayed, the parents lightly and lovingly either tap or rub the standard acupoints from the Basic Recipe.

When difficult thoughts and events are described, the child is clearly "tuned in" to the problem, and the tapping is very likely to at least lighten her or his stress response to what is being brought to mind. Given the bombardment of stimuli that confront a child within a single day—parents, teachers, peers, television, computer games, the Internet—having a way that eases the emotional integration of the most difficult ones can be of tremendous value. Those that go unresolved tend to become the basis of limiting beliefs, unnecessary fears, and unprocessed grief. Some examples of the "bad" things children might bring up are:

> "Daddy scared me when he yelled at me."
> "I saw a monster eating people on television."
> "My teacher doesn't think I'm very smart."
> "I can't run as fast as Jimmy."
> "Roseanne is prettier than me."
> "Reverend Butler said I have to do better or God will be angry with me."

There are, of course, millions of other stimuli that a child might have to process. Alert parents have an opportunity on a daily basis to help see that these experiences, rather than harming the child's self-esteem or confidence, serve constructive ends. The process can be very nurturing for both the parents and the children. Children love to be touched in loving ways. Asking the child questions while gently tapping or lovingly rubbing the various energy points can bring you deeper into issues than normal conversation usually does. A loving ceremonial space can be created each evening, and this also sets an atmosphere where the child will be more receptive to the parents' wisdom or "reframes" of his or her concerns. Introducing the basic Setup phrase "Even though I have this problem, I'm still an awesome kid" or a reframe, such as "Even though I can't run as fast as Jimmy, I'm a great team player"—can also be useful.

In the nighttime review, both difficult and pleasurable events are described. Tapping while a disturbing thought has been activated diminishes its emotional hold, and corresponding changes in the brain's electrochemical activity have been mapped (see inside back cover). Tapping on pleasant memories and goals for the future seems to increase their neurological strength, though the mechanisms involved are less well understood.

Recalling a "positive" memory can take on an interesting twist. Sometimes even remembering a success or a pleasant event will make a child feel worse. A reason for this may be that, like the tail-enders discussed in the previous chapter, some positive statements evoke a subconscious negative comparison. For example, if a child says, "My teacher complimented me today in front of the whole class," the negative comparison behind it might be "But I am afraid she will find out that I didn't do a good job on my English test and will take it all back in front of everyone." So recalling the "good" memory may ultimately hold a negative charge. Tapping while recalling the "good" memory, on the other hand, may simultaneously reinforce the "good" part of the memory *and* reduce the reaction to any automatic negative comparisons.

The nighttime review encourages intimacy between parent and child and much more. It gives the child a forum for reviewing the day, a method for helping to neurologically integrate difficult experiences, and it may also help maximize the impact of positive ones.

A plethora of studies has demonstrated both that a child's emotional intelligence is a critical force in how well that child's life will fare and that children can be educated to increase the essential skills that comprise emotional intelligence. It is within our hands to cultivate the emotional intelligence of our young, as well as in ourselves, and energy psychology offers a powerful supplement to other methods that have already proven to be effective.

IN A NUTSHELL: Emotional intelligence has been studied in detail and is recognized as a key factor in a child's future success—personally, socially, and academically. Children's emotional competencies can be increased in numerous critical areas, including 1) recognizing, understanding, and managing their emotions; 2) marshalling their emotions in the service of a goal; and 3) responding to the emotions of others with accuracy, empathy, and skill. Energy methods can be used, in concert with other techniques, at each step of the way in cultivating emotional intelligence in ourselves and in our children.

# 6

# YOUR BODY'S ENERGIES

The human mind emerges from patterns in the flow of energy.
—DANIEL J. SIEGEL, M.D., *The Developing Mind*

Just as emotional intelligence is vital to a child's ability to thrive personally and socially, skills in understanding and working with your body's overall energies can be vital to your psychological and physical health. Our goal in this chapter is to help you begin to develop those skills.

Our facility with the energies that affect us has, to our detriment, declined dramatically since the times when we lived closer to nature. We understand the flesh far more than we understand the energies that animate it. Understanding the cells and organs is, of course, one of the monumental achievements of our scientific culture. Before human anatomy and physiology were mapped through the dissection of cadavers and later through surgery, X-rays, MRIs, and other imaging techniques, the internal workings of the human body were largely a mystery shrouded in superstition. A parallel situation exists for us today with the "energy body."

A central idea within energy medicine is that just as your anatomy is composed of interrelated parts that have specific functions, your "energy body"—which supports your physical body—has its own "anatomy."[1] The anatomy of the energy body includes various interrelated energy systems (such as the aura, chakras, and meridians), and these energies serve specific functions. The meridians, for instance, are distinct in purpose from the chakras, and the heart meridian performs different tasks than the lung meridian.

Phantom limb pain illustrates the relationship between the physical body and the energy body. Few medical practitioners who have worked with this ailment fail to be impressed by the tenacity and intensity of the chronic debilitating pain that may be experienced in the area of a missing arm or leg. Neurological explanations for phantom limb pain are not altogether convincing, or are at least incomplete. Energy medicine, however, offers an alternative understanding that is both plausible and that has led to successful treatments. The missing limb's counterpart in the energy body is believed to still exist and to still be registered by the person's nervous system. Because of the trauma brought to the area when the limb was lost, this energy may have become severely disrupted, sending distress signals that can cause tremendous pain. Interestingly, such pain has, after all other treatments had failed, many times been rapidly and completely dispelled by holding the air where the limb's acupuncture points *had been*.[2] The fact that the same energy treatment that would reduce pain in an injured limb reduces pain in a phantom limb suggests that the meridians remain active even if the physical structure is no longer there.

From the perspective of energy medicine, your flesh and bones are supported by a "skeleton" of living energy. Your physical structure is built on and animated by the foundation of your energy body's meridian pathways, chakra centers, aura, and other discrete energy systems. Given the complexity of the physical body, it is not surprising that its energetic infrastructure would comprise many kinds of energy as well. It is not just one great big undifferentiated electromagnetic field. And, in fact, people who "see energy" can describe with some precision the *anatomy* of the energy body, and their descriptions tend to corroborate one another.[3]

## THE ANATOMY OF THE ENERGY BODY

These descriptions are now backed by electromagnetic measurements,[4] and they also correlate with descriptions of subtle energies found throughout the world, understood in each culture's own terms and concepts.[5] *Meridians, chakras,* and *aura* are three terms that have entered our language; but other energy systems have been identified as well.

Donna is known for being able to "see," or clairvoyantly read, the body's energies. She describes eight energy systems that impact the body and mind. In addition to the meridians, chakras, and aura, Donna refers to the *basic grid,* the *Celtic weave,* the *five rhythms,* the *triple warmer,* and the *radiant circuits.* We will offer only a brief sketch of each system here to give you an idea of the reality of the energy body as understood by a person who is experienced in healing people by working with it. A far more thorough discussion of each system is available elsewhere.[6]

Even though these descriptions of the energy systems are built around *analogies,* each designed to give you a more concrete sense of a subtle system, please keep in mind that verbal descriptions can go only so far in capturing this elusive realm.

### THE MERIDIANS

In the way an artery carries blood, a meridian carries energy. As the body's *energy bloodstream,* the meridian system brings vitality and balance, removes blockages, adjusts metabolism, and even determines the speed and form of cellular change. The flow of the meridian energy pathways is as critical as the flow of blood: no energy, no life. Meridians affect every organ and every physiological system, including the immune, nervous, endocrine, circulatory, respiratory, digestive, skeletal, muscular, and lymphatic systems. Each system is fed by at least one meridian. If a meridian's energy is obstructed or unregulated, the system it feeds is jeopardized. The meridians include fourteen tangible channels that carry energy into, through, and out of your body. Your meridian pathways also connect hundreds of tiny, distinct reservoirs of heat and electromagnetic energy along the surface of the skin. These are your acupuncture points, and they can be stimulated with needles or physical pressure to release or redistribute energy along the meridian pathway.

## THE CHAKRAS

The word *chakra* translates from the Sanskrit as disk, vortex, or wheel. The chakras are concentrated centers of energy. Each major chakra in the human body is a center of swirling energy positioned at one of seven points, from the base of your spine to the top of your head. Where the meridians deliver their energy *to* the organs, the chakras bathe the organs *in* their energies. Each chakra supplies energy to specific organs, corresponds to a distinct aspect of your personality, and resonates (from the bottom to the top chakra, respectively) with one of seven universal principles having to do with survival, creativity, identity, love, expression, comprehension, or transcendence. Your chakras also code your experiences in their energies, just as memories are chemically coded in your neurons. An imprint of every emotionally significant event you have experienced is believed to be recorded in your chakra energies. A sensitive practitioner's hand held over a chakra may resonate with pain in a related organ, congestion in a lymph node, subtle abnormalities in heat or pulsing, areas of emotional turmoil, or even tune in to a stored memory that might be addressed as part of the healing process.

## THE AURA

Your aura is a multilayered shell of energy that emanates from your body and interacts with the energies of your environment. It is itself a *protective atmosphere* that surrounds you, filtering out many of the energies you encounter and drawing in others that you need. Like a space suit, your aura protects you from harmful energies. Like a radio antenna, it brings in energies with which it resonates. The aura is a conduit, a two-way antenna that *brings in* energy from the environment to your chakras and that *sends* energy from your chakras outward. When you feel happy, attractive, and spirited, your aura may fill an entire room. When you are sad, despondent, and sombre, your aura crashes in on you, forming an energetic shell that isolates you from the world. Some people's auras characteristically reach out and embrace you; others keep you out like an electric fence. A study conducted by Valerie Hunt, a neurophysiologist at UCLA's Energy Fields Laboratory, compared "aura readings" with neurophysiological measures. The auras seen by eight practitioners not only corresponded with one another; they also correlated with wave patterns picked up by electrodes on the skin at the spot that was being observed.[7]

## THE BASIC GRID

The basic grid is your body's foundational energy. Like the *chassis* of a car, the basic grid carries all the other energy systems. For instance, when you are lying down, it would appear to a seer like Donna that each of your chakras sits upon this foundational energy. Grid energy is sturdy and fundamental. But severe trauma can damage and deform the grid, and when this occurs, it does not usually repair itself spontaneously. Rather, the other energy systems adjust themselves to the damaged grid, much as a personality may be formed around early traumatic experiences. Repairing a person's basic grid is one of the most advanced and intense forms of energy therapy. If a grid's structure or a car's chassis is sound, you never notice it is there; if it is damaged, nothing else is quite right.

## THE CELTIC WEAVE

The body's energies spin, spiral, curve, twist, crisscross, and weave themselves into patterns of magnificent beauty. The equilibrium of this kaleidoscope of colours and shapes is maintained by an energy system known by different names to energy healers throughout the world. In the East, it has been called the "Tibetan energy ring." In yoga tradition, it is represented by two curved lines that cross seven times, symbolically encasing the seven chakras. In the West, it is seen in the caduceus, the intertwined serpents—also crossing seven times—found on the staff that is the symbol of the medical profession. Donna uses the term *Celtic weave* not only because she has a personal affinity with Celtic healing, but also because the pattern *looks* to her like the old Celtic drawings of a spiralling, sideways infinity sign—never beginning, never ending, and sometimes forming a triple spiral. Like an *invisible thread* that keeps all the energy systems functioning as a single unit, the Celtic weave networks throughout and around the body in spiralling figure-eight patterns. The double helix of DNA is this pattern in microcosm. The left hemisphere's control of the right side of the body and the right hemisphere's control of the left side are this pattern writ large.

## THE FIVE RHYTHMS

Your meridians, chakras, aura, and other essential energies are influenced by a more pervasive energy system. Donna does not see it as a separate energy but as a *rhythm* that runs through all the others, leaving its vibratory imprint on physical attributes, health patterns, and personality traits. Mapped long ago in traditional Chinese medicine, all of life was categorized into five *elements*, *movements*, or *seasons* (there is no perfect translation—all three terms have been used, suggesting both cyclical and substanative qualities). These energies were considered the building blocks of the universe, which provided a basis for understanding how the world works, how societies organize themselves, and what the human body needs to maintain health. Metaphors for describing these five distinct rhythms have been drawn from concrete, observable elements of nature (water, wood, fire, earth, and metal) and from the seasons (winter, spring, summer, Indian summer, and autumn). Like a movie's background music, a person's primary rhythm, in combination with the changing rhythms of life's seasons, directs the tone and mood of the entire energy system and sets the atmosphere of the life being lived.

## TRIPLE WARMER

Triple warmer is the meridian that networks the energies of the immune system to attack an invader, and it mobilizes the body's energies in an emergency for the fight-or-flight-or-freeze response. In carrying out these critical functions, it operates in ways that are so beyond the range of any other meridian that some consider it a system unto itself. Although the exact reasons for the term *triple warmer* are lost in antiquity, its energies work in conjunction with the hypothalamus gland, which is the body's thermostat. The hypothalamus is also the instigator of the body's emergency response. Like an *army*, triple warmer mobilizes during threat or perceived threat, coordinating all the other energy systems to activate the immune response, govern the fight/flight/freeze mechanism, and establish and maintain habitual responses to threats.

## THE RADIANT CIRCUITS

The radiant circuits function to ensure that all the other energy systems are working for the common good. They redistribute energies to where they are most needed, responding to any health challenge the body might encounter. In terms of evolution, the radiant circuits have been around longer than the meridians: Primitive organisms such as insects move their energies via the radiant circuits rather than through a meridian system, and the radiant circuits can be seen in the embryo before the meridians develop. As in the way that riverbeds are formed, it is as if radiant energies that habitually followed the same course became meridians. Where the meridians are tied to fixed pathways and specific organs, the radiant energies operate as fluid fields, embodying a distinct spontaneous intelligence. Like hyperlinks on a website, they jump instantly to wherever they are needed, bringing revitalization, joy, and spiritual connection. If triple warmer mobilizes your *inner militia*, the radiant circuits mobilize your *inner mum*, showering you with healing energy, providing life-sustaining resources, and lifting your morale. They are the topic of the following chapter.

## ENERGY APTITUDE

The eight energy systems that animate your body are in continual motion and flux, performers in a perfectly choreographed dance with your thoughts, feelings, movements, digestion, and every other physiological process. Because such energies are subtle and invisible, operating "behind the scenes," you are usually unaware of them. Yet knowing how to work with them can put you on an accelerated path towards enhanced physical and mental health.

Donna's approach to healing grows out of her ability to see these energies, assess them, and work with them for increased health and vitality. She has also dedicated herself to teaching people who are not able to *see* energy to nonetheless work effectively with their own energies. She has brought her approach to tens of thousands of people in classes throughout the world, and the remainder of this chapter offers an introduction to some of the methods and concepts that are particularly relevant for psychological well-being.

Your "energy aptitude" (a sort of energy counterpart to *emotional intelligence*) has four components. The first is based on your *awareness* of your body's changing energies. This simply requires that you stay attuned to internal energetic shifts, noticing for example the underlying energy dynamics in familiar experiences. Your body gives you many signs about the state of your energies. For instance, changes in your mood and the way you feel physically reflect underlying shifts in your energies. It is not difficult to develop a self-reflective, almost meditative, attunement to your internal energies. They are always there; you only need to notice them.

The second component for cultivating your energy aptitude is based in your ability to *influence* those energies in ways that benefit you. You can, relatively easily, master the set of basic procedures we are about to present for calming, stimulating, and restoring your energies when they have become disturbed or depleted. Like keeping a machine well oiled, balancing your energies prevents unnecessary wear and damage. It also helps you think more clearly and function more effectively. If illness does occur, addressing it energetically is often the least invasive approach, and energy interventions can also augment other remedies. The underlying principle of energy medicine, in fact, is this:

> Any physical or emotional difficulty you face has a counterpart in your energy system and can be treated at that level.

So the first two components of energy aptitude are an active awareness of the energies that animate you and an ability to work with them for your benefit. These focus on your internal energies. The third and fourth components are the abilities to accurately perceive the energies of others and to harmonize with or impact those energies in mutually beneficial ways. Developing an aptitude both with your own energies and with the energies of others is important, but we will focus on the energies within you. We want to present tools that allow you to influence your body's energies for your overall well-being. As you become more skilled in understanding and working with the energies that are at the foundation of your own thoughts, emotions, and physical health, you will also become more adept with the energies of others.

## KEEPING YOUR ENERGIES HUMMING

You may experience disharmonies in your energies as agitation, their depletion as exhaustion, or their imbalance as pain. People with a high degree of energy aptitude have an early-warning system. Energy imbalances show up in their awareness before progressing into conditions that are harder to reverse. The downside of this is that they are more sensitive and seem more reactive and vulnerable; the upside is that based on this early warning system, they can and often instinctively do take corrective steps to keep problems in their energy system from becoming problems in their physical structure. The little aches and pains of daily life are signals from your body. They are your body's way of asking for attention. If you keep ignoring them, chronic problems are more likely to emerge. If you take steps to reduce pain energetically, the energy imbalance does not have a chance to build.

Intervening energetically whenever you feel pain does not simply suppress the pain like a "painkilling" medication. A secret of energy medicine, rather, is that energy remedies serve both to *alleviate* the pain and to begin to energetically *shift the causes* of the pain. Similarly, intervening energetically whenever you are emotionally upset does not bury your problem but clears your mind so you can deal with it more effectively.

Unlike the Basic Recipe, which concentrates on specific problems or goals, the methods presented here help you in a more general way. They leave you energetically more vibrant and more resilient. The first set of techniques is what Donna teaches as a Five-Minute Daily Energy Routine.

# FIVE-MINUTE DAILY ENERGY ROUTINE

Donna has treated more than ten thousand people in individual sessions during a twenty-five-year period. After a session she typically gave people homework assignments. These were techniques, often invented for the situation, designed to strengthen the energy system in specific ways. She noticed over time that some of these techniques seemed to help nearly everyone. She also noticed which techniques had the greatest impact. From those that had the greatest impact with the greatest number of people, she selected a set designed to systematically strengthen and harmonize the various energy systems within the body. She wanted a five-minute sequence that would not only shift the energy patterns in the body for greater health, vitality, and clarity of mind, it also needed to be sufficiently brief that people would be willing to do it on a daily basis.

Because humans are creatures of habit, the best strategy we have found for helping people establish a daily practice is to encourage them to build it into a routine they already do. If you exercise regularly, it is a great warm-up. If you practice yoga or Tai Chi or qi gong, it can fit right into your routine. Some people do it as soon as they wake up, while still in bed, and they find it helps them start their day on a positive energetic footing. Others do it as a little transition ritual when they get home from work. Some adapt it for their bath or shower, doing the sequence while luxuriating in warm water (this is *not* a "no pain, no gain" operation). The more comfortable and enjoyable, the better your energies will flow. The routine has seven parts and requires only five minutes. You will be well rewarded for the time spent with increased efficiency, greater vitality, and better health. The specific benefits of each method are also listed, and each can be used separately as well as within the routine.

## 1. THE THREE THUMPS

As you have been seeing throughout this book, certain points on your body, when tapped with your fingers, will affect your energy field in predictable ways by sending electrochemical impulses to specific regions of your brain and releasing neurotransmitters. A sequence called the Three Thumps helps to restore you when you are tired, to increase your vitality, and to keep your immune system stronger amid stress. You can tap these points at any time during the day when you need a boost. Do not be too concerned about finding the precise location of each point; if you use several fingers to tap in the vicinity shown, you will stimulate the right spot. Tap firmly, but never so hard as to risk hurting or bruising yourself.

**A. The K-27 Points** You already know these points from the Basic Recipe. They jump-start your energy system, focus your mind, and correct meridian energy that is "flowing backward," which tends to happen when you are physically or emotionally exhausted. To locate these points, place your forefingers on your collarbone and move them inward towards the U-shaped notch at the top of your breastbone (about where a man would knot his tie). Move your fingers to the bottom of the U. Then go to the left and right about an inch and tap. Most people have an indentation

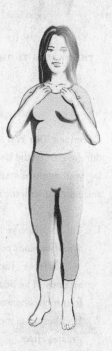

*Figure 6*

THE K-27 POINTS

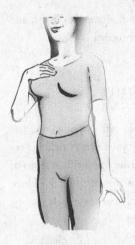

*Figure 7*
THE TARZAN THUMP

or soft spot there. Breathe slowly and deeply as you briskly tap or massage these points for 10 to 12 seconds.

**B. Tarzan Thump** Tapping on the middle of your chest tends to stimulate your energies, boost your immune system, and release stress. This is also called the Thymus Tap.

1. Place the fingers of either or both hands in the centre of your sternum, at the thymus gland.
2. Tap for about 20 seconds, using your thumb and all your fingers.
3. As you tap, breathe slowly and deeply, in through your nose and out through your mouth.

**C. Spleen Tap** You also learned one of the two variations of this procedure as part of the Basic Recipe. The Spleen Tap has the effects of boosting your immune system, balancing your blood chemistry and electrolytes, and helping with the metabolism of food, toxins, and stress.

1. Tap the *neurolymphatic* spleen points firmly for about 15 seconds. The *neurolymphatic points* are beneath the breasts and down one rib.
   *Alternate:* Tap the spleen *acupuncture* points firmly for about 15 seconds. The acupuncture points are on the side of the body about four inches beneath the armpit.
2. If either set is more tender, use those points as they will produce the greater effect.
3. Breathe slowly and deeply, in through your nose and out through your mouth, as you tap.

*Figure 8*

SPLEEN NEUROLYMPHATIC
POINTS

*Figure 9*

SPLEEN ACUPUNCTURE
POINTS

## 2. THE CROSS CRAWL

This simple exercise supports the crossover patterns in your body's energies that are necessary for coordination, healing, and vitality. There is one
important thing to keep in mind: If the Cross Crawl makes you feel tired
rather than vitalized, if it seems like you are pushing upstream, this is an
indication that your energies may not be crossing over at all (they are
forming a "homolateral pattern"), and the Cross Crawl is less likely to be
helpful. An exercise called the Homolateral Crossover can bring your
energies into a crossover pattern so the Cross Crawl, as well as any other
energy intervention, can then be more effective. So, if this seems to apply

to you, chronically or on a given day, substitute into your Daily Routine the Homolateral Crossover (p. 219) instead of the Cross Crawl. To do the Cross Crawl, which is essentially marching in place:

1. While standing, lift your right arm and left leg simultaneously.
2. As you let them down, raise your left arm and right leg. If you are unable to do this because of a physical disability, here is an alternative: While sitting, lift one knee and touch it with the opposite hand. Then lift and touch the other knee.
3. Repeat, this time exaggerating the lift of your leg and the swing of your arm across the midline to the opposite side of your body.
4. Continue in this exaggerated march for at least a minute, again, breathing deeply in through your nose and out through your mouth.

*Figure 10*

THE CROSS CRAWL

## 3. THE WAYNE COOK POSTURE

Originally developed in the 1960s to help people who stutter, this exercise has proven effective with dyslexia, ADD, and other learning disorders. Beyond correcting for dysfunction, it is one of the best single techniques we know for increasing your mental acuity and bringing out your best in a performance or confrontation.

1. Sitting in a chair with your spine straight, place your left foot over your right knee. Wrap your right hand around your left ankle and your left hand around the bottom of your left foot.

2. Breathe in slowly through your nose, letting the breath lift your body as you breathe in. At the same time, pull your leg towards you, creating a stretch. As you exhale, breathe out of your mouth slowly, letting your body relax. Repeat this slow breathing and stretching four or five times.

3. Switch to the other foot. Place your right foot over your left knee. Wrap your left hand around your right ankle and your right hand around the bottom of your right foot. Breathe in the same way.

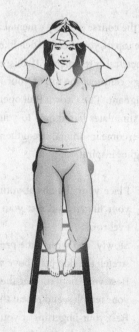

*Figure 11*

THE WAYNE COOK POSTURE

*Figure 12*

THE WAYNE COOK "STEEPLE"

4. Uncross your legs and "steeple" your fingertips together, forming a pyramid. Bring your thumbs to rest on your "third eye," just above the bridge of your nose. Breathe slowly and deeply, in through your nose and out through your mouth, about three or four full breaths. Then as you exhale, allow your thumbs to separate slowly across your forehead, pulling the skin.

5. Slowly bring your hands down in front of you. Surrender into your own breathing.

# 4. THE CROWN PULL

In the course of a day's mental activities, energy naturally accumulates at the top of your head, much like the electrostatic charge that can build on electrical instruments. If this energy doesn't move out through the energy centre at the top of your head, called the crown chakra, it becomes stagnant. The Crown Pull opens the way for such energy to be released. It stimulates blood flow to your head, releases mental congestion, helps overcome insomnia, strengthens memory, and opens the crown chakra to higher inspiration.

1. Place your thumbs at your temples on the side of your head. Curl your fingers and rest your fingertips just above the centre of your eyebrows.

2. Slowly, and with some pressure, pull your fingers apart so that you stretch the skin just above your eyebrows.

3. Rest your fingertips at the centre of your forehead, thumbs still at your temples, and repeat the stretch.

4. Rest your fingertips at your hairline, thumbs wherever comfortable, and repeat the stretch.

5. Continue this pattern, fingers curled, and pushing in at each of these locations:

| Figure 13 | Figure 14 |
|---|---|
| THE CROWN PULL | THE CROWN PULL, CONTINUED |

a. Fingers at the top of your head, with your little fingers at the hairline. Push down with some pressure and pull your hands away from one another, as if pulling your head apart.

b. Fingers at the centre of your head, again pushing down and pulling your hands away from one another.

c. Fingers over the curve at the back of your head, again using the same stretch.

d. Continue down the neck to the shoulders.

e. Repeat each of these stretches one or more times.

6. End with your fingers at the back of your shoulders. Give yourself a little massage, rake your fingers over your shoulders, and drop your hands.

## 5. THE NEUROLYMPHATIC MASSAGE

The neurolymphatic reflex points, located all over your torso, regulate the flow of energy to the lymphatic system. The lymphatic system has the critical job of removing toxins and dead cells from your body. Unlike the bloodstream, your other liquid circulatory system, which is pumped by the heart, your lymphatic system has no pump. Its flow is stimulated by the normal exercise of daily life, walking, stretching, and any other movement. But if toxins accumulate in the lymphatic system, both physical toxins and stagnant energies can become so clogged that physical exercise does not move them. Massaging your neurolymphatic reflex points stimulates the lymph system and breaks apart clogged toxins so they can be eliminated from your body. Sending toxins into the waste-removal systems not only expels physical blocks; it also breaks up energetic blockages and ultimately energizes your body.

While there are charts of where these points are located,[8] you can also find them by simply massaging the front of your torso between your ribs and along the sternum and noting where you are sore. Sore spots indicate clogged energy at these reflex points. While injuries, illness, or strain can also be the cause of soreness, once these are ruled out, soreness generally indicates reflex points that need attention. Here is a basic routine for massaging these points (moving the skin in a circular motion with strong pressure and staying with each point for at least five seconds):

*Figure 15*
MASSAGING
NEUROLYMPHATIC
POINTS

1.  Find the clavicle (collarbone) and deeply massage the points just beneath it (K-27).
2.  Move out to your shoulders. Massage the points along the half circle where

your shoulder meets your torso. K-27 and the arm connection points have so much information moving through them that energy frequently clogs in them, so it is good to clear these on a daily basis.

3. Find another point on your torso that is tender, probably along the sternum or between the ribs or under the breasts. Massage it for at least five seconds. Each day, find two or three points that are tender and massage them. You will find that while one point that was sore yesterday is no longer sore today, another point will demand regular treatment. But even those points will become less sore as you continue to work with them.

## 6. THE ZIP-UP

Central meridian, the energy pathway that moves up the front centre of your torso, teams with bladder meridian to keep your central nervous system functioning at its best. Central meridian, whose path runs directly above and connects with five of your seven chakras, also bridges your body's energies with the environment. When you are feeling sad or vulnerable, central meridian can be like a radio receiver that channels other people's negative thoughts and energies into your own energy centers. It is as if you are open and exposed. Simply running your hand up this meridian weaves tight the energies of central meridian, and this is a natural form of self-protection. Central meridian runs like a zipper from your pubic bone up to your lower lip, and you can use the electromagnetic energies of your hands to "zip it up." The Zip-Up will help you:

*Figure 16*
ZIP-UP BEGINNING

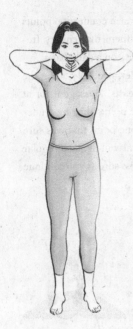

- feel more confident
- think more clearly
- tap your inner strengths
- protect yourself from negative energies that may be around you

The Zip-Up lifts your energies and your spirit. It can also be combined with stating an affirmation or a positive image. You can "zip" the statement or image into your energy system.

*Figure 17*

ZIP-UP AT TOP OF
CENTRAL MERIDIAN

1. Briskly tap the K-27 points to assure that your meridians are moving in a forward direction.
2. Place your hands at the bottom end of the central meridian, which is at your public bone.
3. Inhale deeply as you simultaneously move your

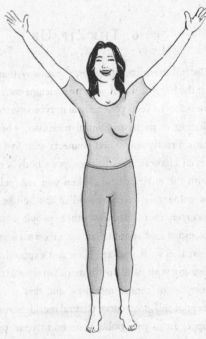

*Figure 18*

ZIPPING UP TO THE SKY

hands, slowly and deliberately, straight up the centre of your body, to your lower lip.

4. Continue upward, bringing your hands past your lips and exuberantly raising them into the sky.
5. Circle your arms back down to your pelvis.
6. Do two more times.

## 7. THE HOOK-UP

This simple routine connects central and governing meridians, increases coordination, and stabilizes the entire energy system. It also strengthens the aura, putting you into a protective energetic cocoon. Because of the neurological power of connecting central and governing meridians, the Hook-Up can help you think more clearly. We have heard several reports of the Hook-Up literally stopping a seizure when applied the moment early signs of the seizure were detected. It is very simple to do:

1. Place the middle finger of one hand on the third eye (between the eyebrows above the bridge of the nose).
2. Place the middle finger of the other hand in the navel.
3. Gently press each finger into the skin, pull it upward, and hold for 12 to 30 seconds.

*Figure 19*
THE HOOK-UP

Doing the Five-Minute Energy Routine on a daily basis gives your body the great benefit of having you consciously attending to the flow of its energies. This can have a cumulative effect as better "energy habits" are initiated and reinforced. Energy medicine is a field unto itself (www.energymed.org), with increasingly sophisticated ways of enhancing health and vitality by working with the body's energies. For our purposes, we will simply provide a few additional basic techniques that have direct application to energy psychology. They address the following issues: 1) if tapping doesn't work or if it has a "paradoxical effect," 2) psychological first aid, and 3) establishing new energy habits.

## IF TAPPING DOESN'T WORK

Estimates we have seen on the various practitioner discussion e-lists are that the client did not respond to tapping for a straightforward, properly formulated psychological issue in about 5 to 15 percent of the cases. Donna, on the other hand, reports that she has never had a client she had the opportunity to work with for a while who was not responsive to energy interventions. The key is to apply the correct technique for that person at that moment. The majority of psychotherapists who have been trained in tapping methods do not have an in-depth understanding of how to work with the entire energy body, and if systems they are not familiar with need attention, the tapping may simply be unable to penetrate a highly disorganized energy field and have the desired effects.

### THREE ROADBLOCKS TO TAPPING

In most cases, the Daily Energy Routine described above will at least temporarily restore the energy system so that tapping on a specific psychological issue can be effective. Some people's energies, however, are simply not receptive to tapping. For most people, gentle tapping on the skin is effective because it speaks the language of the body, where the heartbeat pulsing through the capillaries is one of the body's most basic and familiar rhythms. In cases where the body, for whatever reasons, does not respond well to tapping, the Touch and Breathe method described on page 45 is an excellent alternative. Another is the Neurovascular Hold, described on page 222. If you have experimented with all three methods and are still not getting the results you are hoping for—or if you are witnessing a rare "paradoxical effect" where after tapping you experience greater distress about the issue rather than relief—the most likely culprits are that 1) unresolved *aspects* of the problem are intruding, 2) psychological reversals are at play, or 3) your body's energies are running in a homolateral pattern.

## The Homolateral Crossover

Your energies are designed to crisscross, actually forming *figure eight*-like patterns at all levels of your body, from the double-helix design of your DNA to your cells to your organs to the aura that surrounds you. When energies are not crossing over adequately, whether at the microlevel of the cells and organs or the macrolevel of the torso, head, and limbs, they are referred to as travelling in a "homolateral" pattern. When this occurs, your functioning is compromised. You cannot think as clearly. You cannot find your natural coordination. You cannot heal as rapidly. You cannot assimilate interventions designed to help you, such as tapping or even the Daily Energy Routine.

In fact, if you are ill, your energies tend to be homolateral. If you are chronically depressed or exhausted, your energies tend to be homolateral. If you suffer with an autoimmune illness, your energies tend to be homolateral. These are all clear signs that you need to correct the homolateral pattern before other techniques are likely to benefit you.

Repatterning homolateral energies is, in fact, one of the most frequent interventions used by energy-medicine practitioners. Whatever else you may be doing to improve your health, if your energies are homolateral, the benefits are less likely to last. Getting the energies back into their natural crossover patterning is critical when working with many conditions. The procedure takes about three minutes and a bit of effort. It is almost always effective, *but* because the homolateral pattern may be a deeply ingrained energy habit, the energies may quickly revert again to the homolateral pattern. Donna has seen cases in which the correction holds for only a minute. But this is another situation where persistence pays. In almost all instances, by doing the three-minute procedure two or three times per day, a new energy pattern has been installed within ten days to six months. If you are indeed homolateral, it is not only interfering with your responsiveness to the Basic Recipe; it is also interfering with your general energy level, resilience, and mental acuity. Shifting homolateral patterning can be a godsend. If you are not sure if you are homolateral, it will not harm you to do the exercise. If you feel better afterward, you needed it. The Homolateral Crossover:

1. Begin by tapping or massaging the K-27 points (p. 43), followed by a full body stretch that "reaches for the stars."
2. Next do a "Homolateral Cross Crawl," simultaneously lifting the right arm and the right leg, and then the left arm and the left leg. Do about 12 lifts, deliberately and slowly, more like a walk than a run. (NOTE: These instructions are for performing the exercise while standing. They can readily be adapted for sitting or lying down by simply bringing your elbows or your palms to meet your knees. If you are lying down [and this is an excellent exercise to use when you are ill], you can also ease the process by propping your knees under a pillow.)
3. Then march in place, doing a normal Cross-Crawl (p. 209), lifting your right arm and left leg and then your left arm and right leg.

4. After about 12 lifts of the arms and legs in this Cross-Crawl pattern, stop and return to the Homolateral pattern (lifting the same-side arms and legs) for about 12 lifts.

5. Again, stop and return to a normal Cross Crawl (lifting opposite arms and legs) for about 12 lifts.

6. Repeat the Homolateral/Cross-Crawl sequence two or three more times.

7. Anchor it with an additional dozen normal (left arm to right leg, right to left) cross crawls. End by again stimulating the K-27 points. Doing the Wayne Cook Posture (p. 210) at this point will help reinforce the new pattern.

In stubborn cases of homolateral patterning, the use of poi balls can be a great resource. This produces the same gains as the Homolateral Crossover. It is at least as potent and more fun. You can learn about poi balls and how to obtain and use them by visiting www.Energy MedicineDirectory.com/id8.html.

*Figure 20*

THE HOMOLATERAL
CROSSOVER

## PSYCHOLOGICAL FIRST AID

When a life event throws you off emotionally, it is sometimes very difficult to "think your way" out of the upset, or even to figure out the most constructive first step. Energy interventions can calm your body, mind, and emotions, allowing you to then mentally process the situation more effectively. The Daily Energy Routine, or specific exercises from it it, applied on the spot, is a good place to begin. If your energies are in a homolateral pattern, the Homolateral Crossover is the first step. Four additional methods are suggested here: 1) the Neurovascular Hold, 2) the Sedating Triple Warmer sequence, 3) the Blow-Out and 4) Connecting Heaven and Earth (for additional methods, see Appendix 2).

## 1. THE NEUROVASCULAR HOLD

Your stress reactions are physical responses. When you emotionally "lose it," your reaction often has more to do with physiology than psychology. Here is the loop all of us are caught in at one time or another: The daily stresses of life trigger your primitive brain centres into an emergency response, up to 80 percent of the blood can leave your forebrain, stress chemicals pour into your bloodstream, primitive stress emotions sweep over you, and you proceed through another challenge of the modern civilized world with the biochemistry of an early ancestor in mortal danger. You wind up using the most primitive parts of your brain trying to adapt to the complex surroundings that caused the stress. Your perceptions become distorted. Your capacity to respond creatively or even appropriately is compromised. Realizing these dynamics alone can allow you some extra compassion for yourself and others.

The Basic Recipe is one way of reprogramming your autonomic nervous system so it no longer sets off a crisis response in the face of daily stresses. The Neurovascular Hold is another. Where tapping interrupts the stress response by sending signals to your amygdala, the Neurovascular Hold works directly with the blood flow to your brain. Neurovascular points are specific spots on your head that activate blood flow. Bringing a stress to mind and at the same time touching these points prevents the blood from leaving your forebrain, interrupting one of the primary phys-

Figure 21

THE NEUROVASCULAR HOLD

Figure 22

ALTERNATIVE
NEUROVASCULAR HOLD

iological components of the fight-or-flight response. This suspends the stress reaction, allowing you to think more clearly and cope more effectively, even amid life's ongoing pressures.

1. Sitting or lying down, tune in to a stress you are already feeling or focus on a stressful thought, memory, or situation.
2. Place your thumbs at your temples and the pads of your fingers on your forehead, just above your eyes.
3. Hold here softly for up to three minutes, breathing deeply, in through your nose and out through your mouth.

   *Alternative:* Place the palm of one hand on your forehead and the palm of your other hand at the back of your head. Again, hold softly for up to three minutes, breathing deeply.

## 2. SEDATING TRIPLE WARMER

Triple warmer is the energy system that governs the fight-or-flight response, the immune system, and the body's habitual ways of managing stress or threat. It is continually scanning for danger. Whenever a threat or potential threat is identified, triple warmer mobilizes the body's energies to respond to the threat, building upon inherited defense strategies such as the immune response or the fight-or-flight mechanism. Its essential task is to identify threat and to protect you, both internally (immune response) and externally (fight or flight).

In any given moment, triple warmer's basic "decision" involves only two possibilities: mobilize for threat or don't mobilize. But triple warmer evolved for a fight-or-perish world that no longer exists. As civilization, and technology in particular, have advanced, the ability of triple warmer to sort out what is friend and what is foe has been overwhelmed, so that for many people, triple warmer is on continual alert. Thousands of chemicals are in our foods and atmosphere that did not exist while triple warmer was evolving. We are surrounded not only by the Earth's geomagnetic field, but by human-made frequencies that fill the entire electromagnetic spectrum. It is triple warmer's task to decide which may harm you, but the identities of most of these substances and atmospheric conditions are not preprogrammed into the patrol system that evolved over the eons. We also feel the stress, every day, of processing hundreds of times the amount of information as our ancestors, and facing many times the number of decisions. Simply the pace of modern life can cause triple warmer to set off an emergency reaction.

Triple warmer takes charge of the meridian system and organizes its energies for a life-or-death emergency. The entire response may be triggered not only by actual threat, but it may be set off by any unrecognized stimulus, and it may become conditioned to a host of "false alarms." When you break into a sweat or begin to shake at the thought of entering lift or if you reflexively withdraw whenever another person begins to become a bit intimate, triple warmer is in overdrive. This is the dynamic that explains many of the psychological maladies people suffer, and as we have seen, it is here that energy psychology treatments may excel.

"Triple warmer in overwhelm" is at the root of much of our personal and cultural malaise. Where the Basic Recipe focuses on specific problems and goals, you can also work directly with triple warmer to help this fundamental energy system become more flexible rather than reactive in its responses. We think of this as "evolving your body," assisting it to adapt more effectively to a world where change has far outpaced the capacities of natural selection to help our species adapt.

Adding some or all of the following to your Daily Energy Routine, or using them when you are feeling anxious or unsettled, helps to calm triple warmer. It is as if you are telling it, "Yes, I know you don't recognize all of these substances and conditions, but I am watching out for both of us. You can calm down and do what you do best, which is to respond to clear-and-present danger, rather than going into emergency alert with every passing shape and form that is unfamiliar to our genetic endowment." After all, that is exactly what is happening at the emotional level with phobias, obsessive-compulsive disorders, and all manner of other anxiety-related disturbances. At the physical level this is a dynamic in autoimmune illnesses from allergies to fibromyalgia to cancer. The following four exercises each speak to triple warmer in its own vocabulary, the language of energy, helping it to relax, recenter, and recalibrate.

**A. The Hook-Up** This simple exercise (see p. 217) is fundamental way of aligning the nervous system and it also serves to calm triple warmer.

**B. Smoothing Behind the Ears** The triple-warmer energy pathway moves from the fourth finger up the arm to beneath the ear. It then circles behind the ear and ends at the temple. Tracing a segment of this meridian backward with your hands is soothing to triple warmer and thus calms your spirit.

1.  Place the pads of your fingers on your temples and take a deep breath in through your nose, exhaling through your mouth.

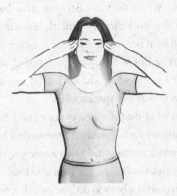

*Figure 23*

SMOOTHING BEHIND
THE EARS

*Figure 24*

SMOOTHING BEHIND
THE EARS, CONTINUED

*Figure 25*

SMOOTHING BEHIND
THE EARS, CONTINUED

2. On another deep inhale, slowly slide your fingers up and over your ears, maintaining some pressure.

3. On the exhale, take your fingers around and behind your ears.

4. Continue down your neck, finally hanging your fingers on your shoulders.

5. When you are ready, push your fingers into your shoulders, drag them across the front of your shoulders, and let them go.

**C. The Triple Warmer/Spleen Hug** The triple-warmer and spleen meridians need to work in harmony. This simple technique provides comfort and reduces emotional stress by balancing the energies between the triple-warmer and spleen meridians. The Crown Pull (p. 212) is a good preliminary to this exercise. Then:

a. Wrap your right hand around the left side of your body, with your fingers underneath your underarm, and your hand around your rib cage.

b. Wrap your left hand around your right arm with your middle finger pressing the indent just above your right elbow.

c. Be still or gently rock. Stay in this position for at least three deep breaths or up to two minutes.

d. Repeat on the other side.

**D. The Fear Tap** The tapping point used in the Nine-Gamut Procedure (p. 47) is a triple-warmer point. It is the simplest single procedure you can have in your "first-aid

*Figure 26*
THE TRIPLE WARMER/
SPLEEN HUG

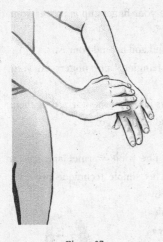

*Figure 27*

THE FEAR TAP

kit" for when you are experiencing irrational fear.

1. Locate the notch on the back side of your hand, just behind the knuckles between your ring finger and little finger.
2. Tap this area with two or three fingers from your other hand for up to a minute, breathing in through your nose and out through your mouth. Switch hands and repeat the process.

## 3. THE BLOW-OUT

Whereas the above four triple warmer techniques help with fears and anxieties, the Blow-Out is designed to release accumulated anger or frustration. It is another vital tool for your emotional first-aid kit, helping to move anger or frustration out of your body, clear congested energies, and free your spirit.

A. Stand up straight. Put your arms out in front of you, bend your elbows slightly, and make fists with your closed fingers pointing up.
B. Take a deep breath in as you swing your arms behind you and up over your head. Hold here for a moment.
C. Turn your fists so your fisted fingers are facing you, and rush your arms down the front of your body as you emphatically release your

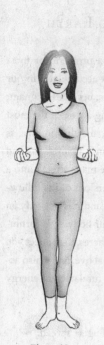

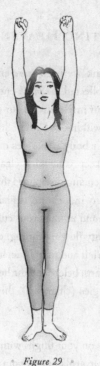

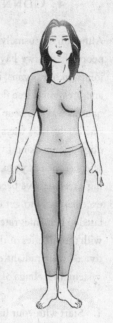

*Figure 28*

THE BLOW-OUT

*Figure 29*

THE BLOW-OUT,
CONTINUED

*Figure 30*

THE BLOW-OUT,
CONTINUED

fists and release your breath, with a "whooooosh" or any other sound that comes naturally.

D. Repeat several times. This will feel good. The last time, take your arms down in a slow and controlled manner, blowing out through your mouth as you go. End with the Zip-Up and Hook-Up (see pp. 215–217).

## 4. CONNECTING HEAVEN AND EARTH

Although we usually think we need *more* energy, a problem for most people is that we have collected *too much* energy. It accumulates in our joints, in our organs, in our meridians, in our chakras; becomes stagnant; and prevents a free flow within our bodies. Stretching is one of the most natural ways to keep your body's energies moving, and this, in turn, is one of the best ways to keep your mind clear. From watching cats and dogs upon waking to practicing disciplines that have made stretch into a science, such as yoga, many models are available. Versions of the following exercise have been found in numerous cultures, and it is not only an excellent way to get energy flowing throughout your body. It is formulated to help integrate the left and right brain hemispheres, to connect you with the energies of the earth below and the heavens above, and it also activates your radiant energies (chapter 7), the most fundamental energy system, in feelings of joy.

1. Start with your hands on your thighs with your fingers spread.
2. Inhale and swing your arms out to your sides, circle them up until your hands meet in front of you, and come into a prayer position in front of your chest. Exhale.
3. With your next inhalation, look up as you bring one arm up and one arm down. "Push" with your palms and hold.
4. Release your breath and bring your hands back into a prayer position.
5. Repeat, switching the arm that goes up and the arm that goes down.
6. Repeat the sequence on each side three times.
7. Finally, drop your arms, lean forward so your waist is bent and the top of your head comes towards the ground, bend your knees slightly, and take two deep breaths.
8. Slowly roll up to a stand.

*Figure 31*
CONNECTING
HEAVEN AND EARTH

*Figure 32*
HEAVEN AND EARTH,
CONTINUED

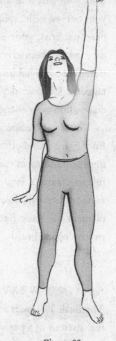

*Figure 33*
HEAVEN AND EARTH,
CONTINUED

*Figure 34*
HEAVEN AND EARTH,
CONTINUED

## ESTABLISHING NEW ENERGY HABITS

Energy moves through your body in ways that are fixed, corresponding with your physical anatomy. It pulses through established pathways in your nerves, cells, synapses, organs, torso, head, and limbs. Beyond these fixed patterns, your energies are *also* enormously creative in the ways they adapt themselves to your body's needs. Adaptations that are repeated become habitual. These energy habits may be more or less advantageous. Chronic depression is an energy habit gone wrong. A joyful disposition is an energy habit worth cultivating.

The Basic Recipe is a powerful tool for changing your energy habits. Energy medicine offers many others, with multiple approaches for shifting the patterns in each of the eight energy systems and addressing the full spectrum of health concerns. It is a vast field of study. From all its methods, we will close this chapter with three techniques that nicely complement the Basic Recipe in establishing new energy habits that support psychological health.

### "WEAVING IN" A POSITIVE STATE

The Basic Recipe is a way you can change your psychological state. You feel anxious in a particular type of situation. You apply the Basic Recipe. You find you remain tranquil the next time that circumstance arises. You are unsure about reaching a certain goal. You apply the Basic Recipe and your confidence increases, along with a tendency to fulfill images of yourself succeeding in the tasks that lead to that goal. These shifts in your psychological state are accomplished by shifting the energies that are associated with a particular thought, image, or situation. Neurological changes follow, almost instantaneously. Such changes often carry over into your daily life. Your energy system and your neurochemistry can be reprogrammed in a single session. Other times, you are working against long-standing energetic habits. You can, however, do a number of things to support a new energetic pattern.

## THE ARM CROSS

When you attain a desired state, the Crown Pull (p. 212) is a simple energy technique that helps anchor the new state into your energy system. After the crown pull, anything that helps the energies cross over from one side of your body to the other also helps to weave in a new energy habit. Simply put the fingers of your right hand under your left armpit, left fingers under right armpit, thumbs facing up and pressing against the area where your arm attaches to your body. Holding this position while at the same time you are feeling confident in your ability to give that next speech or confront that difficult person reinforces the new emotional state at an energetic level. It can be that simple.

## THE AURIC WEAVE

The Auric Weave is a more elaborate technique than the Arm Cross. Unlike the arm cross, it can be used not only while you are already in a positive state, but can also help change your state to make it positive. The human biofield, or aura, is an electromagnetic field that comes several inches out from the skin and surrounds the entire body. It is like an envelope that *contains* your energies. It *protects* you from some of the energies in the environment while *connecting* you with other energies. It also influences energies that are deeper in your body. Because your hands carry an electromagnetic charge, you can use them to smooth, trace, and strengthen your aura. This is almost like giving it a massage. The aura seems to have the best response when "massaged" in figure-eight patterns. When the crossover patterns in your aura are strong, the crossover patterns in every other system of your body are being deepened and reinforced. This supports a positive mental state. If a positive state has already been accessed, doing the Auric Weave tends to make that positive state echo within your energy field.

The Auric Weave is actually much more complex to describe than it is to do. You can do it to music and in much more of a free flow than the directions imply. The more fun it is, in fact, the stronger the results. Find all the ways you can move your arms and hips in figure-eight patterns. By simply glancing over the following directions, you will get the idea.

1. Stand tall, with your hands on your thighs. Throughout the exercise, breathe slowly and deeply, in through your nose and out through your mouth.

2. Swing your arms out to your sides, circle them up until your hands meet in front of you and come into a prayer position in front of your chest.

3. Rub your hands together, shake them out, face your palms towards each other, and see if you can feel the energy between them. Do not be concerned if you cannot feel it; this is a growing sensitivity.

4. Rub your hands together again, shake them out, put them up near your ears, about three inches out, and take a deep breath.

5. With your next inhale, bring your elbows together.

6. On the exhale, cross your arms in front of you.

7. Swing your arms out to the side.

8. Cross them again in front of your body and swing them out to the side again.

9. Do this again, but as you swing your arms out, bend over.

10. Recross your arms in front of your legs.

11. Stay bent. Swing your arms out again, then recross in front of your ankles.

12. Bend your knees slightly. Straighten your arms, turn your hands towards the front, and begin to scoop up that energy.

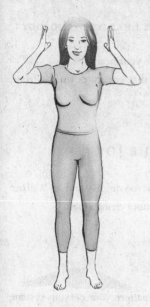

**Figure 35**
AURIC WEAVE

**Figure 36**
AURIC WEAVE,
CONTINUED

**Figure 37**
AURIC WEAVE, CONTINUED

**Figure 38**
AURIC WEAVE, CONTINUED

13. Stand, raising your arms straight above your head.
14. Bring your palms down, pouring all that energy down the front, sides, and back of your body.

## "TAPPING IN" THE JOY

Joy is nature's gift. But moments of joy pass too quickly and, as William Blake warned, clinging to such moments cannot change that:

*He who binds himself to a joy*
*Does the winged life destroy*

But you *can* use a moment of joy to help repattern your nervous system, to make it more harmonious with joyful energy! The nervous system is governed by the bladder meridian and the central meridian. The first acupuncture point on the bladder meridian is at the "third eye," known in many traditions as a powerful point for psychic and spiritual opening. By tapping on the "third eye" while you are feeling joy, you begin to repattern your nervous system around that feeling. This, in Blake's famous words, "kisses the joy as it flies," helping it to reverberate more strongly in your memory and in your neurochemistry.

*Figure 39*
"TAPPING IN" THE JOY

The next time you are feeling joy, the next time your cup runneth over, the next time life is as good as it gets, "tap it in" at your third eye. Tuning in to your joy, tap with the middle finger of either hand, between your eyebrows, above the bridge of your nose. This helps you imprint the good moments in your life into your nervous system, programming your mind to gravitate towards the positive. Two variations on this also promote excellent physical and mental hygiene:

1. It is powerful energy medicine to treasure your body. Thank your body for its amazing service, and as you reach that state of gratitude, "tap it in."
2. It is powerful energy psychology to treasure the good moments in your life. Recall a treasured moment and "tap it in."

## EMOTIONAL INTELLIGENCE, ENERGY APTITUDE, AND THE CAPACITY FOR JOY

The previous chapter focused on "emotional intelligence," this on "energy aptitude," and the following addresses your "capacity for joy." Rather than overwhelm you by suggesting you add three separate and complex themes to your personal development agenda, we want to emphasize that all three are spokes in the same wheel. Cultivating your emotional intelligence, energy aptitude, and capacity for joy is a lifelong journey, and effort in any one area supports all three. Developing the capacity for joy is no frivolous pursuit; it feeds the life of the spirit. Like emotional intelligence, the capacity for joy has an energetic dimension at its core, and that is the topic of chapter 7.

IN A NUTSHELL: In this chapter, you have learned a five-minute sequence for keeping your energies balanced and in a good flow on a daily basis. You have learned alternative methods if the Basic Recipe is not having the desired effects. You have learned a number of "first-aid" techniques you can use when emotional upset or other signals tell you that your energies need attention. You have learned techniques to reinforce positive emotional patterns and to make them more habitual. These tools can serve you for the rest of your life.

# 7

# THE CIRCUITS OF JOY

Happiness is our natural state. . . . Bliss is hardwired.

—CANDACE PERT, PH.D., *The Molecules of Emotion*

The *neurological fact* that your brain is wired for joy[1] and the *social reality* that your world has rewired you for passive entertainment, consumerism, and abstract worries set the stage for our final chapter. We begin by inviting you to consider that it is far from frivolous to fix your sights on recapturing the joy and playfulness that are your natural endowment. When your work is touched by joy, the product radiates. When your relationships are infused with play, love flourishes. When your challenges are met with an eager spirit, you navigate them more effectively. Inner joy is, for certain, a different standard of wisdom than worldly knowledge, a different standard of success than material accomplishment, a different standard of health than the absence of illness, and a different standard of good citizenship than mere obedience. It is a gold standard in each of these areas, capable of bringing a Midas touch into your life. And while we cannot promise you a life of uninterrupted joy any more than we can promise you that you can easily tap away all your problems, we can show you ways to increase the flow of joyful energy through your body.

In one of the saddest ironies of modern times, those in wealthy technological cultures—who have comforts and luxuries that would have been the envy of royalty not so many generations ago—often feel less joy than those in the simplest of circumstances. While our materialistic values, unrelenting pace, and stress-filled lifestyles are obvious contributors to our diminished *levels* of joy, a diminished *capacity* for joy has also become wired into our energy systems. Energy follows habits, and our habitual behaviours tend to create energy patterns that prevent feelings of joy from easily flowing through our bodies. But even while the stresses and pace of your life contribute to these deadening energy patterns, you can counteract their effects by taking direct steps to reinvigorate the energy channels that support feelings of joy. Many of the pursuits we follow, from too much shopping to too much Internet to too much food, are futile substitutes for the joy and deep satisfactions we know we lack. Stimulating the flow of your body's natural joyful energies is more direct, readily accessible, and it is free.

## INCREASING YOUR CAPACITY FOR JOY

Increasing your capacity for joy is a matter of opening natural channels that have become shut down. Even amid stress-filled days, you can rebuild this capacity as surely as you can develop your muscles or your computer skills. This chapter offers tools for reawakening your natural inner joy. While, like a physical exercise program, it requires some effort and intention, remember that the capacity for childlike joy is your birthright. Do you have the time to reclaim it? Your call. But when you review your life in later years, the amount of joy you felt will count for much more than the number of e-mails you answered.

The exercises you will be learning nurture your "radiant circuits."

Your radiant circuits are in gear whenever you feel joy. The ancient Chinese doctors sometimes called these the "extraordinary meridians." They carry an energy that not only supports greater joy and a more positive attitude; their energy keeps you healthy and can also heal you when you are ill. It is the "first arm" of your immune system.[2] Where the processes governed by the triple-warmer meridian use the familiar "search and destroy" strategy for protecting you, the radiant circuits use the more fundamental strategy of protecting you by keeping you vibrant, healthy, and happy. An organism that is healthy fights all potential invaders with its robustness before needing to fight specific invaders that have attacked its vulnerabilities. Keeping you robust in body and spirit is the charge of the radiant energy system.

If you have lost your childhood ability to feel joy, methods for regaining this capacity can literally offer you a new lease on life. The first step is as straightforward and direct as simply tuning in to the radiant energies that already move through your body. Vivid attunement begins to open channels between *their* flow and *your* awareness. That not only allows you to enjoy what is already going *very right* within you; you literally increase the strength of your radiant energies *when you enjoy them*. The more you bask in them, the more they flow. That's how they work.

For many people, stimulating points that activate the flow of the radiant energies makes it easier to tune in and open up to the radiant energies. Stimulating these points can help you sense the radiant pulsation as it moves through you. Be alert for a very pleasant kind of wave radiating from the area focused on in each exercise. It may be very faint in the beginning, but the increased movement of these energies is a neurological response to holding, tracing, or massaging the relevant areas. The radiant circuits activate endorphins. The more freely the radiant circuits move through your body, the more your body produces the chemicals that generate joy. Getting them pumping is a good deal all around.

Unlike the meridian tapping from the Basic Recipe, where your beliefs do not affect the outcome, it helps with the radiant circuit exercises if you *believe* they are activating your radiant circuits. To be clear, the exercises will activate them on their own, whether or not you believe they will. But *if* you believe they will, or can at least temporarily suspend your doubt, you will be more likely to discern their subtle movement and tune in to what is already there. And that jump-starts the system. The more you feel them, the more they flow. Before offering precise instructions, let's take a tour of the radiant energy system.[3]

## THE NATURE OF THE RADIANT CIRCUITS

First described in the *Neijing Suwen* (*The Yellow Emperor's Classic of Internal Medicine*) some 4,500 years ago, the radiant circuits are still used within acupuncture, jin shin do, qi gong, and shiatsu.[4] Like the meridians, chakras, and aura, the radiant circuits are an independent energy system with specific functions. They serve to connect all the other energy systems in the body. Wherever the radiant energies move, they bring strength and resilience, joy and vitality.

Called the "strange flows," "collector meridians," or "extraordinary vessels" in traditional Chinese medicine, they are not exactly flows, meridians, or vessels. More like hyperlinks on the Web, they jump instantly to wherever they are most needed, which is one reason the Chinese found them to be both strange and extraordinary. Through them, all of the body's energy systems are linked and energetic deficiencies and excesses regulated. Beyond doing repair work, these are also primary energies in exhilaration, falling in love, orgasm, hope, gratitude, rapture, and spiritual ecstasy. Because they are also associated with the awakening of psychic abilities and the capacity to channel healing energies into the body, they are sometimes called the "psychic channels."

Given the multitude of terms being used for the same energy system, Donna began to look for an accurate and broadly descriptive name for this critically important force. She felt these energies were largely misunderstood and underappreciated. She chose the term *radiant* because she experiences them as carrying a radiant glow (other people who clairvoyantly see energy have corroborated this), and she chose the term *circuits* because one of their most important functions is to create instant circuits that distribute energies to where they are needed. Just as they literally have a radiant appearance for people who are able to see energies, they bring a radiant, joyful, uplifting quality to all they touch.

The radiant circuits appear to predate the meridians, and they are the first energy circuit to appear in the developing foetus.[5] We believe, in fact, that a meridian is an energy pathway that was once, in the course of evolution, a radiant circuit. Donna, who sees eight human energy systems in varying colours, intensities, and geometric patterns, sees the meridians and the radiant circuits as discrete energies in humans and in animals, but she cannot see meridians in simpler organisms, only the radiant circuits. As creatures became more complex, radiant energies that moved along the same lines day after day, generation after generation, seem to have formed the meridians. Meridians are the energy equivalent of riverbeds, flows of energy movement that have become embedded in the body. A meridian is highly efficient for specific, repetitive tasks. Radiant energy, on the other hand, spontaneously jumps to wherever it is needed.

One study conducted in China is reported to have been suppressed because it found that treatments which focused on the radiant energies were "far more effective than those of the traditional Chinese protocols."[6] A well-designed pilot study at Florida International University in Miami, examining the use of acupuncture to stimulate the radiant circuits in the treatment of major clinical depression, yielded 1) promising results with seven of eight patients,[7] 2) a clinical reference manual for acupuncturists treating depression, and 3) a training program that teaches laypeople the use of magnets and other methods for activating their radiant energies.[8] From her own students and clients, Donna has received perhaps a hundred unsolicited testimonials indicating strong emotional benefits from working with the radiant circuits, and her more sensitive students can readily feel the movement of the radiant circuits both in their own bodies and those of their clients. There is also a scholarly website that examines the radiant energies and probes a wide range of clinical, neurological, philosophical, and empirical issues (www.rebprotocol.net).[9] The descriptions of radiant energy found in this chapter combine the traditional Chinese descriptions with Donna's ability to see and feel these energies and her personal and clinical experiences in working with them.

## CLINICAL EXAMPLES

Two people's experiences with the radiant circuits introduce you to their potential impact. Donna was the practitioner in both cases, and the descriptions are in her words.

### A CRUMBLING PERSONA AND A FAILING MARRIAGE

The pastor of a large progressive church in my town came in for a session. He brought his two sons with him and left them in the waiting room. He was concerned because his ministerial persona was wearing thin. He was desperate inside and had become harsh and brittle with others. His temper was easily provoked, particularly by those closest to him. During this, his first session, a story emerged. He had a third son who had died at age two. He was separated from his wife, and they were deciding whether or not to divorce. He was trying to get his spirit back and to find relief from the pain and anger he was carrying. While he did not think there was a chance for his marriage, he knew his anger was hurting his two remaining sons.

He was talking a mile a minute. When energy spills out like that, the person isn't able to receive. Incoming energies are literally being blocked by the pressured speech. Usually in a situation like this, I begin by "unscrambling" the force fields. But my instinct told me to go right to his radiant energies. I began holding points that stimulate the radiant circuits and connect them with one another so the entire radiant system would become activated. He immediately fell silent and began to relax. It was as if he were taking in the most soothing nourishment. After a time, he began to cry and cry.

The boys came in from my waiting area concerned that I was hurting their daddy. But he was so soft when they came in, which was such a relief from the harshness they'd been living with, that they started laughing and laughing and laughing. And it made him laugh as well. I was just holding points. That's all I was doing. All three of them became relaxed. I got the boys to go back into the other room. Then the man began to shake. His tremors were so violent that it was one of those rare times I wanted to intervene in a natural process. I began to help him stop. He said, "No," so I let him be. He just kept shaking and releasing. Then he became still, and it looked like he was in bliss.

We worked with the radiant energies in each of his next several sessions, but from that first session, his demeanour changed, particularly with his wife. He had never realized why he was so angry at her. But as he softened and they began to communicate, he discovered that he had (irrationally) been holding her responsible for the death of their son. He'd never uttered this thought, even to himself, and this unacknowledged blame and rage was the domino that resulted in his retreat from her and into his brittle shell. From there, he was able to heal and the marriage was able to rebuild.

## INTRACTABLE DEPRESSION

A woman who suffered with periodic bouts of severe depression had been treated over a period of years with unsuccessful talk and drug therapies. She believed that if she were able to heal the torments from her past, her depression would lift. She responded well to an energy approach, particularly work with her chakras. Over several months, distasteful or forgotten scenes from her childhood would emerge and the traumatic energies associated with them were purged.

It seemed she had energetically cleared truckloads of bad memories she had not been able to release through talk therapy, but she was enormously disappointed with the outcome. While she was no longer so entangled with the traumas from her past, they were not replaced by any kind of happiness. When caught in her old story, she at least felt passion when she would cry and wail and go to pieces. Now nothing made her feel alive.

I could see that her energies were gridlocked. Over the years, they had spiraled down into extreme life-negating patterns. Her radiant circuits were hardly even moving, and when I looked at her energies, I could see no radiance anywhere in her body. Her energies had a uniform dull appearance. Even after the significant, desirable healing of her childhood wounds, her body was simply unable to come out of its deadness. Chronic tension and negative thinking had become habitual and were deeply ingrained. She in fact hated the idea of "positive thinking" and was irritated by people like me who seemed "too happy."

She herself certainly wasn't going to look foolish by acting happy, but she longed for more passion and a sense of aliveness. As the inner deadness persisted, she went into greater despair than ever. All treatment progress ceased. Her disappointment and negative thinking began to dominate the sessions. We reached a point where I wouldn't even let her talk during the treatments so she would stop countering the energy work with incessant negative patter. This was more than twenty-five years ago, and I'd not had much experience at that point working with the radiant energies, but I decided to experiment.

As I applied techniques for activating the radiant circuits, the first thing to happen was that tension would leave her body. This allowed the radiant energies to begin to move, which literally began to flush the negative energies from her system. Then she would feel something akin to happiness well up from inside her. It was an odd sensation for her. She knew glimpses of happiness that were caused by external events—such as when she would receive a compliment or something good happened in her life—but this was different. It was coming from within. From one session to the next, the feeling would remain longer. She had been using marijuana and other drugs to make her feel happy and alive. The radiant energies began to give her the same feeling. This amazed her.

I must emphasize that this was hardly an instant cure. Years of depression had created deep patterns in her energies and her lifestyle, as well as her ways of thinking. It is necessary to rebuild the radiant pathways when habitual energies gravitate towards deeply established negative patterns, and it is hard not to feel negative when this is the energetic foundation of your emotions. With persistence, the pathways did rebuild. Her bouts of depression gradually ceased, her pessimism lifted, and her demeanour became more cheerful.

Where the new "positive psychology" perspective in psychotherapy recognizes that an *optimistic outlook* leads to better choices, mood, and health,[10] energy psychology recognizes that optimizing the flow of the radiant energies *leads to* a more optimistic outlook.

## REASONS TO FOCUS YOUR EFFORTS ON THE RADIANT ENERGIES

The radiant circuits, thought of in Chinese medicine as "inner wells of joy," support a vibrancy and a harmony throughout your entire body and its energy systems. Working with the radiant circuits can orient your body towards more joy and less despair. They can be marshalled to overcome self-sabotage and negative thinking. They bring us in contact with our "core self," showing us how healthy functioning felt before life's inevitable woundings.[11] By countering the triple warmer's lock on habitual thought and behavioural patterns (p. 224), they can help people trapped in dysfunctional habits to change them. If you can cause your radiant energies to be activated more consistently, you will experience greater enjoyment of life. In addition to working with the radiant energies to enhance your capacity for joy, consider giving them special attention:

- *If depression or negative thinking are persistent themes in your life.*
  Because the radiant circuits are a distinctly "positive" energy,
  they begin to displace negativity and leave a positive, optimistic,
  hopeful psychological imprint.
- *To overcome resistant habits.* As part of the body's survival strategy, energy habits run deep. So do the radiant circuits. They
  permeate the cells. The information they carry spreads with a
  tuning-fork-like resonance. Working with the radiant circuits
  can initiate changes in the body's energy habits, and you see
  these changes in the health and behavioural patterns that reflect
  them.
- *When caught in the past.* Even if your energy system is holding
  on to a habit, a belief, or a dream that is no longer viable, if you
  think about this old way at the same time you engage the radiant
  circuits, you forge a fresh pathway that allows a new truth to
  emerge.
- *When other corrections won't hold.* When energy treatments result in improvements, but the improvements are short-lived,
  older energy habits may be winning the battle. Activating the
  radiant circuits can weave the corrections into the larger energy
  system. If you can make the radiant energies a more pervasive
  force in an ongoing and consistent manner, you will be less vulnerable to the way other influences tend to engage old habits or
  activate past fears and trauma.

## KEEPING YOUR RADIANT CIRCUITS RADIANT

Many things you do naturally and spontaneously activate the radiant circuits. Joy begets joy. The healing qualities of laughter are well documented. A natural, spontaneous smile sends joy all the way down to your psychic core and back up again. A deep smile is not an ornament or a mask; it engages your radiant energies. So does listening to music you love, being overtaken by beauty, reveling in nature, laughing uncontrollably, abandoning yourself in play, dance, or love—as does anything that moves out negative thoughts, painful emotions, or stagnant energies, including exercise, laughter, or energy techniques such as those found in the Daily Energy Routine.

But it is also true that "if you don't use it, you lose it." The radiant energies can become stagnant and unable to move easily to where they are needed. This is the plight of many of us today where busyness, computer screens, and shopping have taken precedence over deeper pleasures. The good news is that your body is designed to keep your radiant circuits in good repair, and many of your normal activities support them. The more the radiant energies are exercised, the more available they are to you. The radiant energies are regularly stimulated and maintained by:

- any activity that helps make space in the body, such as stretching or yoga
- any activity that crosses the energies from one side of your body to the other, such as walking or swimming
- any activity that engages your spirit, such as watching a beautiful sunrise or hearing an inspiring story
- anything that improves your environment, even something as simple as walking outdoors to get more air and space around you

With so much that you already do supporting your radiant energies, you may wonder why we are suggesting extra effort to engage them. It is somewhat like taking vitamins. Ideally, the food you eat would provide all the vitamins you need; and ideally, the activities in your life would keep your radiant energies flourishing. For most of us, however, neither is the case. We can stay healthier by taking well-chosen vitamin supplements, and we can stay happier by attending to our radiant energies.

Not surprisingly, several of the procedures built into the Daily Energy Routine (p. 206), besides yielding other benefits, strengthen the radiant circuits. These include the Crown Pull, the Zip-Up, and the Hook-Up. Other methods introduced in the previous chapter, including the Blow-Out, the Sedating Triple Warmer sequence, and the Celtic Weave, also directly engage the radiant energies. The following six additional techniques are immediate, direct, and always available—nature's Prozac. Following each exercise, briefly pause and enter a contemplative state, breathe deeply, and carefully observe your experience. You may find warm feelings or other sensations flowing through your body, you might find that your intuition is more open and that creative thoughts or images are coming to you, or you may simply feel deeply and pleasantly relaxed.

Some methods will feel better to you than others, and the ones that *feel* better *work* better. These exercises work best if you enjoy them. That is the nature of the radiant energy system. It is worth keeping a couple of these techniques in your back pocket for daily doses as well as for those moments when your spirit begins to darken.

Begin with the Crown Pull (p. 212). Do it slowly and deliberately, breathing in through your nose and out through your mouth. When you are done, simply notice the sensations that move through your skull. The crown pull is a good place to begin because we all think so much that energies become congested in our heads, blocking the radiant circuits that are involved with the central nervous system. When you are finished, focus on the sensations that are moving through your head, neck, and shoulders, registering that they are the forerunners of joyful feelings. Then do any combination of the following six additional exercises:

## 1. RADIANT IMAGINATION

Recall the sudden glow you feel when you see someone you find attractive. This is how quickly your radiant energies can spring into action. Your internal images can also give an instantaneous boost to your radiant energies. At any given moment, you may become peaceful or anxious, happy or sad, based on what is playing in the theatre of your mind. By focusing your imagination, you can make that program not only enjoyable but also a force that boosts your radiant energies. Use any of the following suggestions, or write your own script:

1.  Imagine that someone who makes you feel alive and happy has just greeted you.
2.  Bring to mind a colour you love and imagine the energy of this colour infusing every cell of your body.
3.  Bring to mind something in your life about which you can feel thankful (gratitude is among the most profound spiritual healers and is the mascot of the radiant energies).

Send this feeling of gratitude through your body. Say thank you to your heart, lungs, kidneys, all your organs; thank your legs for walking you; thank your environment and your loved ones for supporting you.

## 2. AB STRETCH

Just as the head becomes clogged with residue that prevents the radiant energies from linking freely to the mind, energetic residue also tends to

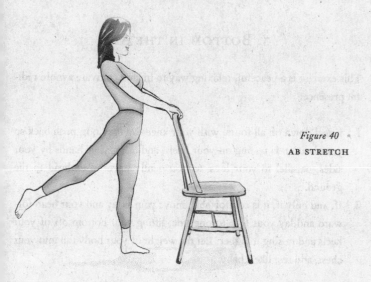

*Figure 40*

AB STRETCH

accumulate at the midline of the body. Most specifically, people tend to accumulate stress chemicals, such as cortisol, in the abdomen. This not only builds excess fat storage in your midsection and puts an extra strain on your heart; it deadens your feelings as well. The Ab Stretch clears this residue, allowing the radiant circuits to flow between the top and bottom halves of the body.

1. Standing straight, grip the back of a chair for support.
2. On an inhalation, lift one leg backward as far as is comfortable without bending at the knees. You will feel a stretch in your abdomen.
3. Lower the leg while exhaling.
4. Repeat with the other leg.

Do several sets, stretching the abdomen with each leg lift. Again, and with each of the subsequent exercises, end by tuning in to the sensations and recognizing them as the precursors of joy.

## 3. BOTTOM IN THE AIR

This exercise is a peaceful, relaxing way to further cultivate a more radiant presence:

1. Kneel down on all fours, with your knees on the floor, push back so your bottom is resting on your heels, and bring your hands by your sides, parallel to your legs, as you gently lower your head to the ground.

2. If, and only if, it is comfortable, move your body and your head forward and lay your face to one side, lifting your bottom off of your heels and raising it higher. Let the weight of your body fall into your chest, and rest like a baby.

Hold this position for two or three minutes. Use the time to meditate, contemplate a positive thought or image, list appreciations, or just let your mind go. As you come back onto all fours, you may find it conducive to do the classic yoga camel pose, arching and then collapsing the back.

*Figure 41*

BOTTOM IN THE AIR

## 4. STRETCH AND BOUNCE

The radiant energies flow naturally, but they can become blocked by tension or stress. Simple physical activities are often enough to revive their movement. A good way to start your day is to scoot down in your bed and stretch your arms as far up as they will go while stretching your legs, feet, and toes downward. Stretch on the inhale; release on the exhale. Repeat twice more.

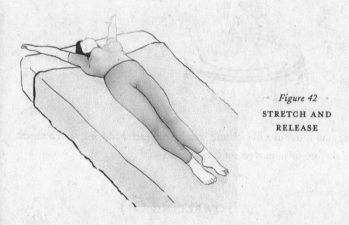

*Figure 42*
STRETCH AND
RELEASE

You can also, at any time of the day, stand and stretch. A dog or cat after a nap models this beautifully. Think of "making space" for your energies to flow. Stretch in all directions. Breathe deeply. Reach high and low. As an option, you can then "jump-start" your energies by bouncing— jumping up and down on the balls of your feet with the rest of your body loose and relaxed. A trampoline-like bouncer is a great aid for getting your radiant energies moving, and it also helps clear your lymphatic system (see p. 213).

One of David's favourite remedies when he is feeling stressed or is

*Figure 43*
BOUNCE AND BREATHE

dragging is to put a five-pound weight into each hand, get on a bouncer, and do free-form movement to dance music.

## 5. TOWELLING OFF

You can trace your meridians and activate your radiant energies every day when you bathe or shower, or when you towel off afterward.

1. Beginning with the bottom of one foot, rub the towel or washcloth up the inside of the leg, over the front of the body, up over the shoulder, down the inside of the arm, and off the fingertips.
2. Repeat on the other side.
3. Then, starting at the back of either hand, travel up the fingers and the outside of the arms to the shoulders.

4. Repeat on the other side.

5. Then reaching behind with both hands and starting as high on the back as you can, rub down the entire length of the back, then down the outer sides of the legs, and off the top of the feet.

6. Finish by towelling or washing your face downward, continuing to the bottom of your neck. Then curl your fingers over the back of your shoulders at the neck and drag them forward and off your body.

## 6. HEAVEN RUSHING IN

This technique is half prayer, half energy work. It connects you with the larger forces that surround you, brings comfort when you are feeling lonely or in despair, and allows you to direct healing energies to specific areas of your body. While this routine can be done anywhere at any time, it is particularly powerful if done in nature or under the night sky.

1. Standing tall, place your hands on your thighs with fingers spread.

2. Inhale deeply and exhale fully.

3. With your next inhalation, slowly draw your hands up into a prayerful position in front of your chest and exhale slowly.

4. With another deep breath, lift your arms straight up. When they are almost as high as you can reach, separate them outward about three feet, so you are reaching to the heavens, palms facing up.

5. Look to the heavens and sense the vastness above you and the energy around you. Receive the energies of the heavens. Allow yourself to open to a larger story. You are not alone. Feel the energies pulsating through your body, or imagine they are there—they are. Allow your hands to accumulate this energy.

6. At the center of your chest, at the level of your heart, is a vortex that is traditionally known as Heaven Rushing In. When you are ready, scoop the energies you have been accumulating in your hands into

*Figure 45*
HEAVEN RUSHING IN,
CONTINUED

*Figure 44*
HEAVEN RUSHING IN

*Figure 46*
HEAVEN RUSHING IN,
CONTINUED

*Figure 47*
HEAVEN RUSHING IN,
CONTINUED

this vortex, placing the palms of both hands over the centre of your chest. Allow your heart to receive this energy. You can then, with your hands, direct this energy to any part of your body that is tired, hurting, or that needs a boost.

You now have a dozen techniques that support your radiant energies. We suggest that you experiment. Find which ones feel the best, and use them frequently or build them into your Daily Energy Routine. Remember to stop after each and receptively notice the sensations, feelings, and intuitions that follow. In addition to knowing techniques for strengthening your overall radiant system, it is also valuable to understand all the individual radiant circuits, their functions, and how to bolster them.

## THE ANATOMY OF THE RADIANT CIRCUITS

Why do you need to know about the specific radiant circuits if you can just stick your butt in the air and activate all of them? One reason is that the radiant energy system can be strengthened by regularly activating its weakest links. Another reason is that radiant circuits that become involved in psychological problems can be targeted to help shift the problems, much as you have learned to do by tapping on the meridian end points. A third reason is that being aware of the structure of this joy-enhancing energy system is in itself reinforcing and empowering.

Eight individual radiant energies have, over evolutionary time, developed in the human body and taken on specific roles and functions (the front and back regulator circuits, the front and back bridge circuits, the belt circuit, the penetrating flow, and the central, governing, spleen, and triple warmer circuits). You can bring about changes in habits that are entrenched in the psyche as well as in the body by focusing on, and strengthening, the action of the related radiant circuit. We will briefly describe each of the radiant circuits, its primary functions, and two or more techniques for supporting it and activating its energies. While more sophisticated methods for assessing the energies in each of the radiant circuits can be found elsewhere,[12] you can make educated guesses about which may need attention based on the following descriptions and experiment with how the techniques for each feel.

## THE REGULATOR CIRCUITS

The back and front regulator circuits influence hormones, chemistry, and circulation as well as the connections among all the systems in the body. These circuits help the body adapt to endless assaults of internal and external changes. Hormonal imbalances and the emotional turmoil that may follow can be addressed by working with the regulator circuits. The following exercise will help activate these circuits.

*Figure 48*

ACTIVATING THE
REGULATOR CIRCUITS

1. Rub your hands together, place them on the sides of your head with your fingers touching over the crown of your head, and slowly pull them down, "smoothing" over and around the ear.

2. Continue down the neck, and to the edge of the shoulders, right hand to right shoulder, left hand to left shoulder.

3. Now with your hands wide open, smooth the energy down your body.

4. As you come off your ankles, pass your hands over the top of each foot, squeeze

the sides of the feet, and then firmly pull the energies off of them.

5. Repeat at least twice.

Another technique for activating the regulator circuits requires a partner.

1. Lie faceup on a bed or massage table, with your partner positioned at your feet.

2. Your partner places his or her thumbs at the bottom of the ball of each foot, between the big and second toes and gradually leans into you, moving your feet at the ankles until your toes point towards your head.

3. Then your partner wraps his or her hands around the top of your feet and leans back, stretching your legs, resembling a water-skier.

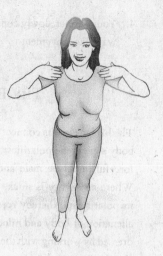

*Figure 49*
REGULATOR CIRCUITS,
CONTINUED

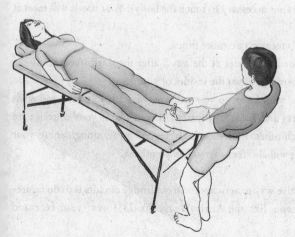

*Figure 50*
REGULATOR
CIRCUITS WITH
PARTNER

4. Your partner slowly continues this, back and forth, until it becomes a wavelike movement.

## THE BRIDGE CIRCUITS

The bridge circuits connect the front and back of the body as well as the body's energetic polarities: positive and negative charges, receptive and forceful impulses, male and female qualities, yin and yang influences. Where an energy is stuck, these circuits function as a bridge across to its polarity and thereby reestablish flow in the system. Inner schisms—alienation of body and mind, head and heart, love and sex—may be addressed by working with the bridge circuits. In the outer world, the bridge circuits support harmony and the exchange of information between people, particularly intuitions about others. Exercises for both the front and back circuits follow.

1. To activate the bridge circuits on the front of your body, place the middle fingers of each hand between your breasts and simultaneously slowly draw a "heart" by circling your hands up and then around each breast (it is not necessary to touch the body). Your hands will meet at the navel.
2. Repeat this motion two more times.
3. When your hands meet at the navel after the third trace, continue, very deliberately, down the insides of your legs.
4. Then bend your knees so you can reach beneath your feet, and wrap your fingers underneath the insteps of your feet so your knuckles are facing each other. Pull your body up and away, straightening your arms. You will also feel a stretch in your back.

Another effective way to activate the front bridge circuits is to do figure-eight movements like the Auric Weave (p. 233) over your face and

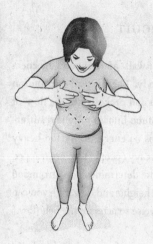

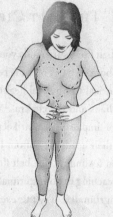

*Figure 51* ·
ACTIVATING THE
BRIDGE CIRCUITS

*Figure 52* ·
BRIDGE CIRCUITS,
CONTINUED

*Figure 53* ·
BRIDGE CIRCUITS,
CONTINUED

then down the front and sides of your body and all the way down to your feet.

1. To activate the bridge circuits that are on your back, start with your arms hanging at the sides of your body, palms facing backwards, and move your hands forward and then behind you in figure-eight patters.

2. If a partner is available, figure-eight movements can be improvised to extend across the width and length of your back, weaving all the way down to your feet. If a partner is not available, doing the figure eights along the sides of your body with both arms simultaneously will still bridge to the energies of your back.

## THE BELT CIRCUIT

The belt circuit, or belt flow, surrounds your waist and connects the energies of the top and bottom parts of your body. This vertical distribution of the energies is critical to physical health and orchestrates the flow of energy in the meridians and the chakras. Much human folly and suffering is a reflection of impairment that keeps us energetically top-heavy (people who live in their heads) or bottom-heavy (people who are trapped in their instincts and feelings). The belt flow determines how grounded you can stay when reaching to your spiritual heights and how high you can reach while staying grounded. Try this exercise to activate the belt flow.

1. Spread the fingers of your right hand and grip your waist, on the left side of your body.
2. Place your left hand behind your right hand, and with pressure, pull your right hand from the back of your waist and all the way across your stomach and to the other side.
3. Your left hand follows your right hand with an equally firm pull.
4. Do this several times. Pull not only at the waist, but above and below it as well.
5. With the last pass, extend the motion across your stomach, and then with both hands open and making firm contact with your body, move down your right leg, and off your foot.
6. Repeat on other side of your body.

*Figure 54*
ACTIVATING THE
BELT FLOW

This procedure feels wonderful for most people, and it re-establishes a top-to-bottom harmony in your body. If you have a partner, you can lie on a bed or massage table so your partner can pull up from behind your waist, allowing more leverage and deeper stimulation.

Another technique for activating the belt flow also stimulates the penetrating flow (see below) and is particularly effective if the energy is cut off at the top of your legs. This one definitely requires a partner.

1. Lie faceup on the floor, bed, or massage table with your partner standing above you.
2. Place either foot against your partner's stomach.

*Figure 55*
BELT FLOW,
CONTINUED

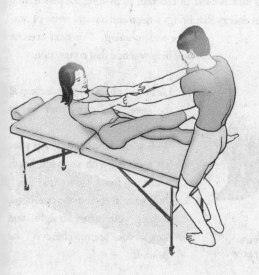

*Figure 56*
THE BELT FLOW/
PENETRATING FLOW

3. Grasp your partner's hands and pull away from each other, keeping your legs straight. Hold this stretch for about 10 seconds.
4. Repeat using the other foot.

## THE PENETRATING FLOW

Whereas the belt and bridge circuits connect up-down and front-to-back energies, the penetrating flow directs energy more deeply inward. When moving freely, its flow penetrates the chakras, the muscles, bones, genitals, and deep into the cells. In the embryo, according to both traditional Chinese and Japanese medicine, the penetrating flow is said to carry the energies of the ancestors and to set the baseline strength of the person's energetic constitution. This energy is vividly experienced in the flowing warmth of an orgasm, and classic mystical experiences can be thought of as moments when the individual is the recipient of the penetrating energies of the universe. When people feel depressed or empty inside, it is often because the penetrating flow is weak or blocked. Activating the penetrating flow connects with an energy that brings a deep and natural sense of purpose and meaning. This next exercise will help you find that connection.

*Figure 57*
ACTIVATING THE
PENETRATING FLOW

1. Lie on your back, bend your legs at the knees, and cross your feet at the ankles.
2. With your right hand, grasp your left foot and with your left hand, your right foot.
3. Pull your feet above your head, keeping your arms straight, and rock so your bottom comes off the ground.

4. Continue rocking as long as it feels good, then rest in the same position.

Another technique requires a partner.

1. Lie facedown and have your partner place one hand on your sacrum, the other at the top of the your back, and then rock you for three to five minutes.
2. When completed, the partner lifts off both hands simultaneously.
3. Bask in the feelings for another minute. This method activates both the governing and the penetrating circuits.

## THE CENTRAL AND GOVERNING CIRCUITS

Four of the body's radiant circuits are also meridians. Unlike the other radiant circuits, their energy is transported along a fixed pathway and accessible through electromagnetically sensitive points on the surface of the skin, the acupuncture points. At the same time, they carry radiant energy and are capable of moving this energy instantly to anywhere it is needed. The central meridian's pathway flows up the front centre of the body, feeding energy to the brain. The governing meridian's pathway flows up the center of the back of the body, feeding energy to the spine and much of the nervous system. The two meridians meet at the back of the throat, creating a single force field, and this is where they begin to behave like radiant circuits. This force field radiates inwardly and outwardly, bringing strength and vitality to the meridians, the chakras, and the aura. When a person is facing confusion or self-doubt, activating the central and governing meridians can pull the cerebrospinal fluid up to the brain and calm the nervous system, eliciting clarity and confidence. When a person is overly sensitive to other people or the environment,

activating the central and governing meridians often lends protection by strengthening the aura. The following exercise can activate these circuits.

1. Begin with a Hook-Up (p. 217) by placing the middle finger of one hand into your navel and the middle finger of your other hand at the third eye point.
2. Push in both fingers and pull them upward towards your head.
3. Hold for about half a minute.

This will usually suffice to activate both circuits, although the Back Hook-Up is a pleasant supplement. The Back Hook-Up requires a partner.

*Figure 58*

ACTIVATING THE
CENTRAL AND
GOVERNING CIRCUITS

1. Lie facedown on the edge of a bed or on a massage table.
2. With his or her arms crossed just below the elbows and palms facing down, your partner stands at your side and places one palm above and one palm below the middle of your spine, with the fingers of one hand pointing towards your feet, and the fingers of the other hand pointing towards your head.
3. Your partner then stretches your spine by pushing his or her hands into your spine and away from each other, creating a stretch.
4. A second stretch is made with the hands slightly farther apart.
5. Your partner continues to move his or her hands in opposite directions, stretching both ends of the back.
6. Hold for at least 15 seconds.

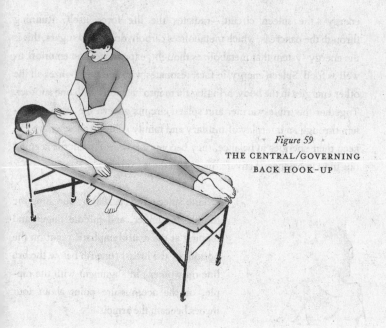

*Figure 59*
THE CENTRAL/GOVERNING
BACK HOOK-UP

## THE SPLEEN AND TRIPLE-WARMER CIRCUITS

The two other radiant circuits that carry the properties of meridians are also paired polarities—triple warmer and spleen. Triple warmer's fixed pathway goes directly from the back brain to the front brain. The back brain is more primal, carrying the survival strategies of millions of years of evolution. Triple warmer feeds the back brain while moving primal survival information into the front brain. It can conscript energy from every other meridian (except the heart meridian) to ensure the body's survival. This is a very serious assignment; triple warmer is the single radiant circuit whose "personality" is more like a general in combat than an upbeat-mum (see p. 203). Meanwhile, the mother of upbeat-mum energy—the spleen circuit—radiates the life force itself. Running through the pancreas, which metabolizes carbohydrates and sugars, this is the energy system that metabolizes thought, experience, and emotion, as well as food. Spleen energy, in fact, resonates with and metabolizes all the other energies in the body, bringing them into harmony with one another. Together the triple-warmer and spleen circuits govern the immune system through an interplay of military and family values, and when we can keep their energies in balance, they become a powerful team for keeping our lives in balance. Activate them with these exercises.

*Figure 60*
THE SPLEEN
NEUROLYMPHATIC TAP

1. Do the Spleen Tap (p. 208) by bunching the thumb, forefinger, and middle finger and tapping at the neurolymphatic point on the bottom of the breast (one rib below the bra line on women) in alignment with the nipple, or the acupressure point about four inches beneath the armpit.

The rule for activating triple-warmer circuit is: *Don't!* It is probably already overactivated by virtue of the culture in which you live. The goal is to reprogram it so its energies will be available when there is a real threat, whether to health, safety, or state of mind. Rather than activated, triple warmer generally needs to be harmonized with the spleen circuit. The Triple Warmer/Spleen Hug (p. 227) has this effect, as does the following method.

1. Open one hand wide so you can lay your thumb on one temple and your fourth fin-

ger on the other temple. Your index and middle fingers will naturally lie on the crown of your head.

2. Place your other hand above your navel, over the solar plexus.

3. Hold for a minute or two as you breathe deeply, in through your nose and out through your mouth.

*Figure 61*
THE TRIPLE-WARMER/
SPLEEN HUG

## HABITS AND THE RADIANT ENERGIES

Habits run deep! Beneath habits of thought and behaviour are habits in the body and its energy system. Many of the developments in energy psychology involve reconditioning the meridian system's habitual response to disturbing stimuli, as you have been doing with the Basic Recipe. Another way to counter the grip of outmoded or otherwise dysfunctional habits is to enlist the radiant circuits:

1. Regularly stimulate the radiant energy system using the *general* techniques presented above.

2. Identify the radiant circuits that seem to be the weakest links for you (either by reading the descriptions of their functions or by noticing which exercises feel best) and use the *specific* techniques presented above to keep those circuits strong.

3. Recondition the radiant energy system by activating vulnerable circuits while bringing to mind the dysfunctional habit or

emotional response. Use the same general approach and Reminder Phrase you used with the Basic Recipe.

Working with the radiant circuits can itself set off waves of energy that feel good. At the same time, they connect the meridian lines, help the chakras spin, and engage all the other energies. But they do not lend themselves easily to formulas, so it is best to adjust the above instructions according to your spontaneous impulses. The "formula," actually, is to model yourself on the radiant energy system itself, which means to be free and spontaneous. The radiant circuits are literally and figuratively the polarity of the meridians' "staying on track." Think of a surge of excitement, falling in love, or becoming enchanted. That is the type of energy you are cultivating.

This chapter has presented general techniques for strengthening the radiant energy system; techniques for working with specific radiant circuits; and a strategy for changing habits by reconditioning the body's energy response to stressful situations, thoughts, and images. When the radiant circuits have been exercised so they stay strong under stressful conditions, they will also feed meridians that tend to be chronically weak. They are an extremely valuable and largely underappreciated system for facilitating positive internal change. While seeing the numerous techniques presented here may at first glance seem formulistic and a bit overwhelming, the techniques are actually easier to do than to read about, do not take much time, and will help you tap into wellsprings of joy. We hope you will experiment with them. Knowledge of how to activate the radiant energies should, in our opinions, be part of everyone's education.

IN A NUTSHELL: The radiant circuits are a discrete energy system. They connect and harmonize all the other energies of the body; and when they do so, the subjective experience is passion and joy. If your radiant energies are compromised, your body is not as able to support you in feeling joy or passion for life, and your overall health is also challenged. In this chapter, you have reviewed six exercises already introduced in previous chapters that boost the radiant energy system and you have learned six new exercises. In addition to these general techniques, you have learned about the eight individual radiant circuits, their roles and actions, and at least two methods to optimize the flow and function of each.

# EPILOGUE

# THE FUTURE OF
# ENERGY PSYCHOLOGY

Energy medicine is the future of all medicine.

—C. NORMAN SHEALY, M.D., FOUNDING PRESIDENT,
AMERICAN HOLISTIC MEDICAL ASSOCIATION

Human history, through one lens, is the story of managing our vulnerabilities. From basic shelter, food production, and communal security to advances such as indoor plumbing, modern medicine, and telecommunications, the twentieth century brought to many people safety, security, and ease that were unimaginable in previous generations.

The twenty-first century, however, opened with inescapable reminders of our vulnerabilities. We are now acutely aware that we may face the unimaginable anguish of biological or nuclear terrorism, that we live on a razor's edge between maintaining our hard-earned lifestyles and environmental destruction, and that the reigning generation can offer little that is reliable for guiding our young into an uncertain future.

The reason for reminding you of our shared vulnerabilities at this late point in the book is not to be grim, harsh, or dramatic. Rather, the fate of our culture may literally hang on *the way we deal with* our vulnerabilities and our anxieties about them. And energy psychology may have a significant role in that global challenge.

Energy psychology is, among other things, a way of managing anxiety. This is not to suggest that energy psychology is the road to world peace or humanity's salvation. But it is to suggest that by helping people recognize the role of anxiety in bad personal and collective decisions and habits, and by giving them tools to reduce the anxious response in their bodies once they've gleaned the message the anxiety is there to deliver, they can make better choices. And that is a substantial contribution to a better life and a better world.

# THE STATUS OF ENERGY PSYCHOLOGY

A hotly debated topic among psychologists is the degree to which the effectiveness of a new therapeutic approach must be backed by empirical research before professionals can responsibly offer it to the public.[1] Some hold that full scientific validation is an impossible criterion—a standard that is usually not even met in the prescribing of medication—and certainly beyond the reach of a field dealing with as many variables as psychotherapy. Others believe that the state of empirical research allows and the public deserves to have such a standard be met. The practical truth, we feel, lies somewhere in between. Our assessment is that there is enough evidence, based on thousands of clinical reports as well as preliminary systematic clinical trials and early research (see Appendix 3), to suggest that the stimulation of selected acupuncture points in energy psychology treatments is:

1. safe and noninvasive,
2. as effective or more effective than other available therapies for a number of mental-health conditions, and
3. also an effective tool in the self-management of emotions and behaviour

# REASONS FOR TREATMENT FAILURES

Among the healthiest ways a therapeutic approach evolves is by examining the cases where it does not work. Based on his own clinical research and extensive contact with the field's practitioners and leaders, David Gruder, Ph.D., the founding president of the Association for Comprehensive Energy Psychology, has distilled five reasons why he believes that energy psychology interventions fail.[2] This rundown is not only instructive for you as you begin to apply the method; it also provides a framework for an important line of future research. The five factors include:

## 1. INCORRECT TREATMENT FOCUS

We have emphasized the importance when your work with a problem or goal is not leading to the desired outcome of identifying the *aspects* of an issue and addressing each of them. In addition to zeroing in on each of the specific aspects of an issue that require attention, Gruder also underscores the importance of 1) initially defining the key issue accurately, 2) focusing first on goals that have leverage for impacting more comprehensive desired changes (identifying what Gruder calls the "top priority issue"), and 3) being sufficiently "tuned into" the problem emotionally and energetically.

## 2. LACK OF READINESS TO BENEFIT FROM TREATMENT

If a person's energy system is severely disrupted in the ways described in chapter 6, stimulating acupuncture points while tuning in to a psychological issue is less likely to be effective. The suggestions presented in that chapter create a greater energetic readiness to focus on specific emotional issues. Similarly, if you select a treatment goal about which you are conflicted—part of you wants to overcome the problem, part of you is invested in the status quo (see discussion of "psychological reversals," p. 59)—you are not likely to achieve the stated goal until you resolve this underlying conflict. Again, relatively straightforward methods (see pp. 216–18) will often achieve such resolution, at least to the extent that treatment can proceed effectively.

## 3. INCORRECT TREATMENT METHOD

Some issues appear to be more responsive to energy interventions than others, and some issues are best treated by using energy interventions in conjunction with other treatments (see discussion on pp. 25–7). In addition, a wide range of methods is used within energy psychology itself. This book has presented a basic approach that when applied correctly appears to be effective with a surprisingly high proportion of people and issues. Where it is not effective, a skilled practitioner will often be able to find the path to the desired outcome by drawing upon a wider range of interventions as well as by having greater facility with the clinical issues at play.

## 4. PREMATURE COMPLETION OF TREATMENT

After your SUD rating is down to 0 or near 0, the next step is to "challenge" the results to assess whether the problem has been fully resolved, whether additional aspects of the issue need attention, and whether the positive results you are feeling are likely to generalize to similar situations in the future. By mentally projecting yourself into a situation that once would have intensely evoked the problematic response, you test the outcome and either fortify it or reveal where further treatment should focus.

## 5. NOT ESTABLISHING A NEW PATTERN
## AFTER ELIMINATING AN OLD ONE

When you successfully overcome a problematic pattern of thought or behaviour but do not replace it with a new pattern that supports more optimal functioning, the odds of defaulting back to the old pattern when you are under stress in the future are much higher. "Peace is not just the absence of war" holds true in psyches as well as in nations. While sometimes simply eliminating a phobia is all that is necessary for a successful treatment outcome, as your goals for personal change become more complex, it is not just about eliminating a problematic response, but also a matter of envisioning new ways of being, behaving, and installing them energetically and psychologically. Ways of accomplishing this were the focus of chapter 4.

# USE OF ENERGY INTERVENTIONS
# BY NONPROFESSIONALS

Teaching powerful psychological methods to the general public is a highly contentious issue. We have obviously cast our vote on the question by writing this book. Two viewpoints are in conflict. One places a "doctor-patient" frame upon any potent psychological intervention that is designed to shift a person's neurochemistry, thoughts, and emotional state. Another holds that an energy-based approach to psychological problems represents a new paradigm where people can readily influence the energies that affect their physical and mental health, and that its methods should have the widest possible distribution. Just as people do not generally need to consult with their doctor to put more protein into their diet, to work out at the gym, or to do stretching exercises to soothe a sore back, those holding this perspective would offer broad access to techniques for better managing one's energies and emotions.

The first consideration for responsibly advocating a new method is to "do no harm." The side effects of surgery, radiation, and medication notwithstanding, this Hippocratic injunction is an ideal to which every health-care provider and energy psychology practitioner can and should aspire. Although formal research findings are still not available, the self-application of the Basic Recipe has been "field-tested" by tens of thousands of people, probably many more, and it is appearing to be a noninvasive measure that is gentle, safe, and often effective with a wide range of emotional concerns. The dictum in the healing profession to first apply the least invasive intervention that might successfully treat a condition, in fact, suggests that in many instances the self-application of the Basic Recipe is a highly appropriate first line of treatment, before psychotherapy or medication. It is easy to learn, it is easy to apply, and it is free.

Nor is widespread access to energy methods about to put professional psychotherapists out of business. The clinical professions could, in fact, be leading the way in setting standards for the responsible application of energy interventions. People who are trained in working with emotional problems and who also know how to work with the energies that impact a person's emotions are simply better equipped. As the fundamentals of energy psychology become more widely understood and practiced, having a base of professionals who can be consulted for applying them more effectively and to more difficult conditions will be an increasingly important resource. The Basic Recipe, as one of various popular protocols, is highly streamlined. A professional's perspective and touch may in many instances provide the interpersonal support and deft application that is the difference between the approach not having the intended effect and having it. The professional's ability to integrate an energy approach within a wide range of other psychological methods is also of incalculable value.

Still, the Basic Recipe and similar protocols are effective so frequently even when self-applied or applied by a non-professional that this, paradoxically, underscores one of their dangers. The fact that anyone can have easy access to these powerful tools should not interfere with people obtaining highly skilled assistance when needed. If you are unable to solve a problem with the tools you have, bringing in other resources is the next step. Psychotherapy is one resource to consider (see Resources, p. 318), and this does not require that you define yourself as mentally ill. Therapists treat a wide range of life issues beyond mental illness.

The other face of the danger inherent in the fact that energy interventions are so often so effective is that many people have been tempted to apply them with others in areas that extend far beyond their competence. Gary summarizes the issue by telling his students, "Don't go where you don't belong." This underscores that you recognize the complexity of emotional problems and psychological concerns and stay within your areas of training and competence. Just because you used the Basic Recipe to help your neighbour overcome her depression after her canary died does not make you a bereavement counsellor or qualify you to treat serious depression. Just because you helped your father-in-law overcome a reaction to strawberries does not make you an allergy doctor. Just because you helped your kid calm down after a bad dream does not qualify you to open a centre for treating PTSD.

Also beware of "the helping hand strikes again" phenomenon, where people with an innovative way to help others become obsessed and intrusive, or simply want to show off their new tools. Attitude counts for a great deal in any relationship, and applying the methods in a manner that is forced or self-aggrandizing will limit their value and may lead to all sorts of unintended tangles.

The bottom line, however, is that it is not possible to stop laypeople from teaching others basic methods for managing their emotions with an energy approach. And while much good can be and has been done, damage has also been done. A number of therapists on various e-lists have reported having had to pick up the pieces after an amateur counsellor applied energy techniques to someone whose emotional vulnerabilities were activated but not skillfully fielded by the practitioner. Steps can be taken to make such unfortunate outcomes—where seeking help leads to additional harm and distress—less likely. The Association for Comprehensive Energy Psychology (www.energypsych.org), for instance, is in the process of articulating standards and training programs for the safe use of energy psychology methods by laypersons.

# PREDICTIONS

As the basic methods of energy psychology become commonplace tools for the self-management of emotions, several predictions can be made.

**Prediction 1:** Empirical investigation will demonstrate that the methods of energy psychology provide a neurologically potent intervention for bringing about desired personal changes. It will be demonstrated that the techniques strengthen mental habits and attitudes that promote psychological well-being and weaken the mental habits and attitudes that interfere with it. Specifically:

- Mentally activating memories that are at the root of negative patterns, while at the same time stimulating selected acupuncture points or other energy centres, reduces the neural connections in the amygdala and other brain centers that trigger problematic responses.
- Activating positive images or affirmations, while stimulating other acupuncture points or energy centers, facilitates the formation of neural connections that empower those images and affirmations.

**Prediction 2:** The second finding above, in particular, will result in laypersons and professionals experimenting with energy interventions in all walks of life, from psychotherapy to medicine to education to sports to business to community life to spiritual pursuits. The experiences that will be gathered will refine the procedures, demonstrate the necessary and sufficient conditions for effective interventions, and identify the powers and limitations of the approach.

**Prediction 3:** Children will be taught energy interventions as a common-sense way of managing their emotions as routinely as "count to ten" before lashing out in anger.

**Prediction 4:** As energy methods become more widely known, adults will generally be expected to have greater competence in managing problematic emotions—such as irrational anger, anxiety, jealousy, and self-hatred—and training in developing that competence will be as readily available as training in CPR and first aid are available from the Red Cross.

**Prediction 5:** Premarital counselling will routinely teach couples how to reduce their reactivity towards one another, help them heal past hurts and resentments that might spill into the marriage, and begin to change family-of-origin patterns that interfere with the current relationship.

**Prediction 6:** Hospitals will routinely have patients use energy interventions prior to surgery to reduce anxiety and cultivate a positive attitude about the procedure. This is just one of many medical applications that can be expected.

**Prediction 7:** Most clinicians, rather than becoming "energy psychotherapists" will, instead, integrate energy methods into their existing repertoire, making their treatment approaches more flexible, powerful, and precise. For instance, energy interventions for increasing empathy will be routinely used to enhance *emotional intelligence*, as discussed in chapter 5; energy interventions for decreasing self-negating thoughts will become standard methods within *cognitive psychology*; and energy interventions for increasing optimism will become a vital element in the new *positive psychology* movement.

**Prediction 8:** Increasingly efficient methods will be developed within the energy psychology field, such as Gary's Borrowing Benefits procedure,[3] allowing the methods to be used with greater effectiveness in large group as well as back-home settings.

**Prediction 9:** Ethical concerns will emerge both in terms of the practitioner's competence as well as blatantly manipulative applications of the methods. For instance, ethical concerns would be involved if energy interventions were used by schools to promote obedience to authority, by businesses to make salespeople less uncomfortable about being coercive, or by the military to make soldiers more cold-blooded in taking life. More subtle ethical concerns will also appear, such as whether a parent's overly routine use of simple physical interventions to clear a child's emotional distress would divert a family from issues that need to be addressed more directly.

**Prediction 10:** The pharmaceutical industry, along with conservative forces within the psychotherapy and medical establishments, will be slow to accept energy interventions and will in fact attempt to discredit research findings that confirm their efficacy. Support from the health-care industry will, however, come from an unexpected source: Insurance carriers, with their eye towards effective low-cost treatments, will make energy interventions a standard of care as the first line of treatment for a range of disorders. Like the 5,000-year-old practice of its direct ancestor, acupuncture, the methods used in energy psychology will prevail.

# THE BASIC RECIPE ON A PAGE

**Preliminaries:** Balance energies, select problem, rate problem from 1 to 10, word Reminder Phrase.

**Part 1—Setup:** Rub chest sore spots or tap karate-chop points while saying three times, "Even though [name problem], I deeply love and accept myself."

**Part 2—Tapping:** Tap the points described below while saying your Reminder Phrase out loud.

**Part 3—Nine-Gamut Procedure:** Tap the point between the little and fourth fingers, wrist side of the knuckle, as you: 1) close your eyes, 2) open your eyes, 3) look down to the right, 4) look down to the left, 5) circle your eyes, 6) circle your eyes in the opposite direction, 7) hum a bar of a song, 8) count to five, 9) hum again. Optionally, end by sweeping your eyes out and up, sending energy through them.

**Part 4—Tapping:** Repeat Part 2.

**Repeat** this sequence until your rating of the problem is at 0 or near 0. Challenge the results by attempting to invoke the disturbing feeling. Once you cannot create the unwanted emotional response, you are ready to test the gains in a "real life" setting.

**If the Problem Is Not Responding,** identify and address 1) other aspects of the problem, 2) psychological reversals, 3) scrambled energies, or 4) energy toxins.

**The Tapping Points:**

Beginning of the Eyebrows
Sides of the Eyes
Under the Eyes
Under the Nose
Under the Lower Lip
K-27 Points

Arm-attachment Points
  (optional)
Thymus Thump (optional)
Under the Arms
Outside of the Legs (optional)
Karate-chop Points

— Beginning of Eyebrow
— Side of Eye
— Under the Eye
— Under Nose
— Under Lower Lip
— K-27 Points
— Under Arm
— Karate Chop Points

Three additional useful points:

Arm Attachment Points
(Half circles at sides of chest)

Thymus Thump
("Tarzan Spot")

Outside of Legs
(midway between hips and knees)

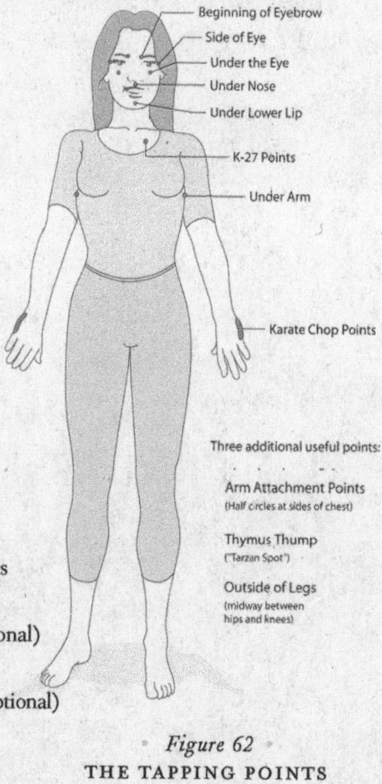

*Figure 62*
THE TAPPING POINTS

## Appendix 2

# IF THE PROGRAM BECOMES UNSETTLING

A delicate issue in presenting the potent methods found in this book is that any useful psychological tool can stir strong emotions or uncover dormant psychological problems. Tapping methods do not, in themselves, seem to have adverse affects. They have been self-applied by, conservatively, tens of thousands of people based on a training manual that is available through Gary's website alone (more than 150,000 copies have been downloaded). Gary has received literally thousands of invited as well as unsolicited outcome reports and has many times followed up when someone did not attain the intended results. While the techniques do not bring about the desired effects for all people or all situations, and on occasion symptoms temporarily get worse before they get better, the general safety of the methods has been strongly affirmed by these interchanges.

Beyond Gary's site, psychotherapists who are on the forefront of energy interventions have for several years been discussing clinical issues on several e-lists. The clear consensus on the lists where we participate is that the vast majority of the people these therapists have worked with experience no adverse emotional reactions following tapping treatments. When the treatment is not going as planned, an analysis almost always points to one of the following:

1. The very process of tuning in to the issue activated a strong or overwhelming emotional response, called an abreaction. This can happen with any therapeutic approach and is particularly true when the issue is connected to an early trauma or involved a bodily injury caused by an accident, physical abuse, or other violence.

2. A psychological reversal (p. 59)—an internal and often unconscious conflict about the treatment goals—may render the treatment ineffective until the conflict has been identified and resolved. This may involve secondary gains for keeping the symptoms (such as disability payments, sympathy, or having an excuse to avoid certain responsibilities) or it may involve a deep fear of addressing and overcoming the problem (such as when having the problem is part of one's identity or is somehow tied to one's sense of safety).

3. Other obstacles to treatment progress might include "scrambled" energies (p. 61), *aspects* of the problem that have not been addressed (p. 55), energy toxins (p. 61), or an overly forceful or overly mechanical (i.e., with no emotional connection) application of the tapping.

The first of these is of the greatest concern in teaching energy methods for use on a self-help basis because beyond the problem not improving, activating a past trauma might make it feel as if the problem is getting worse. Simply bringing to mind an emotional issue or difficult memory or physical trauma can shake one's confidence, open an old wound, or stir up overwhelming feelings. While tapping will not *cause* new emotional problems, any potent experience can bring to the surface underlying issues that have not been resolved. If repressed emotions are on the verge of breaking through one's psychological defenses, a reaction might be triggered by seeing a powerful film, helping one's child through a difficult time, having an argument with a loved one, experiencing a volley of criticism from a friend, entering psychotherapy, opening oneself to the deeper recesses of one's psyche while working with one's dreams, participating in an intensive "personal growth" workshop, or using techniques such as the ones presented in this book. What to do when this occurs is our topic here.

First, we want to emphasize that intense emotional reactions are not a setback. Critical, however, is that when they occur, you find the support and resources so you are able to resolve them and come out stronger, and not with an additional unresolved trauma that leaves you feeling more fragile or defended. There is no question that energy work, like any other psychological approach and many other life experiences, may bring old emotional wounds to the surface. Although this may be challenging, emotional problems that lie beneath the surface often drain a person's vitality and foster defensive thoughts and behavioural patterns. By bringing them into your awareness, doorways open for healing them. With that healing, the energies that had been defending against the old wounds can be oriented towards a more dynamic response to life.

We have made every effort to present the techniques in this book so you can adjust them to your own needs, readiness, and pace. If, however, you should feel disturbed or unsettled as you apply the procedures, and if those feelings persist after you have utilized the suggestions given below, we strongly encourage you to elicit support from family and friends or seek professional assistance (see Finding a Psychotherapist in the Resources section). This program does not attempt to be a substitute for psychotherapy (please review What This Book Can Do and What It Can't Do, pp. 25–27) and, again, there are times when life experiences bring us into a receptiveness where working with a good therapist can yield enormous benefit.

For a first course of action if the program becomes upsetting, you can take any of the following "psychological first-aid" measures. In most cases, one or more of these will suffice. But do not forget that prolonged upset can also be an opportunity, an opening for a highly beneficial course of healing and growth facilitated by focused effort, psychotherapy, a spiritual discipline, or other healing resource. Immediate steps you can take if you find yourself becoming upset include:

**Apply the Basic Recipe to the Reaction You Are Having.** The Basic Recipe is a powerful way to calm yourself. If focusing on your personal issues leads to emotional discomfort, take a step back and apply the Basic Recipe to the emotional discomfort itself. Since you are in the midst of the emotion, begin by simply doing the tapping sequence. It is not necessary to create a Reminder Phrase since you are already tuned in to the feeling. With intense emotional reactions, it may take twenty to thirty excursions through the tapping sequence. During the period when the feelings are intense, it is also not necessary to stop for the Nine-Gamut Procedure or Setup.

**Hold Your Neurovascular Points.** This procedure (p. 222) can have a similar effect, relaxing your body and calming your emotions. A stress reaction sends blood to your arms, legs, chest, and other organs involved in the fight-or-flight response. Holding these points counters the stress reaction by directing blood back to your brain. Simply place the palm of one hand over your forehead and the palm of your other hand over the back of your head just above your neckline. Hold comfortably for two to three minutes, breathing in through your nose and out through your mouth.

**Balance Your Energies.** Do the Five-Minute Daily Routine (p. 206), or a special emotional first-aid sequence consisting of some or all of the following: the Hook-Up (p. 217), the Wayne Cook Posture (p. 210), the Homolateral Crossover (p. 219), the Sedating Triple Warmer sequence (p. 224), the Blow-Out (p. 228), and Connecting Heaven and Earth (p. 230).

**Calm Your Mind.** Shift to a calming activity: listen to music, work in your garden, telephone a friend, take a walk in a natural setting, meditate, watch an entertaining video, do yoga or stretching exercises, breathe deeply.

**Rest Your Body.** Take a break. Take a bath. Take a nap. Take a vacation. Rest your body. Rest your spirit.

**Stimulate Your Body.** Involve yourself in an invigorating physical activity, such as swimming, running, dancing, jumping on a bouncer, cleaning your house, or waxing your car. Regularly discharging pent-up or stagnant energies is an excellent form of emotional self-care.

**Use Your Imagination.** Experiment with imagery that takes you to a protected, beautiful, sacred place—a redwood grove, a mountain stream, a childhood hideaway. Later, cultivate your ability to go there in your mind whenever you feel the need for safety, sustenance, or renewal.

**Tap In to Your Inner Guidance.** Archetypes are forces in the psyche that tap into a greater wisdom than the rational mind. They can often be accessed by going inward and imagining an inner guide who is able to nurture and advise you. Imagine this person vividly, perhaps in the beautiful, sacred setting described above. Ask for the guidance you need. Listen carefully to the response. Cultivate a relationship with this symbol of your inner wisdom.

**Find Support from Another Person.** Share intimately with someone who cares about you. Use this person as a sounding board and a source of support.

**Be Patient with Yourself.** In applying energy psychology to your own life and issues, you are affirming your ability to change and evolve. Appreciate yourself for your intention and efforts, *and* use the Basic Recipe to counter your self-judgments, to increase your ability to accept yourself *just the way you are*.

**Develop a Self-Affirming Perspective for Your Trials and Tribulations.** When deep changes occur, old and familiar ways of perceiving, thinking, and behaving all transform. This by its nature is disorienting and can be destabilizing. Give yourself time and support for adjusting to new information and new ways of being. Use the Basic Recipe to foster optimism, welcome a new perspective, call upon your creativity, and find the humour, ironies, and lessons in the process.

**Bring in New Sources of Inspiration.** From inspirational reading to great movies to sacred ceremonies to worship services to prayer to meditation, we are all fed by experiences that expand our understanding of the invisible patterns behind the visible world, that model for us the courage and vastness of the human spirit, and that call us into a keener relationship with ourselves and our surroundings. Dedicate time to such activities. For a very simple, energetically attuned meditation that can open you to sources of inspiration that transcend your usual ways of thinking, consider the Heaven Rushing In exercise on p. 255.

While we have been focusing here on the possible hazards of self-guided exploration, we want to close by reemphasizing the powerful benefits that can be enjoyed by working directly with the energies that are at the foundation of your habits, thoughts, and feelings. Our lives are shaped, it has been said, by *fate*, *chance*, and *choice*. Energy psychology offers tools you can use to optimize the "choice" part of the equation by artfully crafting your inner responses and your actions in the world.

## Appendix 3
# RESEARCH EVIDENCE[1]

Energy psychology applies principles and techniques for working with the body's physical energies to facilitate desired changes in emotions, thought, and behaviour. "Energy psychology" has been used interchangeably with "energy-based psychotherapy," or simply "energy therapy," and it is also an umbrella term for numerous specific formulations, such as Thought Field Therapy, Emotional Freedom Techniques, Energy Diagnostic and Treatment Methods, and more than two dozen others.

Early empirical studies within energy psychology have been able to build upon a substantial body of research on acupuncture that has appeared in more than a dozen major peer-reviewed Western scientific journals that are devoted largely or solely to acupuncture.[2] Within this context, the manual (non-needle) self-stimulation of acupuncture points (combined with energy psychology's use of cognitive and imagery methods) is beginning to be examined scientifically. While this line of investigation is still in its early stages, preliminary indications are that the methods being investigated are effective in treating a range of psychological conditions.

The first stage of evidence in establishing a new therapy is the accumulation of case studies and anecdotal reports. Here the data are striking, with reports coming in from hundreds of therapists who represent the full spectrum of backgrounds and theoretical orientations. A sampling of these cases can be found in books such as Fred Gallo's anthology *Energy Psychology and Psychotherapy*[3] and on websites that offer both written reports and videotaped treatments, such as www.emofree.com. Estimates based on informal interviews David has conducted with a sampling of the Association for Comprehensive Energy Psychology's 700-plus members are that more than 5,000 "strikingly effective" cases (more rapid *and* more favourable outcomes than the therapist would have predicted had standard treatments for the conditions been employed) are documented in the membership's clinical records alone.

## SYSTEMATIC OBSERVATION

The next step in establishing a new therapy—between case studies and formal scientific research—is systematic observation. This might occur when a therapist simply wants to gather initial data about the effects of a new treatment or when a particular clinic introduces a new therapy and compares its effectiveness with the progress of those receiving the treatments that had been in place, based on chart notes and therapist impressions. Or a new therapy might be used with a particular population under special circumstances. For instance, because energy psychology is believed to be so effective in treating the effects of trauma, several relief teams trained in its methods have been sent to disaster areas, as you saw with the work in Kosovo described in chapter 1.

A number of the field's early studies that did not qualify for peer-reviewed journal publication (for instance, they may not have addressed all the variables that need to be controlled in formal research or may have relied primarily on the clients' self-reports of improvement rather than more objective measures) nonetheless constitute systematic observation that can be very instructive in assessing a new therapy. For example, a study that tracked the clinical outcomes of 714 patients treated by seven therapists using Thought Field Therapy (TFT) in an HMO setting found that decreased subjective distress following the treatment was far beyond chance with thirty-one of thirty-one[4] psychiatric diagnostic categories, including anxiety, major depression, alcohol cravings, and PTSD.[5] Data like this, while not decisive in itself, encourage further experimentation with the method and further research.

# EMPIRICAL RESEARCH

Beyond anecdotal accounts and systematic observation is formal research that meets established scientific standards and that is published in a peer-reviewed professional journal. While respectable research literature does exist in related areas, such as acupuncture and Therapeutic Touch,[6] only a handful of published empirical studies that directly investigate energy psychology have been published at the time of this writing. A number of fundamental questions about energy psychology await further scientific investigation. Are its treatments as rapid and effective as its early proponents are reporting? For what conditions are they most effective? Exactly which procedures constitute the "necessary and sufficient conditions" for therapeutic change? What are the precise mechanisms involved when the tapping of acupoints results in the reduction or elimination of a psychological symptom? Different practitioners have different answers to these and related questions, and far more research is needed to address and eventually resolve many of the areas of confusion and controversy. A few early studies do shed some light on basic issues.

## EFFICACY

For instance, are the reported clinical outcomes due to something intrinsic in the energy psychology procedures or do these outcomes simply reflect a placebo effect due to focusing on the problem with a caring practitioner? This is a fundamental question that must be addressed before any new treatment is credibly established. Doctoral dissertations are often the first wave of research with a new therapy. While their findings often do not make it to publication in a scientific journal, many dissertation studies nonetheless use a rigorous research design.

Three dissertations that have investigated the efficacy of energy psychology procedures found positive treatment outcomes, two based on systematic observation of individuals who received treatment and a third based on a controlled experiment. The first, using objective measures such as standard anxiety inventories, demonstrated significant improvement, after just one hour of treatment with TFT, in forty-eight individuals plagued with public-speaking anxiety. Following the treatment, the subjects reported decreased shyness and confusion and increased poise and interest in giving a future speech. Treatment gains were still present on four-month follow-up interviews.[7] A second dissertation followed twenty patients who had been unable to receive necessary medical attention because of intense needle phobias. After an hour of TFT treatment, they showed significant immediate improvement which held on a one-month follow-up.[8] A third dissertation investigated the effects of TFT on self-concept with twenty-eight subjects who presented with a phobia. Two self-concept inventories were administered a month prior to the treatment and then two months after the treatment. Again, the TFT treatment reduced the phobias substantially, and in this study, significant improvement was also found in self-acceptance, self-esteem, and self-congruency two months after the treatment. A group of twenty-five subjects who were on a waiting list did not show improvement.[9]

A study published in the *Journal of Clinical Psychology* examined whether the effects of energy psychology procedures were due to placebo as well as the question of how much improvement could be gained in a *single session* with individuals who volunteered to receive help with strong irrational fears of insects or small animals, including rats, mice, spiders, and roaches. The energy psychology approach was compared with a relaxation technique that uses diaphragmatic breathing. Significantly greater improvement was found, based on standardized phobia scales and other measures, in the group that received the energy psychology treatment. On follow-ups, six to nine months later, the improvements held.[10] A study conducted at Queens College in New York to see if these findings could be replicated produced markedly similar results.[11] Other studies are in progress, and updated reports can be found at energypsych.org/research.htm, www.eftupdate.com/ResearchonEFT.html, and www.emofree.com/res.htm.

## PROCEDURES

With preliminary evidence suggesting that the procedures used in energy psychology are more effective than no treatment and more effective than relaxation training in the treatment of a phobia, a next logical question is whether it matters which points are tapped. Is there something about simply tapping the body that has a curative effect, or is there really something special about the points that were identified in ancient China?

Here the evidence is mixed. An early investigation of this question suggested that in treating forty-nine people with height phobias, those who tapped the traditional points showed significantly more improvement than those who tapped "placebo" points.[12] In a subsequent study, published in the medical journal *Anesthesia & Analgesia,* treatments that involved stimulating acupoints were applied by a paramedic team after a minor injury and compared with treatments that stimulated areas of the skin that do not contain recognized acupuncture points. Again, the treatments that used the traditional points were more effective, resulting in a significantly greater reduction of anxiety, pain, and elevated heart rate.[13]

A third study used a randomized, controlled, double-blind design in treating thirty-eight women diagnosed with clinical depression.[14] The researchers compared the use of acupuncture points (during twelve treatment sessions over an eight-week period) specifically selected for the treatment of depression with acupuncture points usually used for other ailments (also twelve sessions over eight weeks) and a wait-list control group that received no treatment. Following the acupuncture treatments, 50 percent of patients who received the depression protocol showed no sign of the disorder while only 27 percent of the patients in the other two groups experienced symptom relief. After the initial clinical trial, the women from the other two groups were administered the depression treatment over an eight-week period. Seventy percent of them experienced a *drop* in depressive symptoms, with 64 percent showing *complete remission* according to *conventional psychiatric criteria.* These findings—beyond demonstrating that placebo or expectation effects that might be associated with acupuncture treatment were not the decisive factors in the clinical outcomes—suggest that the targeting of the proper points was an important ingredient of the treatment.

A fourth study, however, did not detect a difference between tapping standard EFT points and non-EFT points in treating fear, though both tapping procedures were more effective than no treatment.[15] While serious questions have been raised about some of the conclusions reached by the authors of this study,[16] there is also clinical evidence suggesting that stimulating certain points not identified in traditional acupuncture may have a therapeutic effect. While this is an area where further study is clearly needed, research in China suggests that the stimulation of many of the traditional acupuncture points—which have lower electrical resistance and a higher concentration of receptors that are sensitive to mechanical stimulation—produces stronger electrochemical signals. Many acupuncture points are also believed to have specific effects, such as increasing serotonin levels or strengthening or sedating the energy flow to a particular organ.

Almost all energy-oriented psychotherapists agree that stimulating at least one of several standard sets of preselected treatment points while a psychological problem is mentally activated will resolve the problem in some proportion of the cases. When it does not, there are strong differences of opinion in terms of what the next steps should be. Some use manual "muscle tests" to determine whether different tapping points would be more effective; some focus on a more precise formulation of the problem; some next look to separate the problem into its aspects; others recheck for psychological reversals, neurological disorganization, or "energetically toxic" substances that might be interfering. Those who use muscle tests to identify which meridians are involved with the problem have developed highly sophisticated procedures to determine which of the many points on those meridians are most likely to correct the problem,[17] and they use these points in the subsequent treatment.

## MECHANISMS

Anyone who has witnessed someone who is terrified of snakes or heights calmly pet a snake or go to the edge of a high balcony after twenty minutes of tapping on certain points while bringing their fears to mind wonders what happened. Brain-scan images provide a dramatic if preliminary scientific response to that question. They are based on readings from a digitized electroencephalogram (EEG).

An EEG provides a visual record of electrical activity of the brain, showing variations in the frequency, amplitude, and voltage of the impulses, known as alpha, beta, theta, and delta rhythms. The colours in such images represent the *ratio* of brain frequencies (specifically, alpha, beta, and theta waves) and subfrequencies within given areas of the brain. At any given moment, different parts of the brain are operating at different frequencies, and different mental states can be distinguished by specific brain-frequency patterns.[18] Anxiety has one such electronic "signature". Depression has another.

Images from Dr Joaquín Andrade's study show that the brain-frequency ratios for the person suffering from generalized anxiety disorder changed markedly over the twelve sessions. As the wave frequencies shifted towards normal levels (from red to blue) in the central and front areas of the brain, the symptoms of anxiety decreased in both their intensity and their frequency. Similar sequences of images and symptom reduction were also typical of other patients with generalized anxiety disorder who received energy-based treatments in this study, and similar findings have been reported by other investigators.[19]

Even if it has been demonstrated that stimulating specific acupuncture points sends electrochemical impulses to areas of the brain that govern fear and the stress response,[20] how do those impulses cure the phobia? An evolutionary twist seems to have made the treatment approach used in energy psychology possible. Simply *bringing to mind* an image that triggers an emotional response creates neurological changes. Depending on what occurs while the image and emotional response are activated, the neural connections between the anxiety-producing image and the emotional response may be increased or decreased—making the response stronger, or weaker—the next time the trigger is encountered.[21] This ability of the brain to alter its structure based on its activity is known as "neural plasticity."

The apparent survival value of this mechanism where simply bringing a fearful object to mind creates an opportunity to rewire the threat response is that, during primitive times, you could readily update your brain's primal reactions to what is life threatening based on more recent experiences. The scent of an animal that was not common in your locale might have been coded as mildly dangerous. But then you see the animal. It looks fiercer than you imagined. You recall a valley some distance from your cave where you had first noticed the scent. Neural connections between the image of the valley and the alarm response are immediately built. But the reprogramming can work in either direction. If the animal turns out not to be a threat, the scent loses its ability to initiate the stress response. Any time a fearful memory is brought to mind, the memory becomes "labile," susceptible to being "consolidated" in a new way. Energy interventions apparently take hold during this moment of *neural plasticity* and calm the response to the image. A paper by Ron Ruden, M.D., that is consistent with this thesis and which presents the neurological mechanisms in much greater detail can be found at www.energypsych.org/article-ruden.htm.

A number of provocative findings suggest that additional electrochemical mechanisms may also be involved in energy psychology treatments. Electronic instruments, for instance, have detected "energy systems" described in the healing traditions of innumerable cultures, but that are not generally recognized in ours, including the *meridians*,[22] the *chakras*,[23] and the *aura,* or *biofield*.[24] People also influence one another electromagnetically. When you are near another person, the electromagnetic field of your heart influences the electromagnetic field of the other person's brain in ways that can readily be detected by an EEG.[25] The electromagnetic field of the heart is, in fact, sixty times stronger than the electromagnetic field of the brain and extends several feet beyond the body.[26] Energy psychology may ultimately investigate these anomalies further as it searches for explanations regarding the mechanisms for the clinical outcomes being reported.

## ELECTROCHEMISTRY OR SUBTLE ENERGY?

The pre- and posttreatment EEG data combine with recent understanding about the brain's "neural plasticity," as discussed above, to yield a plausible explanation regarding the electrochemical mechanisms of tapping treatments. Many energy therapists, however, feel that mapping the neurological steps that occur in the treatment does not tell the whole story. They believe that energy treatments open them to a different realm than the material world of molecules, neurons, and electromagnetic impulses.

While such notions make an already suspect area of clinical investigation vulnerable to outright dismissal by empirically minded observers, clinical reports that cannot be fully explained by conventional neurological and electrochemical mechanisms are not infrequent. And it is no more scientific to dismiss these reports because they don't fit our paradigms than it is to accept them uncritically.

Many of the reports concern "distance healing." The impact of thought in influencing the physical world has actually been well documented. Numerous laboratory experiments have, for instance, demonstrated that some people can mentally influence the growth of plants, fungi, and bacteria.[27] Stanford physicist William Tiller showed that human intention can affect electronic instruments.[28] Other studies have demonstrated, to an extraordinarily high degree of scientific confidence,[29] that some people can, by simply using their intention, impact someone in another room. Through the use of calming or activating imagery, they can influence the relaxation or anxiety level of targeted individuals, unawares, in other locations, as gauged by spontaneous changes in the targeted individual's subjective state as well as galvanic skin-response activity. Prayer and focused intention have been shown to enhance a patient's medical condition in a wide variety of settings.[30] Credible reports of such "distance healing" (called surrogate healing when, for instance, a child's mother is provided an energy treatment with the intention of healing her child—who is not present in the treatment setting), while totally outside the box of conventional understanding, are too numerous among energy psychology practitioners to ignore.[31]

In an effort to explain how thought can influence the physical world, various formulations such as "thought fields" or "subtle energies" have been proposed. Subtle energies and subtle forces, by definition, cannot be detected by mechanical or electrical measuring devices, yet they are known for their effects. Gravity is such a force. The impact of the mind on the physical world, and on healing in particular—if the existing research is confirmed by further study—will require some explanatory mechanism. Subtle energies or other forces are likely candidates. And all this may ultimately fall within the domain of energy psychology. We are only beginning to glimpse the ways intention can be focused to produce desired changes, not only in our own neurons and overall health, but in the environment around us as well. While it is not necessary to believe that subtle forces exist, no less that they play a role in the reported effectiveness of energy treatments, a small proportion of the healings being observed within the field simply do not lend themselves to explanations within generally accepted frameworks.

## ENERGY TREATMENT COMPARED
## WITH OTHER THERAPIES

While there has been little systematic comparison between the outcomes of energy psychology treatments and other psychotherapies,[32] the brain scans discussed in this book come out of a large-scale study, summarized below, that did comparisons among energy psychology procedures, medication, and Cognitive Behaviour Therapy (an action-oriented treatment that focuses on changing the client's thoughts, or cognitive patterns, in order to shift his or her behaviour and emotional state). Patients who were successfully treated for anxiety with Cognitive Behaviour Therapy (a standard treatment for anxiety disorders) showed a progression in their brain scans that was similar to the progression described in Chapter 1. But it took more sessions to achieve the improvements. And more important, on one-year follow-up, the brain-wave ratios for patients who received the Cognitive Behaviour Therapy protocol were more likely to have returned to their pretreatment levels than they were for the patients who received the energy treatments.

Another comparison was done of the brain scans of patients whose primary treatment was antianxiety medication and patients whose primary treatment involved stimulating energy points while tuning in to anxiety-provoking images. Both groups showed a reduction of symptoms. But the brain scans for the medication group did not show noticeable changes in the wave patterns, even though the symptoms of anxiety were reduced while the drug was being taken! This suggests that the medication was suppressing the symptoms *without addressing* the underlying wave frequency imbalances. Consistent with this interpretation is that, in addition to the side effects reported by many in the medication group, symptoms tended to return when the medication was discontinued.

## EMPIRICAL RESEARCH IN OTHER CULTURES

Most of the medical research published in non-Western cultures is not translated for English-language journals, yet vigorous scientific investigation of acupuncture is being carried out in China. Joaquín Andrade, M.D., the principal investigator in the South American studies discussed below, uses acupuncture and frequently goes to mainland China for further study. He reports that in the major hospitals, researchers with doctorates in physiology, biochemistry, and related fields have been scientifically scrutinizing traditional healing methods. They view the ancient theories as valuable precedents to be regarded with respect, but they also recognize that those ideas must be considered within the cultural context and historical period in which they originated and need to be scientifically confirmed before they can be applied with confidence. Andrade estimates that specific, measurable functions have been identified for approximately 15 percent of the acupuncture points (stimulating this point releases that chemical, sends impulses to that brain structure, etc.).

He reports, for instance, having personally witnessed a well-designed study at one of the major hospitals in Beijing with twelve patients diagnosed with severe panic disorder. Various drug and acupuncture interventions were used over a two-week period. Each patient's biochemistry as well as emotional responses were carefully tracked. During a three-day period, the primary intervention was to stimulate six acupuncture points that are believed to increase serotonin, a neurotransmitter involved with depression and other mood disorders. During this period, the intensity and frequency of the panic attacks decreased for all twelve patients (eight of them became asymptomatic), their serotonin levels increased (this is the clinically desirable direction), and their norepinephrine levels decreased, again the desirable direction.

# The First Large-Scale Preliminary Clinical Trial of Energy Psychology

The largest study of energy psychology treatments to date was conducted over a fourteen-year period and involved some 31,400 patients. It was supervised by Dr. Andrade, who introduced energy psychology methods to eleven allied clinics in Argentina and Uruguay after he was trained in the approach in the United States. Dr. Andrade had, as a young man, spent long periods of time in China, where he studied traditional acupuncture, and he had been applying it in his medical practice for thirty years. He was struck with the effectiveness of this new application, which focused directly on anxiety and other psychological disorders, and which did not use needles to stimulate the acupuncture points.

The staff of the eleven clinics met this new procedure with both interest and scepticism. While the group had no funding for research, they decided to track the outcomes of treatments with these new methods and compare them with the treatments currently in place.

Standard record-keeping already maintained a patient's intake evaluation, the interventions used, and the treatment outcomes. Dr. Andrade's team added a simple procedure for briefly interviewing the patient, usually by telephone, at the close of treatment and then one month, three months, six months, and twelve months later. The interviewers had not been involved in the patient's treatment. They had a record of the diagnosis and intake evaluation, but not of the treatment method. Their job was to determine if at the time of the interview the initial symptoms remained, had improved somewhat, or if the person was now symptom-free.

Over the fourteen-year period, thirty-six therapists were involved in treating the 29,000 patients whose progress was followed (even after the initial question of whether the energy interventions were effective had been answered to the satisfaction of the treatment staff, the follow-up calls were continued because they seemed to have clinical value, sometimes leading to further treatment). The impressions of the interviewers, supported by the data they collected, were that the energy interventions were more effective than existing treatments for a range of conditions. The clinics also conducted a number of substudies that allowed more precise conclusions.

The overall investigation did not use a control group. A control group receives a different treatment, or no treatment, so there is a basis of comparison for the outcomes produced by the method being investigated. The substudies, however, did use control groups, comparing energy interventions with the methods that were already in use at the clinics. In the substudies, a "randomized design" (a standard for research that compares treatment modalities) was also employed, which means that any given patient had an equal chance of being placed in the group that received the energy therapy or being in the control group.

The largest of the substudies, conducted over a five-and-one-half-year period, followed the course of treatment of approximately five thousand patients diagnosed with anxiety disorders. Half of them received energy-therapy treatments and no medication. The other half received the standard treatment being used at the clinics for anxiety disorder, which was Cognitive Behaviour Therapy (CBT), supplemented by medication as needed. The interviews at the end of treatment, along with the follow-up interviews at one, three, six, and twelve months, showed that the energy therapy was significantly more effective than the CBT/medication protocol in both the proportion of patients showing some improvement and the proportion of patients showing complete remission of symptoms (see Table 1).

While conducting telephone interviews to place people in one of three categories (no improvement, some improvement, complete remission of symptoms) is not the most stringent way to measure clinical outcomes, various other measures supported these findings, such as pre- and posttreatment scores on standardized psychological tests, including the Beck Anxiety Inventory, the Spielberger State-Trait Anxiety Index, and the Yale-Brown Obsessive-Compulsive Scale. Pre- and posttreatment brain-scan images, as discussed above, also matched the interviewer ratings. However, while these more objective measures did corroborate the interviewers' ratings, they were not consistently applied or tracked.

*Table 1*

## OUTCOME—COMPARISONS WITH 5,000 ANXIETY PATIENTS AT CLOSE OF THERAPY

|  | CBT / MEDICATION | ENERGY ONLY |
| --- | --- | --- |
| Some Improvement | 63% | 90% |
| Complete Remission of Symptoms | 51% | 76% |

In another substudy, the length of treatment was dramatically shorter with energy therapy than with CBT supplemented with medication, as shown in Table 2.

Another question that is relevant for anyone experimenting with the methods presented in this book is whether tapping the acupoints is as effective as the traditional method of placing needles in them. As an acupuncturist, this was of particular interest to Dr. Andrade. A third substudy, while very small, had a surprising outcome, suggesting that tapping the points in the treatment of anxiety disorders may actually be *more effective* than inserting needles into them (see Table 3).

### *Table 2*

## LENGTH OF TREATMENT—COMPARISONS WITHIN A SAMPLING OF 190 ANXIETY PATIENTS

|  | CBT / MEDICATION | ENERGY ONLY |
|---|---|---|
| Typical Number of Sessions | 9 to 20 | 1 to 7 |
| Average Number of Sessions | 15 | 3 |

### *Table 3*

## TAPPING VS. ACUPUNCTURE—COMPARISONS IN THE TREATMENT OF 78 ANXIETY PATIENTS

|  | NEEDLES | TAPPING |
|---|---|---|
| Positive Response | 38 patients | 40 patients |
|  | 50% | 77.5% |

While the results of the overall study as well as the various substudies seem to lend substantial support for an energy psychology approach, we must emphasize that in terms of scientifically establishing the methods of energy psychology, these findings are highly preliminary. The study was initially envisioned as an exploratory in-house assessment of a new method and was not designed with publication in mind. Not all the variables that need to be controlled in robust research were tracked, not all criteria were defined with rigorous precision, the record-keeping was relatively informal, source data were not always maintained, and the degree to which any valid conclusions would generalize to other settings is unknown. Clinical trials of this nature are regarded as "heuristic," or suggestive; they do not prove a case.

Nonetheless, the substudies did use randomized samples, control groups, and "blind" assessment, and the clinical outcomes were striking. If subsequent research corroborates these early findings, energy psychology will become a household word.

# NOTES

## INTRODUCTION: A REVOLUTIONARY APPROACH
## TO PERSONAL CHANGE?

1. The statements in this paragraph are supported by reports from several hundred practitioners. Empirical research is just beginning to be conducted, but early findings also tend to confirm these impressions (see Appendix 3).

2. Among the classic devices that claim to measure the electromagnetic energies of the meridians or acupuncture points are the AMI (Apparatus for Meridian Identification) developed in Japan by Hiroshi Motoyama (the AMI machine, as well as Motoyama's book, *Measurements of Ki Energy Diagnoses & Treatments: Treatment Principles of Oriental Medicine from an Electrophysiological Viewpoint*, 1997, are available through www.cihs.edu) and Reinhold Voll's EAV device for electrodiagnosis and electroacupuncture (see www.eavnet.com). Many other instruments have now been developed and are undergoing experimentation. See for instance, the Centre for Biofield Sciences (www.biofieldsciences.com) and Med-Tronik (www.med-tronik.de/homee.html).

3. David Feinstein and Stanley Krippner, *The Mythic Path* (New York: Tarcher/Penguin Putnam, 1997, www.innersource.net).

4. Phil Mollon, Review of *Energy Psychology Interactive. Clinical Psychology* 42 (2004): 37–39.

5. The review, by Ilene Serlin, appeared in the March 2, 2005, issue of *PsychCRITIQUES* [The American Psychology Association's online *Review of Books*, 50 (9), Article 12].

## CHAPTER 1: YOUR ELECTRIC BRAIN

1. Throughout this book, names of the people presented in the case studies have been changed except in instances where we have been given explicit permission to use the actual name.

2. Available as part of the EFT Foundational Course through www.emofree.com.

3. Carl Johnson, Mustafe Shala, Xhevdet Sejdijaj., Robert Odell, and Kadengjika Dabi-shevci, "Thought Field Therapy—Soothing the Bad Moments of Kosovo," *Journal of Clinical Psychology* 57 (2001): 1237–40.

4. For instance, the prestigious American Psychological Association (APA) took the extraordinarily unusual step in 1999, bordering on censorship, of prohibiting its continuing-education providers from granting psychologists credit for energy psychology courses.

5. To the American Psychological Association's credit, six years after taking the above position, several energy psychology courses were available as APA-approved continuing education, and the organization had published a laudatory assessment of *Energy Psychology Interactive* in its official on-line book-review journal *PsychCRITIQUES* (see p. 8).

6. Ten years after Gary's work at the V.A. Hospital in Los Angeles, Marilyn (Lynn) Garland, L.I.C.S.W., of the Veterans' Healthcare System in Boston, is providing training in energy psychology to other V.A. clinical staff throughout her region. Many of them, she reports, are having "dramatic results in relieving both acute and chronic symptoms of combat-related trauma and other anxiety disorders."

7. Paul B. Fitzgerald et al., "Transcranial Magnetic Stimulation in the Treatment of Depression: A Double-Blind, Placebo-Controlled Trial," *Archives of General Psychiatry* 60 (2003): 1002–08.

8. Michael Rohan et al., "Low-Field Magnetic Stimulation in Bipolar Depression Using an MRI-Based Stimulator;" *American Journal of Psychiatry* 161 (2004): 93–98.

9. Joan Arehart-Treichel, "Efficacy Evidence Builds for Vagus Nerve Procedure," 2003, *Psychiatric News* 38, no. 17 (2003): 26.

10. James R. Evans and Andrew Abarbanel, eds., *Introduction to Quantitative EEG and Neurofeedback* (New York: Academic Press, 1999).

11. O. Bergsmann and A. Woolley-Hart, "Differences in Electrical Skin Conductivity between Acupuncture Points and Adjacent Skin Areas," *American Journal of Acupuncture* 1 (1973): 27–32.

12. Lee Pulos, "The Integration of Energy Psychology with Hypnosis," in *Energy Psychology in Psychotherapy*, ed. Fred P. Gallo (New York: Norton, 2002), 167–78.

13. Among the mental-health conditions the World Health Organization lists as being responsive to acupuncture are anxiety, depression, stress reactions, and insomnia. Energy psychology practitioners report success with the range of conditions listed on pages 23–25. An excellent popular book that suggests which acupuncture points to stimulate for specific emotional benefits is *Acupressure for Emotional Healing*, by Michael Reed Gach and Beth Ann Henning (New York: Bantam, 2004).

14. Z.H. Cho et al., "New Findings of the Correlation Between Acupoints and Corresponding Brain Cortices Using Functional MRI," *Proceedings of National Academy of Science* 95 (1998): 2670–73.

15. K. K. S. Hui et al., "Acupuncture Modulates the Limbic System and Subcortical Gray Structures of the Human Brain: Evidence from MRI Studies in Normal Subjects," *Human Brain Mapping* 9, no. 1 (2000): 13–25.

16. This study is discussed in *Energy Psychology Interactive: Rapid Interventions for Lasting Change* (Ashland, Ore.: Innersource, 2004), 199–214.

17. Many of the probable neurological mechanisms have been mapped by Ron Ruden, M.D. See www.energypsych.org/article_ruden.htm.

18. Martin Lotze et al., "Activation of Cortical and Cerebellar Motor Areas During Executed and Imagined Hand Movements: An MRI Study," *Journal of Cognitive Neuroscience* 11 (1999): 491–501.

19. K.A. Martin, S.E. Moritz, and C. Hall, "Imagery Use in Sport: A Literature Review and Applied Model," *Sport Psychologist* 13 (1999): 245–68.

20. Fred P. Gallo, ed., *Energy Psychology in Psychotherapy* (New York: Norton, 2002).

## CHAPTER 2: A BASIC RECIPE

1. The basic procedures presented in this and the following two chapters are derived from Gary Craig's Emotional Freedom Techniques (EFT). EFT is a revised formulation of Roger Callahan's Thought Field Therapy (TFT) that is particularly well-suited for self-help applications. Callahan's method traces back to George Goodheart's Applied Kinesiology, which was one of the first Western systems to use the stimulation of acupuncture points to promote healing. While numerous approaches have since emerged that apply acupoint stimulation to psychological problems, EFT is the most widely known and used.

2. Australian psychiatrist John Diamond, another pioneer of energy psychology, reports independently having observed this phenomenon.

3. Callahan's account of discovering psychological reversals is described in Gary Craig's *Emotional Freedom Techniques: The Manual*, 4th ed. (2002), 49.

4. You can learn more by visiting the websites of the International College of Applied Kinesiology (www.icak.com), the Association of Energy Kinesiology (www.energyk.org), the Kinesiology Network (www.kinesiology.net), or the Touch for Health Kinesiology Association (www.tfhka.org).

5. Controlled laboratory investigations have used mechanical devices to exert pressure on the muscle and have determined that, under different conditions, different degrees of pressure are needed to overcome the muscle. For instance, more pressure will be required to overcome the muscle after you make a statement you believe to be true than after you make a statement you believe to be false. See, for instance, Dan Monti et al., "Muscle Test Comparisons of Congruent and Incongruent Self-Referential Statements," *Perceptual and Motor Skills* 88 (1999): 1019–28.

6. Developed by psychologist John Diepold, Ph.D. www.tftworldwide.com

7. Fred Gallo named these "Criteria-Related Psychological Reversals" and has mapped them in some detail in his *Energy Diagnostic and Treatment Methods* (New York: Norton, 2000).

8. You can learn more about this approach at www.eft-innovations.com/Articles/collection.htm.

9. Doris Rapp, *Our Toxic World: A Wake-up Call* (Buffalo, N.Y.: Environmental Research Foundation, 2003).

10. See, for instance, www.allergyantidotes.com.

## CHAPTER 3: FOCUSING ON PROBLEMS

1. Because energy interventions can create precisely targeted neurological changes, we do not want to close the door on the possibility that energy methods may be devised that will have benefits similar in effect to those of antipsychotic medications, and without the side effects. But we know of no instances at this point where chronic schizophrenia was permanently cured using energy interventions.

2. Alan Batchelder was the therapist.

3. Betty Moore-Hafter was the therapist.

4. Blair Hornbuckle was the practitioner.

5. Stephani Fried was the therapist.

6. The positive effects of optimism on success, health, and happiness are a central principle within the recent trend towards "Positive Psychology" (www.positivepsychology.org).

7. A description of the "Tell the Story" technique can be found at http://www.emofree.com/tutorial/tutorltwelve.htm.

8. Avshalom Caspi et al., "Influence of Life Stress on Depression: Moderation by a Polymorphism in the 5-HTT Gene," *Science* 301 (2003): 386–89.

9. Again, we do not want to close the door on the possibility that energy interventions that create neurological change may one day be developed for overcoming longstanding endogenous depression, but we do not know of any practitioners who are reporting consistent positive results using only energy interventions with this condition.

10. M. B. Keller et al., "A Comparison of Nefazodone, the Cognitive Behavioural-Analysis System of Psychotherapy, and Their Combination for the Treatment of Chronic Depression," *New England Journal of Medicine* 342 (2000): 1462–70.

11. R. M. Hirschfeld et al., "Does Psychosocial Functioning Improve Independent of Depressive Symptoms? A Comparison of Nefazodone, Psychotherapy, and Their Combination," *Biological Psychiatry* 51 (2002): 123–33.

12. Reported in Patricia Carrington's "Divide and Conquer with EFT: A New Way of Handling Major Depression," *EFT News & Innovations*, March 2002, www.eft-innovations.com.

13. The inventories he uses can be found in Dennis Greenberger and Christine A. Pedasky's *Mind over Mood: Change How You Feel by Changing the Way You Think* (New York: Guilford, 1995).

14. Ron Ruden's *The Craving Brain* (New York: HarperCollins, 2003) is a superb intro-

duction to the neurochemistry and treatment of addiction. Our discussion follows Ruden's model.

15. Ibid.

16. Ibid., Chapter 6, for an introduction to the use of neurofeedback training in the treatment of addictions.

17. Personal communication, February 21, 2005.

18. A promising five-stage model for using EFT with addictions can be found at www.emofree.com/addictions/five-stages-addictions.htm.

19. Visit www.carollook.com to learn about Dr. Look's workbooks and training videos for working with these issues.

20. In a study of medical clinic patients, "only 16% of their complaints were explained by biophysical paradigm of disease" (p. S-4), reported in *Academic Medicine* 66, no. 9, S4-S6, 1991.

21. Silvia Hartmann was the therapist.

22. Mary Kuriger provided this report of her experience.

23. Larry Stewart was the practitioner.

24. Pamela Ney-Noyes was the practitioner.

## CHAPTER 4: FOCUSING ON POTENTIALS

1. Beyond the case examples offered in this book, viewing actual treatment sessions can help you further develop these skills. The EFT Foundational Course (www.emofree.com) includes dozens of demonstration sessions on audio- or videotape. Another source is the two-DVD set *Introduction to Energy Psychology*, available through www.EnergyPsychEd.com.

2. This session was conducted over the telephone. A complete transcript of the forty-five-minute session can be found on the *Energy Psychology Interactive* CD (see Embedded Topics, "EFT Session Transcript"). It is interesting to follow the questions Gary asked and the statements he formulated, sometimes deviating from the exact format of the Basic Recipe. While you can still get to the desired outcome without these on-the-spot modifications, they get you there more quickly. This is part of the art of the technique in the hands of an advanced practitioner.

3. Robert Kegan, *The Emerging Self: Problem and Process in Human Development* (Cambridge, Mass.: Harvard University Press, 1982).

4. Brian Reid, "The Nocebo Effect: Placebo's Evil Twin," *Washington Post*, April 30, 2002. The various published scientific studies mentioned in this and the following paragraph are described in this article.

5. Norman Cousins, "Beliefs Become Biology," *Advances in Mind-Body Medicine* 6, 20–29, 1989.

6. Deborah Mitnick is the therapist.

7. Edmund J. Bourne, *The Anxiety & Phobia Workbook*, 3rd ed. (Oakland, Calif.: New Harbinger, 2000). Chapter 9 of this superb self-help resource focuses on self-talk.

8. Ibid, pp.174–75.

9. Ibid, p. 220.

10. Variations of this research design have been used many times and produced similar outcomes. See, for instance, K. A. Martin, S. E. Moritz, and C. Hall, "Imagery Use in Sport: A Literature Review and Applied Model," *Sport Psychologist* 13 (1999): 245–68.

11. Patterned on the "Outcome Projection Procedure" developed by Fred P. Gallo, Ph.D. See his *Energy Diagnostic and Treatment Methods* (New York: Norton, 2000), 175–77.

12. Introduced by Ryan Harrison, Turbo Tapping is described at http://www.emofree .com/articles/turbo-tapping.htm.

## CHAPTER 5: CULTIVATING "EMOTIONAL INTELLIGENCE"

1. Three studies following into middle age the lives of 95 Harvard students, 450 boys from low-income schools in nearby Somerville, Massachusetts, and 81valedictorians and salutatorians in Illinois high schools all came to this conclusion. See Daniel Goleman, *Emotional Intelligence* (New York: Bantam, 1995), 35.

2. Psychologists Peter Salovey and John D. Mayer—who introduced the term in their article "Emotional Intelligence," *Imagination, Cognition, Personality* 9 (1990): 185–211— have developed a detailed model of *emotional intelligence*. A related concept, social intelligence, was used as early as 1920 by the eminent psychologist E. L. Thorndike, but not widely embraced. Psychologist Robert J. Sternberg revived this concept in his *Beyond IQ* (New York: Cambridge University Press, 1985), where he emphasized "people skills" and "practical intelligence."

3. Goleman, 1995, op. cit.

4. Goleman, 1995, op. cit., xiii.

5. Jeffrey Sachs, *The End of Poverty: Economic Possibilities for Our Time* (New York: Penguin, 2005).

6. From the Resolving Conflict Creatively Program's website: www.esrnational.org/ about-rccp.html.

7. For a description of the Child Development Project and an overview of the research data, visit www.devstu.org/cdp/index.html.

8. Daniel J. Siegel, *The Developing Mind: How Relationships and the Brain Interact to Shape Who We Are* (New York: Guilford Press, 2001).

9. From a lecture by Ann Adams, "Using EFT for Emotionally Disturbed Children," contained in the CD-based "EFT Specialty Series I" and available through www.emofree.com.

10. Anders Ericsson, "Expert Performance: Its Structure and Acquisition," *American Psychologist* 49 (1994): 725–47.

11. Denise Wall was the therapist.

12. Martin Seligman, *Authentic Happiness* (New York: Free Press, 2002).

13. Counsellor's name withheld to further ensure confidentiality.

14. Michael Carr-Jones was the counsellor.

15. Jim Sharon was the therapist.

16. See, for instance, the Choices Method, www.eft-innovations.com/Articles/collection.htm.

## CHAPTER 6: YOUR BODY'S ENERGIES

1. Caroline Myss, *Energy Anatomy* (Audio CD Set, Boulder, Colo.: Sounds True, 2002).

2. Donna Eden, *Energy Medicine* (New York: Tarcher/Penguin, 1999), 31–34.

3. Richard Gerber, *Vibrational Medicine,* 3rd ed. (Santa Fe: Bear & Co., 2001).

4. See footnote 1 of the Introduction to this book and footnotes 5 and 19 through 21 of Appendix 3.

5. Most cultures have concepts for subtle energies that are equated with the "life force," such as *chi* (in China), *ki* (in Japan), *prana* (in India and Tibet), *baraka* (in Sufism), *waken* (in the Lakota Sioux tradition), *megbe* (in the Ituri Pygmy culture of the northeastern Congo forests), and *ruach* (in Jewish Kabalistic tradition).

6. Eden, 1999, op. cit.

7. Valerie Hunt, *Infinite Mind: The Science of Human Vibrations.* (Malibu, Calif.: Malibu Publishing, 1995).

8. Eden, 1999, op. cit., 84–85.

## CHAPTER 7: THE CIRCUITS OF JOY

1. The capacity for delight is higher on the evolutionary scale than the inclination to avoid pain. According to neurochemist Candace Pert, we humans have evolved with a greater concentration of endorphin receptors—the chemical basis for the experience of pleasure—than any other creature, and these receptors are ingeniously paired with our capacities to love and to learn. As Pert summarizes it, "We are wired for pleasure!" (from "Your Body Is Your Subconscious Mind," a CD published by Sounds True, 2004, www.soundstrue.com).

2. Donna Eden, *Energy Medicine* (New York: Tarcher/ Putnam, 1999), chapter 8.

3. This is not to imply that happiness is merely a matter of getting your energies in line. While strengthening your radiant energies supports happiness, psychological factors that have been identified by researchers and clinicians include a mindset that "prompts you to revel in small delights; makes it easier to like yourself; promotes more fulfilling relationships, more rewarding social activities, and greater social support; enhances physical fitness, rest, personal solitude, and a persent-centered absorbtion in the flow of

life; highlights that which realistically gives you greater control over your destiny; [and] supports 'learned optimism' rather than 'learned helplessness'" (from David Feinstein and Stanley Krippner, *The Mythic Path* [New York: Tarcher/Putnam, 1997], 196).

4. Further references, along with a more detailed treatment of the radiant circuits, can be found in Donna Eden and David Feinstein's "Radiant Circuits: The Energies of Joy," in Fred P. Gallo (ed.), *Energy Psychology in Psychotherapy.* New York: Norton, 2002.

5. Jerry Alan Johnson, *Chinese Medical Quigong Therapy: A Comprehensive Clinical Text* (Pacific Grove, Calif.: International Institute of Medical Qigong, 2000), 157.

6. Ibid, 157.

7. L. E. Blitzer, Daniel J. Atchison-Nevel, and Maureen C. Kenny, "Using Acupuncture to Treat Major Depressive Disorder: A Pilot Investigation." *Clinical Acupuncture and Oriental Medicine 4* (2004): 144–47.

8. For additional information, Laura E. Blitzer, Ph.D., of Florida International University in Miami, may be contacted at blitzerl@fiu.edu.

9. The developer of that website, Phillip W. Warren, has written: "While attending an energy psychology conference in the spring of 2001, I had an epiphany. I discovered that Donna Eden's Radiant Circuits are the most efficient way to work with the body's energy system. With my colleague, Janet Nestor, I spent the next 3 years researching, developing, and refining what I now call the Radiant Energies Balance protocol (REB). REB can be used as both a sophisticated professional therapeutic system incorporating mainstream and cutting edge therapeutic methods as well as an easily applied self-help procedure. It is one of the most user-friendly approaches in the field of energy psychotherapy."

10. See www.positivepsychology.org.

11. Arnold Porter, "Recipes for Magic," in *A Complete Guide to Acupressure*, ed. Iona M. Teeguarden (Tokyo/New York: Japan Publications, 1996), 122–29.

12. David Feinstein, *Energy Psychology Interactive: Rapid Interventions for Lasting Change* (CD), www.EnergyPsychologyInteractive.com.

## EPILOGUE: THE FUTURE OF ENERGY PSYCHOLOGY

1. Gerald P. Koocher, "Three Myths about Empirically Validated Therapies, *Independent Practitioner* (Bulletin of Psychologists in Independent Practice, American Psychological Association Division 42) 24(2).

2. Presented in a talk delivered by Dr. Gruder at the First European Conference on Energy Psychology, July 6, 2001, Fürigen, Switzerland, these ideas are elaborated in "Five Keys to Successful Treatment," a paper that can be found on the *Energy Psychology Interactive* CD. Visit www.willingness.com for additional resources from Dr. Gruder.

3. For an overview of "Borrowing Benefits," visit www.emofree.com/tutorial/tutorkeleven.htm. A study investigating the phenomenon found a statistically significant decrease ($p < .0005$) in all measures of psychological distress based on scores on a stan-

dardized test given before and after the experience to 105 subjects. The changes had held at a six-month follow-up. Jack E. Rowe, "The Effects of EFT on Long-Term Psychological Symptoms," *Counselling and Clinical Psychology* (in press).

## APPENDIX 3: RESEARCH EVIDENCE

1. This Appendix draws heavily on David Feinstein's program for professional psychotherapists, *Energy Psychology Interactive: Rapid Interventions for Lasting Change* (Ashland, Oreg: Innersource, 2004).

2. Among the English-language journals are *Acupuncture & Electro-Therapeutics, American Journal of Acupuncture, Acupuncture in Medicine, Clinical Acupuncture & Oriental Medicine, International Journal of Clinical Acupuncture, Journal of Chinese Medicine, Journal of Traditional Chinese Medicine, Medical Acupuncture,* and the *Oriental Medical Journal.*

3. Fred P. Gallo, ed., *Energy Psychology in Psychotherapy,* 2nd ed. (New York: Norton, 2002).

4. The reported improvements reached a .001 "level of confidence" with twenty-eight of the conditions and .01 for the other three.

5. The positive changes identified in the treatment group (n=714) reached a very strong statistical "level of confidence" (.001). While not submitted to peer review, a report of this study was carried in a special issue of the *Journal of Clinical Psychology* that focused on Thought Field Therapy. Caroline Sakai et al., "Thought Field Therapy Clinical Applications: Utilization in an HMO in Behavioural Medicine and Behavioural Health Services," *Journal of Clinical Psychology* 57 (2001): 1215–27.

6. Dorothea Hover-Kramer, *Healing Touch: A Guide Book for Practitioners,* 2nd ed. (Albany, N.Y.: Delmar, 2001).

7. Beverly Schoninger, *TFT in the Treatment of Speaking Anxiety.* Unpublished doctoral dissertation (Cincinnati: Union Institute, 2001).

8. Dale Darby, *The Efficiency of Thought Field Therapy as a Treatment Modality for Individuals Diagnosed with Blood-Injection-Injury Phobia.* Unpublished doctoral dissertation (Minneapolis: Walden University, 2001).

9. Joel F. Wade, *The Effects of the Callahan Phobia Treatment Techniques on Self Concept.* Unpublished doctoral dissertation (San Diego: Professional School of Psychological Studies, 1990).

10. Steve Wells et al., "Evaluation of a Meridian-Based Intervention, Emotional Freedom Techniques (EFT), for Reducing Specific Phobias of Small Animals," *Journal of Clinical Psychology* 59 (2003): 943–66.

11. A. Harvey Baker and Linda S. Siegel, "Can a 45 Minute Session of EFT Lead to Reduction of Intense Fear of Rats, Spiders and Water Bugs?—A Replication and Extension of the Wells et al. (2003) Laboratory Study." Paper submitted for publication, 2005.

12. Joyce Carbonell, "An Experimental Study of TFT and Acrophobia," *The Thought Field* 2, no. 3, (1997): 1–6.

13. A. Kober et al., "Pre-hospital Analgesia with Acupressure in Victims of Minor Trauma: A Prospective, Randomized, Double-Blinded Trial," *Anesthesia & Analgesia* 95 (2002): 723–27.

14. John J. B. Allen et. al., "The Efficacy of Acupuncture in the Treatment of Major Depression in Women," *Psychological Science* 9, no. 5 (1998): 397–401.

15. Wendy L. Waite and Mark D. Holder, "Assessment of the Emotional Freedom Technique: An Alternative Treatment for Fear," *Scientific Review of Mental Health Practice* 2, no. 1 (2003).

16. A. Harvey Baker and Patricia Carrington, "A Comment on Waite and Holder's Research Supposedly Invalidating EFT," paper submitted for publication, 2005.

17. Fred P. Gallo, *Energy Diagnostic and Treatment Methods* (New York: Norton, 2000).

18. Daniel G. Amen, *Images into Human Behaviour: A Brain SPECT Atlas* (Newport Beach, Calif.: MindWorks, 2003).

19. A study by Peter Lambrou and George Pratt, presented at the Eleventh Annual Conference of the International Society for the Study of Subtle Energy & Energy Medicine, June 15, 2001, in Boulder, Colorado, reported significant pre- and posttreatment improvement in autonomic nervous system function based on computerized biofeedback equipment with four patients treated with TFT for claustrophobia. An unpublished report by John H. Diepold and David Goldstein, *Thought Field Therapy and QEEG Changes in the Treatment of Trauma: A Case Study,* showed that the subject's brain-wave patterns normalized after TFT treatment and remained in the normal range at an eighteen-month follow-up. Another unpublished study, by Paul G. Swingle and Lee Pulos, showed that the brain-wave patterns of four subjects who had been involved in motor-vehicle accidents and suffered PTSD following the accidents normalized in the sensory motor cortex, the right frontal cortex, and the occipital region of the brain following EFT treatment.

20. K. K. S. Hui et al., "Acupuncture Modulates the Limbic System and Subcortical Gray Structures of the Human Brain: Evidence from MRI Studies in Normal Subjects," *Human Brain Mapping* 9, no. 1 (2000): 13–25.

21. This observation emerges from a research program conducted at New York University by Joseph LeDoux. See, for instance, Karim Nader, Glenn E. Schafe, and Joseph E. LeDoux, "The Labile Nature of Consolidation Theory," *Nature Neuroscience Reviews* 1, no. 3 (2000): 216–19. We are grateful to Joaquín Andrade, M.D., for pointing out the significance of LeDoux's work in explaining some of the neurological mechanisms of energy psychology.

22. A discussion of various investigations into the meridian system, such as injecting solutions with radioactive isotopes into traditional acupuncture points and finding that the liquid's flow paralleled the ancient descriptions of the meridian pathways, can be found in Richard Gerber's *Vibrational Medicine,* 3rd ed. (Santa Fe: Bear & Co., 2001), 122–27.

23. Neurophysiologist Valerie Hunt carried out a series of meticulous investigations over a twenty-year period at UCLA's Energy Field Laboratory. In one study, electrical oscillations in the skin above the areas where the chakras are traditionally believed to be located were shown to have frequencies of 100 to 1,600 cycles per second, as contrasted with 0 to 100 in the brain (and usually in the 0-to-30 range), up to 225 in the muscles, and up to 250 in the heart. Reported in Gerber, Ibid., p. 133.

24. Another study coming out of UCLA's Energy Field Laboratory compared descriptions by those who could "see" auras with neurophysiological measures. Descriptions by eight "aura readers" not only corresponded with one another, they correlated *exactly* with electromyography (EMG) wave patterns picked up by electrodes on the skin at the spot that was being observed. Valerie Hunt, *Infinite Mind: The Science of Human Vibrations* (Malibu, Calif.: Malibu Publishing, 1995).

25. Rollin McCraty, "The Energetic Heart: Bioelectromagnetic Communication Within and Between People," in *Bioelectromagnetic Medicine,* ed. Paul J. Rosch and M. S. Markov (New York: Marcel Dekker, 2004), 541–62.

26. Ibid.

27. Daniel Benor, *Spiritual Healing: Scientific Validation of a Healing Revolution* (Southfield, Mich.: Vision Publications, 2001).

28. William A. Tiller, *Science and Human Transformation: Subtle Energies, Intentionality and Consciousness* (Walnut Creek, Calif.: Pavior, 1997).

29. William G. Braud, "Human Interconnectedness: Research Indications," *ReVision: A Journal of Consciousness and Transformation* 14 (1992): 140–49. The significance level was $2.6 \times 10^{-14}$.

30. Larry Dossey, *Healing Words: The Power of Prayer and the Practice of Medicine* (San Francisco: Harper, 1993).

31. A case study documenting a surrogate healing treatment between a mother and her son can be accessed from the "Embedded Topics" area of the *Energy Psychology Interactive* CD. Also see: Nick Arrizza, "A Shared Memory Case Study: The Mind Resonance Process and Evidence for Non-Local Consciousness," *International Journal of Healing and Caring* (online), Jan. 2005, Vol. 4, No. 1.

32. An early study by Joyce Carbonell and Charles R. Figley compared four treatments that were in use for PTSD: TFT, EMDR (Eye Movement Desensitization and Reprocessing), "traumatic incident reduction," and "visual/kinesthetic dissociation" (V/DK). All four treatments resulted in improvement based on self-reports, with EMDR, V/DK, and TFT showing substantially stronger results than traumatic-incident reduction. TFT was the most efficient of the methods, requiring only an hour of treatment, and it seemed to work on fragile clients that the EMDR team refused to treat. This study is thoughtfully discussed in John G. Hartung and Michael D. Galvin, *Energy Psychology and EMDR: Combining Forces to Optimize Treatment* (New York: Norton, 2003), 71–72.

# RESOURCES

## AFTER THIS BOOK—FURTHER HOME-STUDY

Class with Demos on 2 DVDs (*Introduction to Energy Psychology*) www.EnergyPsychEd.com
Gary Craig's Free Downloadable EFT Manual: www.emofree.com/downloadeftmanual.htm
Gary Craig's Basic and Advanced Video Training Programs: www.emofree.com/products.htm
Donna Eden's *Introduction to Energy Medicine* DVD: www.energymed.info
David's Home Study Course for Professionals: www.EnergyPsychologyInteractive.com
Professional Home Study Programs in the Energy Therapies: www.EnergyHomeStudy.com

## FREE INFORMATION-PACKED WEBSITES

www.emofree.com (Gary Craig's Emotional Freedom Techniques Site)
www.eftsupport.com (Pat Carrington's Emotional Freedom Techniques Support Site)
www.EnergyPsychEd.com (includes free papers and various training programs and products)
www.energypsych.org (ACEP—Association for Comprehensive Energy Psychology Site)
www.wholistichealingresearch.com (Wholistic Healing Research Site)
www.handoutbank.org (the Energy Medicine Institute's Free Handout Bank)

## FREE E-MAIL NEWSLETTERS AND DISCUSSION GROUPS

www.emofree.com/email.htm (Gary's Emotional Freedom Techniques Newsletter)
www.eftupdate.com (Pat Carrington's *EFT 1-Minute News* twice-monthly free newsletter)
http://groups.yahoo.com/group/meridian-energy (Meridian Therapy Discussion Group)
http://groups.yahoo.com/group/energym/ (Energy Psychotherapists' Discussion Group)

## FINDING A CONVENTIONAL PSYCHOTHERAPIST

www.4therapy.com (guidelines for seeking a therapist, thousands of listings worldwide)
www.psychologytoday.com (guidelines for seeking a therapist, thousands of listings)

www.1-800-therapist.com (a service designed to help you choose the right therapist for you)

1-800-964-2000 (The American Psychological Association's public-information line)

www.psych.org/public_info (The American Psychiatric Association's public-information page)

www.naswdc.org (The National Association of Social Workers' website)

## FINDING A PSYCHOTHERAPIST SPECIALIZING IN ENERGY TREATMENT

www.emofree.com/practitioners/referralmain.asp (Gary's EFT Practitioner List)

www.eftsupport.com/practstatelist.htm (Pat Carrington's EFT Practitioner List)

www.energypsych.com ("Energy Diagnostic and Treatment Methods" Practitioner List)

www.seemorgmatrix.org (Practitioners Trained by Asha Clinton)

www.energytherapy-AAMT.info (lists of therapists and trainers worldwide)

## FINDING AN ENERGY MEDICINE PRACTITIONER

www.innersource.net/links/links_practitioners.htm

## NONPROFIT ORGANIZATIONS CONCERNED WITH ENERGY PSYCHOLOGY

www.energypsych.org (ACEP—Association for Comprehensive Energy Psychology)

www.theamt.com (Association for Meridian Therapies)

www.energymed.org (Energy Medicine Institute)

www.issseem.org (International Society for the Study of Subtle Energies and Energy Medicine)

www.energytherapy-AAMT.info (Association for the Advancement of Meridian Energy Techniques)

# ABOUT THE AUTHORS

**DAVID FEINSTEIN, PH.D.**, is a clinical psychologist who serves as national director of the Energy Medicine Institute. Author of six books and over fifty professional papers, he has taught at The Johns Hopkins University School of Medicine and Antioch College. His multimedia *Energy Psychology Interactive* program was a recipient of the Outstanding Contribution Award from the Association for Comprehensive Energy Psychology. Among his other books are *The Mythic Path*, *Rituals for Living and Dying* and *Energy Medicine*, written with his wife, Donna Eden.

www.EnergyPsychEd.com

**DONNA EDEN** has, for more than a quarter century, been teaching people how to understand their body's energies. As Caroline Myss wrote in her foreword to Donna's classic book, *Energy Medicine*: "The contribution Donna Eden has made will stand as one of the backbone studies as we lay a sound foundation for the field of holistic medicine." Donna is widely recognized for her inborn ability to clairvoyantly see the body's energies, to track down the causes of physical and psychological problems based on the state of those energies, and to devise highly effective

treatments. A deeply loving and joyful personality, Donna has treated more than ten thousand clients individually and has taught hundreds of classes, speaking to packed houses throughout the United States, Europe, Australia, New Zealand, and South America.

www.EnergyMed.info

**GARY CRAIG,** born in 1940, holds a degree in metallurgical engineering from Stanford University (1962). However, his passion has always been in the field of personal-improvement psychology. He is the founder of Emotional Freedom Techniques (EFT), the most widely used of all the techniques within the burgeoning new field of energy psychology. He is the author of the *EFT Manual* and six detailed video sets aimed at teaching EFT (*The EFT Course, Steps Towards Becoming the Ultimate Therapist, From EFT to the Palace of Possibilities, EFT Specialty Series 1 & 2,* and *Borrowing Benefits*) that have been sold in nearly every country in the world. He has a large, library-like website on EFT and authors *EFT Insights,* a popular e-mail newsletter.

www.emofree.com